Rethinking Peace and Conflict Studies

Series Editor
Oliver P. Richmond
University of Manchester
Manchester, UK

This agenda-setting series of research monographs, now more than a decade old, provides an interdisciplinary forum aimed at advancing innovative new agendas for approaches to, and understandings of, peace and conflict studies and International Relations. Many of the critical volumes the series has so far hosted have contributed to new avenues of analysis directly or indirectly related to the search for positive, emancipatory, and hybrid forms of peace. New perspectives on peacemaking in practice and in theory, their implications for the international peace architecture, and different conflict-affected regions around the world, remain crucial. This series' contributions offers both theoretical and empirical insights into many of the world's most intractable conflicts and any subsequent attempts to build a new and more sustainable peace, responsive to the needs and norms of those who are its subjects.

More information about this series at
http://www.palgrave.com/gp/series/14500

Roberto Belloni

The Rise and Fall of Peacebuilding in the Balkans

palgrave
macmillan

Roberto Belloni
Department of Sociology and Social
Research
University of Trento
Trento, Italy

Rethinking Peace and Conflict Studies
ISBN 978-3-030-14423-4   ISBN 978-3-030-14424-1   (eBook)
https://doi.org/10.1007/978-3-030-14424-1

Library of Congress Control Number: 2019932932

Cover design by MC Richmond

This Palgrave Macmillan imprint is published by the registered company Springer Nature
Switzerland AG
The registered company address is: Gewerbestrasse 11, 6330 Cham, Switzerland

ACKNOWLEDGEMENTS

The intention of this book is to appraise twenty years of peacebuilding in the Balkans. The actions of different international and domestic players are all evaluated against the overarching liberal framework which has influenced peacebuilding since the end of the Cold War and which involved primarily, but exclusively, rapid democratization and marketization. In this context, corruption and civil society—both key elements cutting across the liberal peacebuilding agenda—are recurring themes across all chapters, thus providing the focus around which the analysis is structured. Some of the individual chapters rework material from a wide range of my research over the last decade or so.

I began working on peacebuilding in the Balkans more than 20 years ago, first as a practitioner and then as an academic researcher. Over that time, I have benefited from the help of dozens of friends, colleagues, officials working for international organizations, civil society activists and, most importantly, family members. Any list would be too long, since it would lose the individuals in a ridiculously long stream of names. At the same time, it would likely be too short since, because of the poor state of my records, it would neglect mentioning at least a few people who contributed to the book. Accordingly, let me just say: Thanks to all of you (you know who you are).

However, I cannot skip mentioning four special debts. First, Oliver Richmond was the first who encouraged me to pursue this project at a time when I was not sure I would be able to bring it to fruition, and later accepted it in his book series. Second, some of the ideas discussed in Chapter 3 evolved from a paper I wrote with Francesco Strazzari (Corruption in Post-Conflict Bosnia-Herzegovina and Kosovo: A Deal Among Friends, *Third World Quarterly*, 35 (5), pp. 132–148). Likewise, Chapter 8 develops issues I first explored with Stefanie Kappler and Jasmin Ramović (Bosnia-Herzegovina: Domestic Agency and the Inadequacy of the Liberal Peace, in Sandra Pogodda and Oliver P. Richmond, eds., *Post-liberal Peace Transitions*, Edinburgh: Edinburgh University Press, pp. 47–64). I am greatly indebted to the three of them for their help in developing my thinking on peacebuilding in the region. Third, for many years Sarajevo represented my research hub in the region. I cannot mention all the friends and colleagues who helped me navigate both the city and Balkan politics, but I want to single out Simone Ginzburg, whose friendship and warmth have been incredible. Finally, the writing of this book coincided with perhaps the most difficult period of my life thus far. I doubt it I could get through it without the help of Anna, Ilaria and Luce. I will always be grateful for all of their help and understanding.

This book is dedicated to Anna, my mother: *Vivamus dum licet esse bene.*

CONTENTS

ACRONYMS

ACCOUNT	Anti-Corruption Civic Organizations Unified Network
BiH	Bosnia-Herzegovina
CEE	Central and Eastern European
CEFTA	Central European Free Trade Area
CFSP	Common Foreign and Security Policy
CSOs	Civil Society Organizations
DPA	Dayton Peace Agreement
DPs	Displaced Persons
EU	European Union
EUFOR	European Union Force
EULEX	European Union Rule of Law Mission in Kosovo
EUSR	European Union Special Representative
FYROM	Former Yugoslav Republic of Macedonia
GDP	Gross Domestic Product
ICB	International Commission on the Balkans
ICO	International Civilian Office
ICR	International Civilian Representative
ICTY	International Criminal Tribunal for the Former Yugoslavia
IMF	International Monetary Fund
IPA	Instrument for Pre-Accession Assistance
KLA	Kosovo Liberation Army
KTA	Kosovo Trust Agency
LGBT	Lesbian, Gay, Bisexual and Transgender
MBOs	Member Benefit Organizations
NATO	North Atlantic Treaty Organization
NGOs	Non-Governmental Organizations

NSS	National Security Strategy
OECD	Organisation for Economic Co-operation and Development
OHR	Office of the High Representative
OSCE	Organization for Security and Cooperation in Europe
PBOs	Public Benefit Organizations
RCC	Regional Cooperation Council
RS	Republika Srpska
SAA	Stabilization and Association Agreement
SAP	Stabilization and Association Process
SFOR	Stabilization Force
UN	United Nations
UNMIK	United Nations Mission in Kosovo
USAID	United States Agency for International Development

CHAPTER 1

Peacebuilding in the Balkans

1.1   INTRODUCTION

In the summer of 2017, when I was in Sarajevo to participate in a seminar on Bosnian politics, a Bosnian friend told me a joke which went roughly like this:

A man is grazing his sheep when another individual shows up:

> 'I know exactly how many sheep you have in your flock. Do you want to bet? If I win I'll leave with one of your sheep'.
> The shepherd is puzzled by the question, but decides to go along.
> 'Ok, let's see if you know the exact number'.
> 'Well, you have 132 sheep in your flock'.
> 'Wow, that's quite impressive, you won!' The man picks up a sheep and starts walking away, when the shepherd calls him back.
> 'Well, let's do it again: I bet I can guess your job. If I win, you give me my sheep back'.
> 'Ok, go ahead'.
> 'You are an international official working for a peacebuilding organization'.
> 'That's right! This is amazing! How could you guess?'
> 'You see, it was easy: you came to me uninvited, you told me something I knew already, and then you left with my dog'.

© The Author(s) 2020
R. Belloni, *The Rise and Fall of Peacebuilding
in the Balkans*, Rethinking Peace and Conflict Studies,
https://doi.org/10.1007/978-3-030-14424-1_1

As with most jokes, this one is unfair. Since the 1990s thousands of international officials have worked in Bosnia-Herzegovina, and elsewhere in the region, contributing in very significant ways to processes of stabilization, reconstruction and peacebuilding. The overwhelming majority of these officials are extremely smart, hardworking, and committed individuals who have dedicated their time and energies to address often very complex problems in an extremely challenging environment. At the same time, while certainly one sided, this joke expresses a widespread sense of frustration among Bosnian citizens for the glaring gap between the promises of liberal peacebuilding activities undertaken since the mid-1990s and the realities of everyday life (Sheftel 2011). This book examines the peacebuilding evolution from the initial optimistic belief that international intervention in the Balkans would build liberal and democratic states modelled on their western European neighbours to the growing disappointment with external involvement in the region. Peacebuilding's focus on formal institutions, political elites and externally driven policy frameworks has led to various levels of stability but at the cost of increasing citizens' dissatisfaction.

Thus, mocking expresses the disappointment with the outcome of more than two decades of liberal peacebuilding. In Bosnia-Herzegovina a peace agreement, internationally brokered in 1995, was followed by the deployment of both international military and civilian forces. This large community engaged in a number of very familiar activities typical of liberal peacebuilding, including the organization of internationally monitored elections, the protection of human rights and of minorities, the promotion of gender equality, the restructuring of the economy along neo-liberal lines, the promotion of rule of law and security sector reform, and the containment and restraint of the use of force by parties to the conflict (Jarstad and Sisk 2008; Mac Ginty 2015). In addition to Bosnia-Herzegovina, at least some of these activities have been carried out in most states which emerged from the process of violent dissolution of Yugoslavia since the early 1990s, including Croatia, the Former Yugoslav Republic of Macedonia (FYROM), Kosovo, Montenegro, Serbia and Slovenia.

Peacebuilding in the Balkans began with so much promise, only to fall to cynical calculations about stability by international actors and widespread popular disappointment by local communities. Since the early 2010s a wave of protests putting forward social, economic and political demands have erupted throughout the region. In Slovenia, Croatia, and Bosnia-Herzegovina, protests have denounced the political system, political elites, corruption, mismanagement, and deteriorating economic and social conditions. Similar instances of discontent, but with a different intensity, emerged in Kosovo, Montenegro and Serbia. In some of these protests, Europe has been the direct target of public scorn and on a few occasions, the European Union (EU) flag has been burned. More commonly, protests have been directed against various governmental levels, which are seen locally as implementing the EU's state-building and peacebuilding agenda.

These instances of discontent reflect the deteriorating economic, political and social conditions that the region has been experiencing at least since the outbreak of the global economic and financial crisis in 2008. A decade later, the economy continues to stagnate, while unemployment leads many young people to leave the region. Institutions are seen locally as either unrepresentative or corrupt—or both. The Transparency International Corruption Perception Index regularly ranks states in the region among the most corrupt in Europe. Patterns of semi-authoritarian political rule involving the exercise of power through party dominance and patron–client networks are ever more common (Bieber 2018). The process of Euro-Atlantic integration (i.e. EU and NATO membership) has not significantly changed the structural political and economic dynamics of the region (Mujanović 2018).

The EU's foreign policy uncertainties, which ultimately are expressed in its inability to provide a reliable enlargement perspective to the Balkans, have facilitated the rise of Turkey, China, the Gulf states and, above all, Russia as realistic competitors for influence. Most notably, Moscow has been supporting the Bosnian Serbs' challenge to the authority of the central state in Bosnia-Herzegovina; it has engaged in a profound security and defence cooperation with Serbia—the only country in the region not seeking full NATO membership; and, according to the government in Podgorica, it even supported a failed coup in Montenegro in October 2016 aimed at disrupting the country's accession to NATO.

Why has internationally led liberal peacebuilding failed to live up to expectations? There are several reasons for this, including liberalism's narrow focus on political institutions, a complacent and paternalistic attitude by external interveners, the presence of domestic clientelistic structures preserving inequality and privilege, and the limited attention to the socio-economic needs of the population. These limited results of liberal peacebuilding in the Balkans are similar to disappointing peacebuilding outcomes elsewhere in the world, and have given rise to extensive critiques. A 'problem-solving' approach has sought to improve the efficiency of peacebuilding activities. Accordingly, a large number of 'lessons learned' exercises aim at 'fixing failed states', in particular by attempting to identify the timeliness and the correct sequencing of liberalization policies (Grimm and Mathis 2015; Paris 2004; Langer and Brown 2016). A 'critical theory', or paradigm-shifting approach, has criticized the ideological foundations of liberal peacebuilding, arguing that intervention in conflict areas is dominated by western neo-colonial interests that reproduce the sources of conflict intrinsic to the existing, and unequal, international economic order (Duffield 2007; Pugh 2005; Richmond 2014). While this critique shed light on the structural inequalities of liberal peacebuilding and its prioritization of western interests and agency, it has been rebutted by 'problem-solvers' for not identifying viable policy alternatives (Paris 2010; for a reply, see, Cooper et al. 2011).

This chapter discusses both the rise of liberal peacebuilding to the centre of international policy concerns since the early 1990s and how the Balkans became a target for liberal interventionism. Liberal peacebuilding in the region went through several phases, from an initial optimistic belief that liberal institutions and norms could be spread everywhere, to a gloomy assessment about the possibility of influencing the deeper political, economic and social structures of Balkan states. What follows does not aim to provide a full account of the rise of peacebuilding and the related debates and counter-debates on the liberal peace. Rather, it shows how peacebuilding, while progressively losing its transformative edge, has become a powerful discourse institutionalized in the activities of international organizations, states and non-governmental organizations (NGOs) (Jabri 2013), and has emerged as the conceptual reference point for international actors intervening in the region.

1.2   The Rise of Liberal Peacebuilding

The end of the Cold War led to a widespread optimism among western political elites about the possibility of exporting liberal values and institutions to states emerging from decades of socialist rule. In the transition from totalitarianism to democracy, several of these states became engulfed in vicious wars with often significant international dimensions threating the stability and prosperity of neighbouring states, such as migration flows, illegal trade, human trafficking and the like. Thus, the post-Cold War world order was still menaced by nonliberal actors, institutions and practices, which required an active and purposeful effort to achieve the universal realization of liberal norms and principles. No longer was the main obstacle to the realization of these norms and principles the alternative model of society advanced by the Soviet Union but so-called 'weak and failing states' (Woodward 2017).

In his 1992 Agenda for Peace, then UN Secretary General Boutros Boutros-Ghali provided the normative justification for intervention in this type of state: 'the time of absolute and exclusive sovereignty... has passed; its theory was never matched by reality' (Boutros-Ghali 1992: para. 17). Accordingly, the UN (as well as other actors subscribing to the liberal template, including security organizations, international financial institutions and NGOs) claimed it could legitimately intervene in the domestic affairs of formally sovereign states in order to support post-war transitions and the development and strengthening of democratic institutions. The assumption that democracy offers a non-violent way of managing domestic conflict through rule-based political competition (Bobbio 1990) made the development of democratic institutions a core component of UN operations during the 1990s. Alongside the UN, both the World Bank and the International Monetary Fund vigorously promoted liberal economic policies, including the liberalization of markets, the deregulation of trade and the privatization of public assets (Paris 2004).

By the early 2000s, the policy attention towards fragile states in the Global South was at its peak. Domestic, sovereign borders were perceived as insufficient to provide protection in a global context where risks and threats emerging from the world's peripheries could quickly spread elsewhere. The vast and growing number of transnational ills involving, for example, economic crises, environmental pollution, crime, drugs, terrorism, and so on, turned the stable and prosperous states of the western hemisphere into 'risk societies' (Beck 1992). The terrorist attacks of 11 September 2001 both confirmed this sense of vulnerability and elevated the peacebuilding agenda, above all its commitment to building democratic and prosperous states, to the top of the list of international policy concerns. As articulated by the 2002 US National Security Strategy (NSS), 'America is now threatened less by conquering states than we are by failing ones' (NSS 2002: Sect. 1). Accordingly, the NSS pledged to 'extend the benefits of freedom across the globe.

We will actively work to bring the hope of democracy, free markets, and free trade to every corner of the world… Poverty does not make poor people into terrorists and murderers. Yet, poverty, weak institutions, and corruption can make weak states vulnerable to terrorist networks and drug cartels within their borders' (ibid.: Sect. 2).

Motivated by very realist security concerns, peacebuilding drastically altered established patterns of international relations. In the Westphalian world order states enjoyed sovereign equality and political legitimacy. By contrast, the liberal internationalist framework developed in the course of the 1990s and embodied in the peacebuilding agenda challenged the prohibition to interfere, directly or indirectly, in the internal affairs of other states. The institution of sovereignty and its prerogatives became increasingly linked to liberal credentials, including arguments in favour of gradations of sovereignty (Keohane 2003). External intervention was justified by the public goods it promised to achieve such as democratic development, economic recovery and prosperity, and the protection and promotion of human rights. The structural impediments that made it impossible for a people to determine their own future associated peacebuilding with various forms of paternalism and assertiveness (Barnett 2016), including the direct control of conflict-affected states by international organizations.

This 'Liberalism of Imposition' (Sørensen 2011) focused on the rights of individuals, not of states. States in the Global South were no longer considered to be either able or willing to guarantee the safety, protection and well-being of their own citizens, and thus the international community claimed that intervention to uphold the rights of those individuals exposed to violence and discrimination and to build democratic institutions was legitimate. The United States, with its strong, established belief in the virtuousness of both its political institutions and its motives, played a predominant role in promoting a Liberal Empire where its values could be furthered (Bishai 2004). For Washington, democracy promotion served to stabilize the control of fragile polities in the Global South during the unstable process of transition to a post-communist era (Robinson 1996). As a result peacebuilding, and more generally liberal interventionism, led to an increasing blurring of the boundaries between international and domestic politics and, in the process, undermined the institution of sovereignty with its corollaries of (formal) equality and non-intervention in the domestic matters of sovereign states (Chandler 2017; Mearsheimer 2018).

Liberal principles provided peacebuilding with the ideological underpinning to interfere in the domestic affairs of sovereign states (Joshi et al. 2014). Needless to say, liberalism is a highly heterogeneous political and philosophical tradition (see, for example, Evans 2001; Doyle 1997; Hobson 2012; Jahn 2013; Richardson 2001). Recurrent themes commonly found in most liberal theories and approaches include the focus on the individual as a sovereign actor and primary reference point; trust in the possibility of progress and people's ability to reform both themselves and institutions; the importance of the rule of law in shaping the relationship between institutions and citizens and contributing to influence foreign policy; the centrality of economic policies in supporting private property, the market and free trade; the emphasis on tolerance, diversity and equal opportunity; the acceptance of unequal power relations and their maintenance through economic, political, ideological and military means.

While liberal approaches present different emphases on and combinations of these themes, actors involved in the practice of peacebuilding regularly refer to one or more of the key liberal ideas in order to justify intervention. No matter which liberal component is emphasized, peacebuilding follows a positivist 'cause and effect' model based on the belief that causes of violent conflicts can be identified and eliminated, and conflict-affected societies can be socially engineered. The neo-liberal variant which prevailed since the early 1990s focused on the development of state institutions, the market and civil society; it stressed the importance of security and human rights; and it underscored the centrality of the rule of law in shaping the relationship between the state and its citizens. Other liberal modes such as social democracy, material redistribution and rights, as well the interventionist role of the state in the economy have been largely neglected, not to mention the emancipatory gradation of the liberal peace based on care, needs, welfare and social justice (Richmond 2011).

Liberals have identified a number of different tools to support the building of peaceful coexistence, most notably the rule of law, the internal democratic character of states, trade and international institutions (for a good discussion, see, Brown et al. 1996). The current debate on liberal peacebuilding has been decisively shaped by an article by Michael Doyle (1983), who revitalized the discussion about the relationship between democracies (which he defined as 'liberal states') and war. Drawing from Kant, he argued that democracies are valuable not only for the advantages they bring about internally but also because they guarantee a more trustworthy and peaceful foreign policy.[1] This insight led to the development of ever more sophisticated versions of Democratic peace theory scrutinizing the claim that democracies do not engage in armed conflict with other democracies.

Empirical evidence has confirmed that democratic regimes prefer to solve their controversies through peaceful means. According to Doyle (1983), this is so because citizens pay the price of war in terms of lives, material destruction, and taxes. Others argue that democratic decision-making constrains the conduct of foreign affairs, that internal conflict resolution norms are projected externally (Russett 1996), or that peaceful international relationships are socially constructed through a process of mutual recognition (Williams 2001). Either way, liberal democratic states are associated with a pacific domestic and international order. The peaceful character of liberal states leads to peaceful international relations among them.[2] The case of Europe, which for centuries experienced recurrent and bloody wars, shows how democratic states which are economically interdependent and share membership in international organizations can re-structure their international relations from a Hobbesian condition of *bellum omnium contra omnes* to a state of Kantian peace and security (Belloni 2016).

On the footsteps of democratic peace theory, liberal peacebuilding posits that the rule of law, institutional checks and balances, economic interdependence and institutional density are peace-enabling elements. Accordingly, liberal peacebuilding aims at managing conflict and insecurity both within and between states on the basis of liberal democracy and market economics. The promotion of political and economic liberalization is expected to lead to internal and external stability and peace (Paris 2004: 19–35). Needless to say, while liberal democracies may be more domestically peaceful than illiberal states, they are not immune from conflict, or even violence. By its nature, liberalism tolerates even large economic inequalities and thus can be subjected to contestation from below. As Chapter 8 will show, economic crisis and uneven wealth distribution create the conditions for the underprivileged to revolt and to challenge both liberal principles and their policy implementation (de Heredia 2018).

More generally, the relationship between liberalism and democracy is complex and does not necessarily involve continuity or identity (Bobbio 1990). Liberalism posits a conception of the state in which the state is considered to have limited powers and functions. Democracy, by contrast, indicates one mode of government in which power is not vested in the hands of a single individual or of a few, but lies with the majority. Accordingly, a liberal state is not necessarily democratic. There are historical instances of liberal states where participation in government was limited to the wealthy classes, as well as cases of illiberal, or partly liberal democratic states where there are limited checks on rulers and thus individual rights are not guaranteed. Thus, liberal democratic regimes can vary considerably depending on whether the emphasis is placed on liberalism or democracy. The emphasis may be placed on the liberal side, thus stressing the importance of autonomy, individual rights, and self-regulating markets, or can be placed on the democratic side, with its focus on popular participation and the attempt to achieve fundamental political and social change (Sørensen 2011: 57–58).

Since liberal peacebuilding became a reference point for international intervention in conflict areas from the early 1990s onwards, its advocates have frequently stressed the importance of rights over democracy, and the prerogatives of intervening actors over the agency of local ones (Paris 2004). External actors are believed to possess the expertise to transplant liberal institutions in fragile states. Rather than understanding institutions as embedded within specific cultural settings, peacebuilders have conceived of institutions as both essentially autonomous from these settings and capable of shaping them. Because the competition spurred by both elections and a market economy can be destabilizing and even trigger violence (Mansfeld and Snyder 2005), some analysts argued in favour of intrusive and long-term forms of intervention further undermining the democratic character of states emerging from civil strife. Fearon and Laitin (2004) proposed the creation of 'new trusteeships'; Krasner (2004) argued in favour of international involvement and control of some domestic governing functions in 'shared sovereignty' arrangements. Perhaps most influentially, Paris (2004) sponsored a policy of Institutionalization before Liberalization (IBL) whereby international actors can suspend democratic processes, impose regulatory liberal frameworks, stabilize fragile states and then move gradually towards liberal forms of market democracy.

Because of peacebuilding's tendency to privilege rights over democracy, critics have argued that liberal peacebuilding was never as 'liberal' as often deemed to be (Chandler 2010). In addition to being illiberal, peacebuilding also frequently protected capitalist or statist interests (Pugh et al. 2008; Selby 2013). While these critical arguments are useful in drawing the attention to the apparent contradiction presented by self-proclaimed liberal agents acting illiberally, they also tend to exaggerate the extent to which liberal interventionism conflicts with liberal norms and practices. To begin with, critical perspectives downplay the extent to which all states, while putatively sovereign and autonomous, in practical terms participate in an international system of norms, monitoring and compliance within an increasingly interconnected world (Sisk 2013: 62–63). In addition, the non-democratic and apparently illiberal nature of western interventionism is not necessarily in contradiction with its liberal principles. Liberalism includes a wide range of perspectives and practices, including the use of coercive tools, which can be selectively adopted and deployed in the process of implementation of liberal policies. From the perspective of external interveners, the development of liberal norms and institutions in nonliberal contexts can necessitate the use of political oppression of nonliberal actors (Jahn 2013: 99). Despite its presumed normative appeal, liberalism has to be enforced.

Unsurprisingly, the relationship between intervening peacebuilding actors and local players and constituencies is inherently difficult. As this book will show, liberal interveners have a paradoxical relationship with domestic elites, who are seen both as indispensable counterparts and obstacles to the implementation of liberal policies. The difficulties of peace implementation have been often explained by the uncompromising attitude of local nationalist leaders who 'capture' the peacebuilding process, undermine liberal goals, and perpetuate patrimonial relationships with their constituencies. In order to satisfy demands of local power-holders, international actors have adopted a pragmatic approach and frequently have compromised their liberal mandates and reduced their transformative ethos (Barnett et al. 2014). Perhaps more importantly, the sense that elites constitute the main problem in states recovering from war has led peacebuilders to adopt a 'problem-solving' attitude and conclude that only a more assertive intervention could 'free' populations from the yoke, keeping them disenfranchised and hostage to narrow political and economic interests.[3]

Not only have elites been frequently singled out as responsible for keeping the peacebuilding process hostage to narrow, vested interests, but also ordinary citizens have shared the blame for their lack of cultural promptness to take advantage of the presumed benefits offered by international actors implementing the peacebuilding agenda. International peacebuilders have identified the 'local' as the key barrier to the goal of transplanting western institutions, norms and practices because of the lack of cultural capacities required for liberalism to take root (Chandler

2017: 31–32). Intervention at the level of civil society thus became necessary to guarantee that the population at large could learn the values of liberal democracy and thus make democratic institutions workable (Donais 2012: 77). This approach stemmed from the disillusionment with the non-liberal other, seen as incapable of acting in a rational way, in particular at the ballot box, and thus requiring international technical expertise to diffuse pluralist and civic values.

Needless to say, this apologetic account of liberal peacebuilding policies has come under close scrutiny. Drawing from Robert Cox's critical theory (Cox 1981), several analysts have criticized the limited problem-solving approaches adopted by policy-makers in the implementation of liberal programmes. These approaches have neglected the power relations and interests underpinning intervention, preferring instead to present policy as neutral or even as reflecting the interests of those intervened upon (Hameiri and Jones 2017; Pugh 2005; Pugh et al. 2008). However, from the viewpoint of the 'beneficiaries'—the subjects of intervention—peacebuilding often looks like neo-colonial practice aimed at legitimizing western interests (Richmond 2016: 10), above all regulatory and controlling concerns vis-à-vis unruly peripheries marginalized by global economic dynamics (Duffield 2007; Robinson 1996). Critics have also highlighted how liberalism's universalizing ethos has ontologically and methodologically prioritized international interveners over local actors and largely neglected domestic agency, in particular if expressed as acts of defiance, resistance or subversion of external frameworks (Richmond 2016). Most damaging for the liberal peacebuilding framework is its empirical record: most peacebuilding intervention did not achieve the objectives of establishing peace and stability nor did they instigate a democratic process (Paris 2004; Woodward 2017). Even when successful at the macro level, peacebuilding did not trickle down to the local level (Autessere 2017). Most commonly, liberal policies, such as the introduction of elections and structural adjustment programmes, contributed to the consolidation of new nonliberal institutions and to the generation of new inequalities and of social and economic crises.

1.3   ENTERING THE BALKANS

The Balkans represent a crucial case in the application of the liberal peacebuilding doctrine and related debates and counter-debates. International peacebuiliding in the Balkans has involved several international organizations (in addition to the UN, NATO, and the EU, most notably the World Bank, the International Monetary Fund, the Organization for Security and Cooperation in Europe, the Council of Europe, and the United Nations specialized agencies), bilateral donors (primarily, but not exclusively, from Europe and North America), and a countless number of international NGOs (Paris 2004: 22–35). The violent break-up of Yugoslavia and the interventions that followed it allowed all of these actors to implement the new peacebuilding doctrine on an unprecedented, vast scale. After the establishment of the UN mission in Cambodia in 1992–1993, the UN mandate was further extended both geographically and substantively: the creation of new protectorate powers in Bosnia-Herzegovina, Kosovo, and East Timor constituted the 'logical conclusion' (Chandler 2017: 51) of the expansionist drive of liberal internationalism.

As with the UN, also for NATO the Balkans represented the region where the new interventionist drive was both rationalized as necessary and vigorously implemented. NATO's involvement in the area has been a 'central hallmark of the transformative efforts made by the alliance in the last twenty years' (Mulchinock 2017: 141). NATO's new 'strategic concept', presented at the Alliance 50th Anniversary Summit in Washington in April 1999, certified NATO's willingness to expand both the geographical area of interest, and the circumstances requiring its involvement. No longer was NATO limited to ensure the protection of its members according to the conditions described in art. Five of its Charter, but rather NATO took on the self-assigned task of intervening to provide stability anywhere it deemed necessary.

At the fringes of the EU, the Balkans constituted a good arena to apply the new interventionist drive. Initially, international actors were drawn into the region reluctantly (Ramet 2005). During the violent process of Yugoslav dissolution, and the resulting wars in Slovenia, Croatia and in Bosnia-Herzegovina, where about 100,000 people died as a result of the war, the international community engaged in a number of mediation and humanitarian efforts, but resisted the use of force for fear of being drawn into open warfare with any of the conflict parties. Only in the summer of 1995, after news about the massacres in the eastern Bosnian town of Srebrenica, where more than 8000 Bosniaks, mainly men and boys, were killed in cold blood, NATO bombed Bosnian Serb positions around the city of Sarajevo. The changing military balance on the ground, together with NATO's assertiveness, created the conditions for the negotiation of a peace agreement. The details of the agreement were hammered out at the Wright-Patterson Airforce base in Dayton, Ohio, between 1 and 21 November 1995. In a few weeks, about 60,000 NATO troops were deployed to guarantee post-war military stabilization, while dozens of international organizations and NGOs initiated, or strengthened, their operations in the country.

International organizations were called on to support the implementation of a peace agreement that contained difficult-to-reconcile contradictions: it simultaneously endorsed group rights and the ethnicization of territory, while recognizing the individual right of displaced persons to return home; it preserved the formal territorial integrity of the country, but divided it into semi-autonomous 'entities;' and, most importantly from the perspective of intervening actors, it allowed the same ethnonationalist elites responsible for the war to maintain power as a result of the organization of rapid elections (Belloni 2008).

After the termination of the war in Bosnia-Herzegovina, rising tensions in both Kosovo and Macedonia motivated international diplomacy to further extend its intervention in the region. In Kosovo, the Albanian majority of the population was marginalized and excluded from political and economic life by Serb dominated institutions. Starting from early 1996 rising tensions between Albanians and Serbs escalated in a cycle of attacks and retaliation. In March 1999, NATO began a bombing campaign against Serb strategic positions both in Kosovo and Serbia. After 78 days of NATO's bombing, Security Council Resolution 1244 marked the end of the war. The Resolution re-affirmed the sovereignty and territorial integrity of the Federal Republic of Yugoslavia, while calling for 'substantial autonomy and meaningful self-determination for Kosovo', and established the United Nations Interim Administration Mission in Kosovo (UNMIK) with a mandate, among other issues, to facilitate a political process to determine Kosovo's future status (Bellamy 2002).

The war in Kosovo exacerbated ethnic tensions in neighbouring Macedonia. In early 2001 Albanian rebels attacked Macedonian police installations, provoking a military reaction by the government in Skopje. A timely diplomatic intervention by the EU contributed to defusing tensions and to supporting the reaching of a settlement between the parties (Schneckener 2002). With the Ohrid Framework Agreement, the Macedonian government committed itself to guarantee the rights of the Albanian minority. The Albanian language was recognized as one of the two official languages of the country, and the participation of

Albanian citizens in public administration, the police and the army were improved. By the early 2000s large peacebuilding missions operated in Bosnia-Herzegovina and Kosovo, while all other states emerging from the process of Yugoslav dissolution were subjected to extensive external economic and diplomatic influence, in particular as a result of the EU's growing role in the area.

1.4   Peacebuilding's Three Phases

Against this background, the following chapters focus on the implementation of the liberal peacebuilding paradigm. This paradigm is adopted, implemented, contested and/or rejected by a number of different actors, including international organizations, NGOs, domestic elites, and ordinary citizens. Needless to say, this multiplicity makes it difficult, perhaps impossible, to examine exhaustively the role and agency of all actors involved in the peacebuilding process taking place in the region for over two decades. Accordingly, the book is divided into three parts, each focusing primarily on a set of actors, while maintaining the liberal peacebuilding paradigm as overall theme.

Part I discusses the rise of peacebuilding intervention since the signing of the Dayton Peace Agreement (DPA) in November 1995, which ended the brutal 1992–1995 Bosnian war. It considers a range of actors, but concentrates primarily on the Office of the High Representative in Bosnia-Herzegovina and UNMIK in Kosovo. Much has been written on this initial period, characterized by the establishment of de facto protectorates in both countries. Despite some achievements in pacifying these troubled areas, peacebuilding intervention came with a cost. Several scholars have highlighted, among other issues, how external assertiveness has led to the creation of domestically unresponsive and scarcely legitimate institutions (i.e. Chandler 2010). Peacebuilders' focus on democratization through elections and marketization has contributed to both the state's capture by ethno-nationalist elites and the dismantling of the state's assets (Keil 2018). Rather than rehearsing these quite well-documented developments, this first part focuses on the largely neglected but central role of corruption in entrenching the rule of ethno-nationalist parties. It shows how, contrary to the rhetoric of peacebuilding agencies, international intervention through its focus on 'stability' has legitimated both the rise of ethno-nationalists to power and the closure of any political space amenable to civic alternatives. While contributing to guarantee the structural conditions that favoured mismanagement, clientelism and corruption, international peacebuilding agencies have attempted to address the symptoms of flawed domestic governance systems through civil society building programmes.

Part II focuses on the role played by the EU in advancing the peacebuilding agenda. In the early 2000s, the EU committed itself to accept Western Balkan states as potential candidates for EU accession and, as a result, became the key international peacebuilding player in the region. Since 2002 the positions of the High Representative of the International Community and EU Special Representative in Bosnia-Herzegovina have been filled by a single international official with closely related mandates. After Kosovo's declaration of independence in February 2008, the EU adopted extensive supervisory responsibilities. In addition to raising its diplomatic status both in Bosnia-Herzegovina and Kosovo, through its promise of membership the EU hoped to provide a positive reforming influence in all other Western Balkan states. The basic template of institutional reform throughout the region became the Stabilisation and Association process with the EU (Pippan 2004). The EU's regional approach aimed at improving the cross-border relationships among former enemies, while providing concrete support for the restructuring along liberal lines of domestic political, economic and judicial institutions. Most significantly, the EU's promise of enlargement drastically changed the relationship between international interveners and domestic political actors. Rather than blatantly imposing policy frameworks on recalcitrant domestic leaders, as during the initial peacebuilding phase, the new EU approach was expected to stimulate domestically driven reforms. The broader peacebuilding goals involving democratization and marketization objectives did not change but they were tailored to meet the benchmarks established by the EU enlargement process. Reporting, monitoring and self-discipline were elevated to essential components of this peacebuilding phase. The EU's celebrated 'normative' or 'transformative' power (Grabbe 2006), in addition to a large amount of economic aid, contributed to several positive developments in the region, in particular by sustaining post-war reconstruction, the development of infrastructure projects, and the establishment of regional links and new security structures. On balance, however, numerous obstacles remained to hinder further peacebuilding progress. Above all, the EU approach proved unable to provide domestic leaders with sufficient incentives to support the democratization process and did not meaningfully involve citizens in the peacebuilding transition.

Part III examines citizens' (re)action to and views about the effects of liberal interventionism. Since the early 2010s, it has become increasingly evident that aspiring new EU member states have developed various forms of Euroscepticism which, in turn, have paved the way for geopolitical competitors such as Russia to play a more assertive role. In addition, growing dissatisfaction with political, economic and social conditions across Western Balkan states have contributed to the emergence of various forms of protests. Citizens have denounced the costs of the seemingly endless peacebuilding transition and have demanded the defence of the commons (that is, cultural and natural resources accessible to all members of a society) and the fulfilment of long-neglected citizens' needs. In response, the EU has reacted by (re)affirming its commitment to the status quo dominated by ethno-political leaders while attempting to re-launch 'a credible enlargement perspective' for the region (European Commission 2018). Although this approach achieved some short-term success, in particular by containing migration flows, in the long run it could actually undermine stability by fuelling popular discontent, damaging the appeal of European institutions (which are seen by pro-democracy movements in the region as an impediment to democratization) and thus opening the way for other geopolitical actors such as Russia to gain further influence.

Each of these three Parts is titled after a city which, respectively, epitomizes the rise of peacebuilding, followed by stalemate and then fall. Part I is named 'Dayton', the city which marks the beginning of large scale peacebuilding intervention in the region; Part II is called 'Brussels' to symbolize the beginning of the transformative expectations which have accompanied the process of EU enlargement in the region; Part III is named 'Tuzla', the Bosnian town where large scale protests against governmental inefficiency, poor governance and corruption broke out in February 2014. While different actors are the primary focus of each Part, their actions are all evaluated against the overarching liberal peacebuilding framework. In particular, corruption and civil society—both key components of the liberal peacebuilding framework—are recurring themes across all chapters, thus providing the focus around which the analysis is structured. As of international actors, their role in the rise (Dayton), stalemate (Brussels) and fall (Tuzla) of peacebuilding is ultimately driven by the attempt to manage the existing reality rather than transforming it, while experimenting with a variety of more or less intrusive intervention tools.

In moving from one phase to another, international peacebuilders have engaged in 'experimentalist governance' under conditions of prolonged uncertainty and crisis. While experimentalism is deeply rooted in any political activity, the concept underscores the importance of procedural open-endedness and the desire to overcome frustration about policy failure. Sabel and Zeitlin define experimentalist governance as 'a recursive process of provisional goal setting and revision based on learning from the comparison of alternative approaches to advancing them in different contexts' (2012b: 411). Experimentalist governance involves four elements linked in an iterative cycle. First, broad framework goals and measures for gauging their achievements are provisionally established by a combination of 'central' and 'local' units in consultation with relevant civil society stakeholders. Second, local units are given broad discretion to pursue these goals as they see fit. Local/lower-level units have sufficient autonomy in implementing framework rules. Third, in return for this autonomy, they report regularly on their performance and, if they are not making good progress against the agreed indicators, they have to show they are taking appropriate corrective measures. Finally, the goals, metrics and decision-making procedures are periodically revised in response to the problems and possibilities uncovered by the review process, and the cycle repeats (Sabel and Zeitlin 2012b: 413).

Examples of experimentalist governance can be found in many jurisdictions, including the United States and Europe, in domains ranging from the provision of public services to the regulation of food and air-traffic safety as well as in transnational regimes regulating, for instance, global trade in food (Sabel and Zeitlin 2012a). In addition, experimentalist governance can be applied to peacebuilding interventions. First, peacebuilding interventions develop both broad frameworks and joint efforts involving authorities at different territorial levels (although supranational authorities may predominate over national and subnational ones). These frameworks comprise of a set of consultation arrangements, decision-making procedures, and performance expectations. Second, peacebuilding interventions give both public actors and, to an extent, private ones, the opportunity to organize, to defend and to promote their own interests. Crucially, while supranational authorities may possess more power and leverage to influence the peacebuilding process, national and subnational levels have some discretion in terms of implementation, and thus they can delay, obstruct, ignore, subvert, or otherwise shape policy. Third, peacebuilding interventions aim at supporting the implementation of a number of closely related policies, while fostering political responsibility and diagnostic monitoring. The peacebuilding framework generates procedures and requests for responsible behaviour against (often changing) benchmarks. Failure with meeting these benchmarks and disappointment with policy implementation motivate a re-evaluation of both the broader peacebuilding framework and the policies composing it. Accordingly, based on the experience with the implementation, the framework is altered and adjusted, and the cycle can repeat itself. As a result, peacebuilding is inherently adaptive and pragmatic and has to be viewed as a process involving elements of both continuity and change (see, in general, Pospisil 2019).

The three Parts of this book testify to the experimentalist character of peacebuilding intervention in the Balkans. Since the mid-1990s, peacebuilding has developed on the basis of a general liberal framework involving the transition from authoritarian institutions to democratic and accountable ones, as well as a passage from a state-led to a market economy. While this framework has involved multiple political and territorial levels, international institutions generally maintained a decisive authority in shaping policy contents, decision-making and implementation procedures and in inducing expectations about what constitutes proper behaviour. Both public and private actors, including extra-legal ones, have mobilized to influence the process according to their own interests and, when they considered it as necessary, they obstructed or otherwise delayed policy implementation. Although domestic political elites, empowered by their international counterparts, have played a key role in this process, citizens have also mobilized and expressed their views and needs, most notably by protesting against the socio-economic structures that emerged as a result of peacebuilding intervention, or by leaving the region in search of better opportunities and living standards.

1.5   Overview

The next chapter examines the key characteristics of each of the three peacebuilding phases and accounts for the debate that the obstacles in the implementation of the liberal peacebuilding in the Balkans have prompted. Then, the book's three parts assess the evolution of peacebuilding in the region. While this evolution is sustained by forms of experimentalist governance, there is no systematic attempt to test in detail the dynamics of experimentalism, by specifying the influence of each intervening actor and the debates and dilemmas of external intervention. Rather, experimentalism is used as a heuristic device to highlight the adaptive character of peacebuilding, including elements of both continuity and change as well as resilience in the face of failure (Pospisil 2019).

Part I ('Dayton') discusses the first peacebuilding period. Chapter 3 shows how the spread of corruption in both Bosnia-Herzegovina and Kosovo has been implicitly legitimized by international actors who have pressured local parties to accept the formal architecture of good governance, including anti-corruption legislation, while turning a blind eye to those extra-legal structures and practices that were perceived as functional to political stability. Chapter 4 zooms in on Bosnia-Herzegovina in order to examine the failure to support the development of domestic civil society, including NGOs working as corruption watchdogs.

Part II ('Brussels') focuses on the peacebuilding role of the EU. Chapter 5 examines the reasons why, by the early 2000s, both analysts and policy-makers believed that the EU could play a positive peacebuilding role in the Balkans by putting forward European integration as a strategic approach to solve the region's problems. Brief illustrations are drawn from Bosnia-Herzegovina, Kosovo and Macedonia. Chapter 6 examines economic, security and political developments in the Western Balkans throughout the year 2000, when the EU became the key peacebuilding player in the region.

Part III ('Tuzla') investigates the decline of peacebuilding. Chapter 7 examines domestic views about the EU, arguing that a growing level of Euroscepticism has helped Russia to emerge as a competitor for influence. Chapter 8 examines citizens' protests against corruption, poor governance, and difficult socio-economic conditions, with particular attention to the February 2014 uprising in Bosnia-Herzegovina. Not only did these protests challenge both domestic ethno-national leaders and their international counterparts, but also they called into question those NGOs nurtured by peacebuilding donors, and widely considered locally as belonging to an elite detached from common citizens, which were analysed in Chapter 4. In order to suggest the close connection between these two chapters devoted to Bosnia-Herzegovina I describe peacebuilding actors in Chapter 4 as engaged in building a 'first Bosnia' while illustrating the events in Chapter 8 as resulting from a 'second Bosnia' composed of ordinary citizens (including the unemployed, the elderly, and the youth) who have been marginalized in the course of more than two decades of peacebuilding.

These two chapters focus on Bosnia-Herzegovina because this country is a key test case to examine the liberal peacebuilding framework and its implementation over time. Not only is this the first instance where peacebuilding has been applied on a large scale, but also it is the state where citizens have most violently protested against the endless peacebuilding transition. To most accounts, it remains also a dangerously volatile state, whose stability is important for the entire region. According to Marko Attila Hoare, who expresses a widely held perspective among analysts, 'If Bosnia-Herzegovina collapses, the entire order in the Western Balkans could collapse with it' (Hoare 2010: 50).

Having examined the rise and fall of peacebuilding, the concluding chapter goes back to a regional perspective in order to discuss growing illiberal tendencies. The EU's acceptance of semi-authoritarian regimes in the region has been described as 'stabilitocracy' (BiEPAG 2017). The chapter takes this analysis further by showing how the EU's current emphasis on promoting resilience may further downplay the transformative ethos of the liberal peacebuilding paradigm.

Throughout the book, the terms 'international community', 'liberal peacebuilders', and 'external interveners' are used interchangeably. In essence, these are short-end expressions to describe primarily European and North American states, multilateral political, economic and security organizations, as well as international NGOs engaged in the process of building peace in unruly world peripheries. Needless to say, both the 'international' and 'the local' are composed of a multiplicity of actors with often conflicting agendas, interests, needs, and values. Moreover, the interaction between the international and the local, the outside and inside, and the related feedback loops, blur the distinction between the internal and external (Björkdahl and Höglund 2013).

However, the international–local divide still has analytical weight, particularly in identifying distinct roles within the peacebuilding process. When I refer to the 'international' I do not endorse its supposed liberalism; as the remainder of this book will make clear, external actors often pursue very realist agendas that have very little to do with liberalism and its values. I simply suggest that liberal norms remain the normative reference for external interveners, even when these norms are violated in practice. Similarly, the 'local' includes a wide range of different actors, such as political and economic elites, NGOs, youth, war veterans, the elderly, the unemployed, and so on. While some of these actors have very nationalist and conservative views, others strive to implement liberal peacebuilding values such as equality, non-discrimination and account-ability. It is precisely the contention of this book that the binary inter-national/liberal vs. local/illiberal is misplaced. Not only do international actors frequently compromise their liberal ideals, as mentioned above, but also, in an attempt to maintain stability, they can subscribe to unwrit-ten pacts with local authoritarian elites.

Finally, it is worth recalling how international actors have repeatedly defined, classified and categorized the region where they intervene. Since the early twentieth century, as a result of the 1912–1913 Balkan wars, the term 'Balkans' came to be increasingly associated with lawlessness, primitivism, and violence (Todorova 1997). By the early 2000s, however, the EU began referring to the region as the 'Western Balkans', essentially to indicate the former Yugoslav states, minus Slovenia, plus Albania, en route to European integration. Because the word 'Balkan' still carries implied negative connotations, some analysts prefer to use the expres-sion Southeastern Europe. In the following chapters when referring expressively to the EU enlargement policy towards the region I adopt the administrative term 'Western Balkans'. Otherwise, I use 'Balkans' and 'Southeastern Europe' interchangeably, even though I am aware of the disagreements about exactly what these rubrics refer to. With these terms, I refer to European countries that were at one time part of the Ottoman Empire. Likewise, I use 'European Union', 'Europe' and the 'Old Continent' interchangeably, both to make the prose more readable and in recognition of the fact that the EU has effectively occupied the identity space of Europe as a political community.

Notes

1. While Doyle focused his analysis on Kant, it was Giuseppe Mazzini, the father of the Italian Risorgimento, who expressed the idea of a separated 'democratic peace' less ambiguously, theorizing its emergence from the initial alliance and gradual deepening of a federation among democracies (Recchia 2013: 244–245).
2. For a scathing assessment of liberal theories of peace from a realist perspec-tive, see, Mearsheimer (2018: 188–216).
3. Accordingly, Timothy Donais (2012: 15) argued that peacebuilding's habit-ual focus on capacity building should be combined with capacity disabling, that is, 'efforts to disable, marginalize, or co-opt those domestic politi-cal structures that stand in the way of the effective establishment of new institutions'.

REFERENCES

Autessere, S. (2017). International peacebuilding and local success: Assumptions and effectiveness. *International Studies Review, 1*(1), 114–132.

Barnett, M. (2016). Peacebuilding and paternalism. In T. Held, U. Schneckener, & T. Debiel (Eds.), *Peacebuilding in crisis: Rethinking paradigms and practices of transnational cooperation* (pp. 23–40). London and New York: Routledge.

Barnett, M., Fang, S., & Zürcher, C. (2014). Compromised peacebuilding. *International Studies Quarterly, 58*(3), 608–620.

Beck, U. (1992). *Risk society: Towards a new modernity.* London: Sage.

Bellamy, A. J. (2002). *Kosovo and international society.* Houndmills: Palgrave.

Belloni, R. (2008). Civil society in war-to-democracy transitions. In A. K. Jarstad & T. D. Sisk (Eds.), *From war to democracy: Dilemmas of peacebuilding* (pp. 182–210). Cambridge: Cambridge University Press.

Belloni, R. (2016). Peace in Europe. In S. Pogodda, O. P. Richmond, & J. Ramovic (Eds.), *The Palgrave handbook of disciplinary and regional approaches to peace* (pp. 411–423). Houndmills: Palgrave.

Bieber, F. (2018). Patterns of competitive authoritarianism in the Western Balkans. *East European Politics, 34*(3), 337–354.

BiEPAG (Balkans in Europe Policy Advisory Group). (2017). *The crisis of democracy in the Western Balkans: An anatomy of stabilitocracy and the limits of EU democracy promotion.* Graz: BiEPAG.

Bishai, L. S. (2004). Liberal empire. *Journal of International Relations and Development, 7*(1), 48–72.

Björkdahl, A., & Höglund, K. (2013). Precarious peacebuilding: Friction in global-local encounters. *Peacebuilding, 1*(3), 289–299.

Bobbio, N. (1990). *Liberalism and democracy* (M. Ryle & K. Soper, Trans.). London and New York: Verso.

Boutros-Ghali, B. (1992, June 17). *An agenda for peace: Preventive diplomacy, peacemaking and peacekeeping* (Report of the Secretary-General UN Doc. A/47/277-S24111).

Brown, M. E., Lynn-Jones, S. M., & Miller, S. E. (Eds.). (1996). *Debating the democratic peace.* Cambridge: MIT Press.

Chandler, D. (2010). *International statebuilding: The rise of post-liberal governance.* London: Routledge.

Chandler, D. (2017). *Peacebuilding: The twenty years' crisis, 1997–2017.* Houndmills: Palgrave.

Cooper, N., Turner, M., & Pugh, M. (2011). The end of history and the last peacebuilder: A reply to Roland Paris. *Review of International Studies, 37*(4), 1995–2007.

Cox, R. W. (1981). Social forces, states and world orders. *Millennium: Journal of International Studies, 10*(2), 126–155.

de Heredia, M. I. (2018). The conspicuous absence of class and privilege in the study of resistance in peacebuilding contexts. *International Peacekeeping, 25*(3), 325–348.

Donais, T. (2012). *Peacebuilding and local ownership: Post-conflict consensus-building.* Abingdon: Routledge.

Doyle, M. (1983). Kant, liberal legacies and foreign affairs. *Philosophy & Public Affairs, 12*(3), 205–235.

Doyle, M. (1997). *Ways of war and peace.* New York: W. W. Norton.

Duffield, M. (2007). *Development, security and unending war: Governing the world of peoples.* Cambridge: Polity.

European Commission. (2018). *A credible enlargement perspective for an enhanced EU engagement with the Western Balkans.* Strasbourg, 6.2.2018, COM (2018) 65 final.

Evans, M. (Ed.). (2001). *The Edinburgh companion to contemporary liberalism.* Edinburgh: Edinburgh University Press.

Fearon, J. D., & Laitin, D. (2004). Neotrusteeships and the problem of weak states. *International Security, 28*(4), 5–43.

Grabbe, H. (2006). *The EU's transformative power: Europeanization through conditionality in Central and Eastern Europe.* Houndmills: Palgrave.

Grimm, S., & Mathis, O. L. (2015). Stability first, development second, democracy third: The European Union's policy towards post-conflict Western Balkans, 1991–2010. *Europe-Asia Studies, 67*(6), 916–947.

Hameiri, S., & Jones, L. (2017). Beyond hybridity to the politics of scale: International intervention and 'local' politics. *Development and Change, 48*(1), 54–77.

Hoare, M. A. (2010). Bosnia-Herzegovina—The crumbling Balkan keystone. *Democracy and Security in Southeastern Europe, 1*(1), 50–55.

Hobson, C. (2012). Liberal democracy and beyond: Extending the sequencing debate. *International Political Science Review, 33*(4), 441–454.

Jabri, V. (2013). Peacebuilding, the local and the international: A colonial or a postcolonial rationality? *Peacebuilding, 1*(1), 3–16.

Jahn, B. (2013). *Liberal internationalism: Theory, history, practice.* Houndmills: Palgrave.

Jarstad, A. K., & Sisk, T. D. (Eds.). (2008). *From war to democracy: Dilemmas of peacebuilding.* Cambridge: Cambridge University Press.

Joshi, M., Lee, S. Y., & Mac Ginty, R. (2014). How just liberal is the liberal peace? *International Peacekeeping, 21*(3), 364–389.

Keil, S. (2018). The business of state capture and the rise of authoritarianism in Kosovo, Macedonia, Montenegro and Serbia. *Southeastern Europe, 42*(1), 59–82.

Keohane, R. O. (2003). Political authority after intervention: Gradations in sovereignty. In J. L. Holzgrefe & R. O. Keohane (Eds.), *Humanitarian intervention: Ethical, legal and political dilemmas* (pp. 275–298). Cambridge: Cambridge University Press.

Krasner, S. D. (2004). Sharing sovereignty: New institutions for collapsed and failing states. *International Security, 29*(2), 85–120.

Langer, A., & Brown, G. K. (Eds.). (2016). *Building sustainable peace: Timing and sequencing of post-conflict reconstruction and peacebuilding*. Oxford: Oxford University Press.

Mac Ginty, R. (2015). *Routledge handbook of peacebuilding*. Abingdon: Routledge.

Mansfeld, E. D., & Snyder, J. (2005). *Electing to fight: Why emerging democracies go to war*. Cambridge and London: MIT Press.

Mearsheimer, J. J. (2018). *The great delusion: Liberal dreams and international realities*. New Haven and London: Yale University Press.

Mujanović, J. (2018). *Hunger and fury: The crisis of democracy in the Balkans*. London: Hurst & Company.

Mulchinock, N. (2017). *NATO and the Western Balkans: From neutral spectator to proactive peacemaker*. Houndmills: Palgrave.

NSS. (2002). *The national security strategy of the United States of America*. Washington, DC: The White House.

Paris, R. (2004). *At war's end: Building peace after civil conflict*. Cambridge: Cambridge University Press.

Paris, R. (2010). Saving liberal peacebuilding. *Review of International Studies, 36*(2), 337–365.

Pippan, C. (2004). The rocky road to Europe: The EU's stabilisation and association process for the Western Balkans and the principle of conditionality. *European Foreign Affairs Review, 9*(2), 219–245.

Pospisil, J. (2019). *Peace in political unsettlement: Beyond solving conflict*. Houndmills: Palgrave.

Pugh, M. (2005). The political economy of peacebuilding: A critical theory perspective. *International Journal of Peace Studies, 10*(2), 23–42.

Pugh, M., Cooper, N., & Turner, M. (Eds.). (2008). *Whose peace? Critical perspectives on the political economy of peacebuilding*. Basingstoke: Palgrave.

Ramet, S. P. (2005). *Thinking about Yugoslavia: Scholarly debates about the Yugoslav breakup and the wars in Bosnia and Kosovo*. Cambridge: Cambridge University Press.

Recchia, S. (2013). The origins of liberal Wilsonianism: Giuseppe Mazzini on regime change and humanitarian intervention. In S. Recchia & J. M. Welsh (Eds.), *Just and unjust military intervention: European thinkers from Vitoria to Mill* (pp. 237–262). Cambridge: Cambridge University Press.

Richardson, J. (2001). *Contending liberalisms in world politics*. Boulder, CO: Lynne Rienner.

Richmond, O. P. (2011). *A post-liberal peace*. London: Routledge.

Richmond, O. P. (2014). *Failed statebuilding: Intervention, the state and the dynamics of peace formation*. New Heaven and London: Yale University Press.

Richmond, O. P. (2016). *Peace formation and political order in conflict affected societies*. New York: Oxford University Press.

Robinson, W. I. (1996). *Promoting polyarchy: Globalization, US intervention, and hegemony.* Cambridge: Cambridge University Press.

Russett, B. (1996). Why democratic peace? In M. Brown, S. Lynn-Jones, & S. E. Miller (Eds.), *Debating the democratic peace* (pp. 58–81). Cambridge: MIT Press.

Sabel, C. F., & Zeitlin, J. (2012a). Experimentalist governance. In D. Levi-Faur (Ed.), *Oxford handbook of governance* (pp. 169–183). Oxford: Oxford University Press.

Sabel, C. F., & Zeitlin, J. (2012b). Experimentalism in the EU: Common ground and persistent differences. *Regulation and Governance, 6*(3), 410–426.

Schneckener, U. (2002). *Developing and applying EU crisis management: Test case Macedonia.* Flensburg: European Centre for Minority Issues.

Selby, J. (2013). The myth of liberal peace-building. *Conflict, Security & Development, 13*(1), 57–86.

Sheftel, A. (2011). 'Monument to the international community, from the grateful citizens of Sarajevo': Dark humour as counter-memory in post-conflict Bosnia-Herzegovina. *Memory Studies, 5*(2), 145–164.

Sisk, T. D. (2013). *Statebuilding.* Cambridge: Polity.

Sørensen, G. (2011). *A liberal world order in crisis: Choosing between imposition and restraint.* Ithaca and London: Cornell University Press.

Todorova, M. (1997). *Imagining the Balkans.* Oxford: Oxford University Press.

Williams, M. C. (2001). The discipline of the democratic peace: Kant, liberalism and the social construction of security communities. *European Journal of International Relations, 7*(4), 525–553.

Woodward, S. L. (2017). *The ideology of failed states: Why intervention fails.* Cambridge: Cambridge University Press.

CHAPTER 2

The Evolution of Peacebuilding

2.1 Introduction

This chapter traces the evolution of liberal peacebuilding in the Balkans. It introduces the three main peacebuilding phases experienced by Balkan states since the mid-1990s onwards. In the first phase, the international community intervened *en mass* to pursue a radical reform agenda aimed at restructuring political, economic and social life along liberal lines. This agenda focused predominantly, but not exclusively, on Bosnia-Herzegovina and Kosovo, arguably the most vulnerable and politically unstable states in the region.[1] Liberal peacebuilders did not hesitate to impose legislation, remove elected officials, and establish vetting mechanisms and institutions to enforce their views on domestic actors.

In the second phase, starting from the early 2000s, the EU began to play an increasingly prominent role. Through its promise of future membership, the EU became the most important political actor not only for those states experiencing large-scale peacebuilding interventions, such as Bosnia-Herzegovina and Kosovo, but for all Balkan states. While the EU remained firmly committed to the general liberal peacebuilding framework discussed in Chapter 1, it put forward a different method of intervention based not so much on external imposition, but on domestic participation and responsibility (Denti 2018).

By the early 2010s a third phase, still ongoing, has begun. Although the EU remains the most consequential external actor, the interests,

R. Belloni, *The Rise and Fall of Peacebuilding in the Balkans*, Rethinking Peace and Conflict Studies, https://doi.org/10.1007/978-3-030-14424-1_2

views, needs, actions and strategies of domestic players, including the politico-economic elites, social movements, and marginalized groups such as the youth, the unemployed and the elderly, have been acquiring a more visible presence within the peacebuilding process. In particular, marginalized groups have contested domestic and international authorities for their responsibilities in the persisting economic and social crisis which affects the region and have challenged the real or perceived failures of peacebuilding. However, in general they have not rejected liberal political and economic principles. Rather, they have demanded that the implementation of these principles does not benefit only a small clique of people well positioned to take advantage from the laissez-faire post-war environment, but that they take into account the needs and expectations of the population at large.

The international community moved from one phase to the other not based on accomplishment, but on failures (Woodward 2017; Visoka 2017). In turn, each failure provided the entry point for pragmatic transitions (Pospisil 2019). The workings of experimentalist governance transformed disappointment and frustration with international intervention into a search for a different approach which later created unintended consequences and new exploration for alternatives. In this process, new actors emerged or gained prominence. While in the first phase multilateral institutions such as the Office of the High Representative in Bosnia-Herzegovina and the UN Mission in Kosovo (UNMIK) prevailed, in the second phase the EU set the boundaries within which the search for sustainable peace was carried out. By the early 2010s, inefficient and unresponsive domestic institutions and persisting socio-economic problems opened the way to a third phase where a variety of domestic actors (often with competing views and mobilization strategies) challenged the shortcomings of EU-led peacebuilding and engaged in both open and hidden forms of resistance. As a result, the entire peacebuilding process in the Balkans has been driven by the difficulties with delivering those benefits promised by external interveners, by the related critique of prevailing approaches and practices, as well as by the quest for alternative avenues of intervention.

2.2   Peacebuilding's Rise, Stalemate, and Fall

The Balkans have provided a crucial test case for liberal peacebuilding policies. Since the early 1990s, international interveners have been involved massively to support the transition from war to peace, from authoritarian to democratic institutions and from a state-led to a market economy. The perception that western powers failed to prevent the outbreak of violence and to intervene effectively to stop the bloodshed in Bosnia-Herzegovina in the first half of the 1990s has contributed to a large-scale political, economic and financial international commitment to the post-war peacebuilding process. In addition, the cross-border consequences on European states of instability in the region have further prompted the deployment of all available tools to stabilize the Balkans and bring them within the European political and economic mainstream.

From the early stages of their involvement, international interveners engaged in forms of experimentalist governance (Sabel and Zeitlin 2010). While experimentalism has been originally developed to examine EU internal governance mechanisms with reference to framework goals as varied as full employment, social inclusion, 'good water status' and a unified energy grid, among others, it can also be applied to peacebuilding intervention in the Balkans. Indeed, experimentalist governance is occasioned by three scope conditions—strategic uncertainty, interdependence and the polyarchic distribution of power (Sabel and Zeitlin 2010: 2) —which are well in place in the peacebuilding governance system in the Balkans. Intervening actors established peacebuilding goals such as developing democratic institutions, privatizing public economic assets, supporting domestic civil society, and encouraging the establishment of free media, together with measures for assessing their realization. Lower level local units, including governments, ministries, and bureaucracies were given freedom to pursue these goals as they deemed appropriate. At the same time, they had to report regularly on their performance and participate in peer reviews and monitoring exercises led by external interveners. Finally, the framework goals and decision-making procedures were periodically revised by the actors who initially established them, if necessary augmented by new participants whose views were seen as indispensable for the realization of the objectives.

Experimentalist governance draws attention to the provisional and developmental character of the political process, its procedural open-endedness, and actors' development of institutional innovation as a result of disappointments with policy implementation. In the case of peacebuilding in the Balkans, three main phases of the experimentalist governance cycle, corresponding to the rise, stalemate and fall of liberal peacebuilding, can be identified. Below the general characteristics of each phase are recognized, and their key features are examined, while later chapters discuss each phase in detail.

2.2.1   Phase 1: Dayton, or Liberal Imposition

Liberal peacebuilding evolved rather chaotically after the end of the war in Bosnia-Herzegovina in late 1995. In the second half of the 1990s international organizations, bilateral donors and international NGOs raced to Bosnia-Herzegovina to contribute to its stabilization. NATO intervention in defence of the rights of Albanians in Kosovo in 1999 provided an additional entry point to reform domestic institutions and societal structures along liberal lines. After a first large-scale operation in Cambodia in the early 1990s, with the peacebuilding missions in Bosnia-Herzegovina and in Kosovo, 'peacebuilding had... properly come of age' (Chandler 2017: 63). The UN and NATO placed both Bosnia-Herzegovina and Kosovo under international administration for an indeterminate period of time. They assertively imposed institutions and policies even by suspending democratic procedures. They justified the use of undemocratic means as indispensable in order to achieve broad liberal goals such as the establishment of democratic structures and the strengthening of domestic sovereignty, the development of market economies, and the defence of human rights and multi-ethnic coexistence.

In pursuing these objectives, a loose hodgepodge of international organizations, powerful states, and international NGOs contributed to an extension of governing authority on all aspects of life. The 1995 Dayton Peace Agreement (DPA) provided the High Representative of the International Community in Bosnia-Herzegovina with the 'final authority in theatre regarding interpretation of this agreement' (Annex 10, art. 5) and contributed to make the country 'the world capital of interventionism' (Donais 2012: 85). This clause offered the legal and political basis to establish a de facto protectorate in December 1997 through the adoption of the so-called Bonn Powers. International actors assumed unprecedented prerogatives which extended beyond security matters to involve civil and governing responsibilities, including the right to remove from office elected local officials, effectively transforming the country into a 'protectorate democracy' (Pugh 2001). For instance, Lord Paddy Ashdown made use of the Bonn powers more than 400 times during his four years as High Representative of the International Community (Chivvis 2010: 62). The DPA also institutionalized forms of 'shared sovereignty' between external actors and domestic institutions, most notably through the establishment of institutions composed by both Bosnian nationals and foreign experts (Belloni 2008).

Similarly, the UN Interim Mission to Kosovo (UNMIK) was established in 1999 to provide the region with the safety and security to administer itself. Between 1999 and 2008, while UNMIK was engaged in building political institutions, the EU focused on shaping Kosovo's economic system. After the declaration of independence in February 2008, Kosovo's authorities invited the EU to deploy a rule of law mission. The mandate of the EULEX Mission included both non-executive and executive tasks, such as the fight against high-level organized crime and court rulings by EULEX judges (Dijkstra 2011).

In both Bosnia-Herzegovina and Kosovo, international administrations were granted extensive powers to shape the peace process and build domestic institutions. For liberal peacebuilders assertive intervention in places such as Bosnia-Herzegovina and Kosovo were legitimized by the public goods they provided, above all 'good governance' and greater respect for human rights (Ignatieff 2003). Paradoxically, in order to provide these public goods, international administrations relied heavily on the same ethno-nationalist leaders whose commitment to the peacebuilding process was dubious. In Bosnia-Herzegovina, liberal peacebuilders legitimized the political-economic elites who emerged from the war, endorsing 'acceptable' political leaders while attempting to marginalize those individuals blatantly opposing the implementation of the peacebuilding agenda. In Kosovo, for the sake of short-term stability UNMIK collaborated with the 'men with guns' and initially failed to engage with both civil society and, at least in part, with minorities (Wolfgram 2008). The stubborn presence of unpalatable ethnic elites provided international peacebuilders with a justification for international rule, and an opportunity to exteriorize failure. In general, as Chapters 3 and 4 will demonstrate, the peacebuilders' policy was more concerned about managing the status quo and preventing future crisis than rooting out the causes and drivers of conflict. Despite the transformative rhetoric and the use of executive powers, 'peacebuilding appeared to be a damage-control mechanism' (Visoka 2017: 6).

As a result of assertive international activism, domestic political processes came to be essentially controlled by outsiders. International intervention undermined self-determination and political autonomy, and thus contradicted some basic tenets of liberalism. The autonomous liberal rights-holder metamorphosed from a subject of rights to an object of regulation (Chandler 2010). In addition, despite the rhetoric on building the capacity of states in the region, international intervention focused on developing outsiders' capacities rather than local ones (Woodward 2017: 70–125). As a result, the reality of assertive intervention led to a 'capacity sucking out' (Fukuyama 2004: 139). Rather than strengthening legitimate and effective local institutions, international peacebuilders crowded out weak domestic capacities. Moreover, when outsiders assertively promoted democratization, the domestic political process did not operate according to the established constitutional order. In order to undermine, subvert or manipulate external governance frameworks, domestic players increasingly operated outside of formal institutional channels. Paradoxically, outside imposition pushed the political process underground—and thus reinforced illiberal, and even illegal, domestic interests.

External assertiveness not only undermined the formal domestic political process but also raised problematic questions about the democratic credentials of foreign interveners (Caplan 2005). International officials claimed that they knew better what was in the interest of the people and the country than local elites selected through (reasonably) free and fair elections. Extensive governing prerogatives, with no accountability mechanisms, carried the obvious risk of arbitrary and unregulated power. In Bosnia-Herzegovina, because the High Representative is unaccountable to, and his powers are largely unchecked by the local population, his prerogative was worryingly reminiscent of the European colonial experience (Knaus and Martin 2003). In March 2005 the Venice Commission of the Council of Europe pointed out the incompatibility of the Bonn Powers with the rule of law and democratic principles, and suggested that such powers should have been gradually abandoned (Venice Commission 2005). Likewise in Kosovo, the executive powers vested in international administrators made local authorities accountable to the international community, instead of their own community (Lemay-Hébert 2013).

Because of the unintended consequences of external imposition, which led to accusations of imperial control, international interveners looked for alternative ways to influence the peacebuilding process. The interest in civil society building as a key component of liberal peacebuilding emerged from the workings and dynamics of experimentalist governance. The progressive disillusionment with the speed and direction of change achieved through external imposition motivated the search for different targets and intervention tools (Belloni 2001). The contradictions of externally driven political processes, as well as the inherent difficulties of transplanting democratic institutions and procedures in divided and sectarian contexts, did not lead to the reassessment of liberal peacebuilding strategies but rather encouraged ever-greater external regulation. Domestic actors were deemed not capable of self-governing and, accordingly, responsible international engagement was thought to require moving beyond institution-building to engage in ever intrusive interventionism at the level of society. Civil society building, discussed in Chapter 4, became a core component of liberal peacebuilding. In sum, experimentalist governance both externalized failure and stimulated an expansionist dynamics. The internal working of liberal principles and practices have led Beate Jahn to explain external intervention as 'tragic' (Jahn 2007a, b), continuing unabated despite its unintended consequences, including counterproductive outcomes.

2.2.2   *Phase 2: Brussels, or the Power of Attraction*

By the early 2000s both policy and academic analyses increasingly drew attention to the limits of external regulation. The assertive peacebuilding framework implemented in the Balkans (and elsewhere, most notably in East Timor), resulted in the artificial institutionalization of weak states with limited domestic legitimacy, sustained primarily by external policy-making and resources (Chandler 2010). Because the liberal hubris of the 1990s ultimately undermined domestic sovereignty, a new approach came to be seen as necessary. The phasing out of executive powers emerged from the dynamics of experimentalist governance. This new approach was not motivated by the real or perceived success of previous interventionism but, on the contrary, by the growing awareness of its limits and the related need to find alternative avenues to pursue the goals envisaged within the peacebuilding framework. From the perspective of external peacebuilders, local institutions had not yet achieved political maturity, and thus it remained unlikely that the domestic political process could generate legitimate and enforceable policies. However, the heightened awareness that domestic processes could not be controlled from the outside led to the assessment that the effectiveness of the coercive policy style had reached its limits (World Bank 2011). While the broad objective of intervention did not change, the tools deployed in this new phase evolved significantly to take into consideration the peacebuilding lessons of the 1990s.

The coercive power of outside imposition gave way to forms of 'supervisory interventionism' (Visoka 2017) which refrained from intervening directly and imposing solutions on recalcitrant domestic elites. Since 2001 the EU adopted the ownership principle as the main principle of its approach to peacebuilding. It was through ever-growing domestic ownership of reform that local institutions were expected to develop their legitimacy and ability to address societal needs (Donais 2012). Perhaps more importantly, the progressive transfer of governing responsibilities to domestic institutions also allowed foreign interveners to posit that functioning and stable democracies were developing in both Bosnia-Herzegovina and Kosovo. Tautologically, the non-use of executive powers served as an indicator of peacebuilding success (Visoka 2017: 35). Moreover, domestic ownership of reform could also serve the purpose of shifting blame for policy failures towards local actors, and thus implicitly justifying prolonged international intervention.

In sum, liberal peacebuilding was re-conceptualized as an exercise aimed at strengthening state sovereignty through domestic ownership and the building of its administrative capacities. As a result, 'good governance' and 'capacity building' became the mantra of international organizations operating in the Balkans. This 'peacebuilding-as-statebuilding' model (Chandler 2017; Woodward 2017: 52–69) aimed at creating the bureaucratic and administrative machinery required to enable states to develop a fruitful two-way relationship with their societies. Accordingly, state-building became 'the *telos* (or end goal) of consolidating peace' (Sisk 2013: x). Needless to say, despite the rhetoric on domestic ownership, the focus on building 'capacity' and 'good governance' was premised upon the presence of a major power imbalance between the international and the local.

The EU assumed the lead of this new peacebuilding phase. The gradual withdrawal of the United States from the Balkans towards more critical regions (i.e. Asia) paved the way to the EU's growing assumption of responsibilities. In Bosnia-Herzegovina, the EU took over a number of policy responsibilities previously assigned to either the UN or NATO (NATO 2005). At the end of 2002, for 10 years, the EU monitored, advised and inspected local police forces. At the end of 2004, the EU replaced NATO in the task of overseeing the military implementation of the DPA, while still using NATO's headquarters in Belgium as its own operational headquarters, and working through the Deputy to NATO's Supreme Allied Commander in Europe. In Kosovo, extensive powers vested in the international administrators between 1999 and 2007 were replaced by a focus on Europeanization (Visoka 2017).

While keeping its intervention focus on both Bosnia-Herzegovina and Kosovo, perceived to be the most problematic states in the region, the

EU planned to bring all Western Balkan states closer to the European mainstream by inviting them to join the Union. EU policy-makers understood EU enlargement as a peacebuilding project (Blockmans 2010; Chandler 2007). Accordingly, at the Feira European Council in June 2000 the EU offered all states in the region, and thus not only war-ravaged Bosnia-Herzegovina and Kosovo, the prospect of European membership. With this offer, the international peacebuilding strategy progressively changed from external imposition to an emphasis on the domestic ownership of the process of transition towards ever-greater inclusion into European institutions (Denti 2018).

The ultimate objective of intervention remained the same one identified by external actors during the rising phase of liberal peacebuilding throughout the 1990s. Peacebuilders still envisaged the construction of democratic states modelled on a western, Weberian template. However, given its politically pluralist nature, the EU left the conceptual meaning of democracy undefined, avoiding the formulation of a single liberal democratic model. This conceptual indeterminacy, and resulting heterogeneity, is occasionally described as a problem because of the lack of a specific state model to base the reforms and transformations on (Keil and Arkan 2015b: 236), but is also a strategic asset because it increases the EU's leeway without appearing to impose one specific governance model over another when dealing with third countries (Kurki 2015: 35–37). In this framework, civil society continued to have an important role, although its importance remained largely instrumental. European peacebuilding actors saw civil society as helpful to secure domestic consensus for external policies, in particular with regard to the enlargement process.

The EU's approach also required a semantic change in the way the region was described. No longer perceived as the 'the Balkans'—an ostensibly violent and uncivilized area outside of European civilization—the region came to be identified as the 'Western Balkans'—an administrative term to identify those states en route to EU integration, or 'South-eastern Europe', that is, a peripheral part of the European civilization core which, with the appropriate external support, could rightfully join the 'European family' (Jeffrey 2008).

The EU's strategy involved both external intervention through a system of incentives and avoidance of direct control of domestic political, economic and social processes. Rather than blatantly imposing policy frameworks, the EU adopted more covert forms of peacebuilding focused on inducing and supporting the 'proper' behaviour by local elites. In particular, conditionality tools were deployed to stimulate domestic reform processes. They involved a wide range of rules, norms and procedures drawn from the general Copenhagen criteria (political, economic, and *acquis*-related), the 1997 Regional Approach, the 1999 Stabilisation and Association Process, country-specific conditions, conditions related to individual projects and the granting of aid, grants and loans, conditions arising out of peace agreements and political deals (Anastasakis and Bechev 2003: 1). Through a combination of 'carrots and sticks', the EU expected that states would comply with these conditions and gradually move closer to Brussels (Anastasakis 2005: 83).

As Schimmelfennig and Sedelmeier (2004: 670) argued, EU conditionality was based on a strategy of 'reinforcement by reward, under which the EU provides external incentives for a target government to comply with its conditions'. This new, institutionalist approach aimed at putting in place a functional framework able to constructively shape social and political interaction in states emerging from the process of Yugoslav dissolution (Lemay-Hébert 2009). It aspired to draw these states closer to the European mainstream by making them increasingly compatible with the EU's own economic and governance system (Denti 2018). Conditionality and the membership perspective were meant to stimulate a pro-Europe, bottom-up, reformist zeal in both political elites and citizens desiring to join the European club. In a memorable sentence by Lord Paddy Ashdown, the then High Representative of the International Community in Bosnia-Herzegovina, with the integration perspective and the related unleashing of the EU's power of attraction, 'the pull of Brussels will replace the push of Dayton' (Ashdown 2004).

The EU's approach has been frequently described as 'member state building' (i.e., Denti 2018; ESI 2005; Keil and Arkan 2015a). This expression was first referred to as a strategy in an influential 2005 report by the International Commission on the Balkans (ICB) titled *The Balkans in Europe's Future*. After noticing the continuing presence of weak states and protectorates in the region, the ICB identified Brussels' challenge in the Balkans as that of '[b]uilding functional member states while integrating them into the EU' (ICB 2005: 29). For the ICB, the member state-building approach should have rested on four interrelated pillars. First, the EU should have exploited the leverage of the accession process to induce domestic change, and 'capacity building' should have become the 'principal and explicit objective of both the Stabilisation and Association Process (SAP) and negotiating framework' (ICB 2005: 30).

Second, Brussels should have fostered the economic integration of the region through the development of a free trade area leading to a customs union with the EU. Third, through its novel approach allowing for greater domestic policy responsibilities, the EU should have attempted to fill the gap between state and society in the region—which emerged as one of the most problematic unintended consequence of the first phase of liberal peacebuilding. Finally, 'a smart visa policy' should have allowed the youth to travel to the EU, thus consolidating pro-European and liberal attitudes in the new generation. As discussed in Chapters 5 and 6, the EU largely subscribed to the analysis presented in this report, and implemented its recommendations. The EU, for the most part, respected the power and control of local elites. The rhetoric on domestic ownership was complemented by the concept of partnership, which became a centrepiece of European involvement in the region. European officials presented themselves as partners in a common peacebuilding effort, rather than emissaries of a coercive external project.

Overall, the most important characteristic of this peacebuilding phase lay in the shift from the powers and prerogatives of intervening states to those of domestic political actors who, however, were still expected to conform to the broader set of policies and expectations emanating from Brussels. By refraining from the external authoritative imposition of institutions and policies, the EU moved from a 'Liberalism of Imposition' to a 'Liberalism of Restraint' (Sørensen 2011) aimed at putting domestic elites in the 'driver's seat' of reform. Accordingly, governance evolved from the top-down external imposition of decisions taken from afar to a focus on domestic ownership. Simultaneously, the new peacebuilding approach aimed at strengthening domestic processes by elevating the social contract between local institutions and citizens to the forefront of international priorities. By answering citizen demands and addressing their needs through the delivery of services, local institutions were expected to gain political legitimacy and root themselves in the domestic context. In the absence of adequate responses to citizen needs, domestic processes of accountability were envisaged to lead to democratic changes in government.

For critics, the states being constructed via EU conditionality mechanisms in the Western Balkans still lack de facto, Westphalian authority and served as a mechanism to implement external regulation. The EU has been blamed for producing post-liberal states with limited sovereignty that will be amenable to integration into the Union in due course

(Chandler 2010). Although institutions and policies were no longer coercively imposed on local actors, they were still channelled through international organizations in an outside-in process. Behind the façade of culturally sensitive and depoliticized democracy, the EU actually promoted institutions coherent with its own economic interests based on economic liberalization and private sector development (Tuerkes and Goegoez 2006), while ignoring different histories of state formation and alternative ways of governing (Woodward 2011: 316). As a result, the EU failed to recognize both that improving public sector governance does not respond to universal recipes or technical fixes and that informal institutions are at least as important as formal ones in determining the quality of governance (Grindle 2017).

Furthermore, critics have also highlighted the contradictions involved in the implementation of the domestic ownership principle. While rhetorically assigning the driver's seat of reform to local institutions, the EU took upon itself a prominent supervisory role that shaped indirectly key developments in all states in the region (see, for example, Džankić 2015; Kacarska 2015). The EU operationalized ownership as internal responsibility for external objectives. Top-down, paternalistic practices were disguised through a language of domestic ownership and responsible policy-making. Accordingly, critics argued that, despite the rhetoric, the EU's engagement in the Western Balkans involved techniques of governmentality and practices of domination and exclusion that, by assigning responsibility to local actors and avoiding the imposition of policies and institutions, aimed at disguising the power imbalance underpinning international intervention (Chandler 2010; Ejdus 2017; Juncos 2018). Local ownership turned both into a technique of governing populations at a distance and a sort of maturity test for local authorities, whereby an authoritative judge—the EU—assessed the reliability and trustworthiness of domestic leaders in implementing external frameworks.

The focus on the responsibility of local actors developed hand in hand with the reluctance to openly impose solutions to domestic problems, as for example in the case of the unsuccessful attempt at constitutional reform in Bosnia-Herzegovina between 2006 and 2010 (Sebastian Aparicio 2014). Similarly, until 2013 EULEX's executive role in Kosovo was characterized by a policy of passivity (Capussela 2015: 74–81). Overall, since the EU promised the Western Balkans a future membership and thus unleashed its celebrated 'transformative power' (Grabbe 2005), a risk-averse, hands-off attitude has become the standard operating procedure of European institutions (Venneri 2010). This approach left more space to domestic agency and the possibility that local leaders could shape the peace process in the pursuit of their own interests. The consensus-seeking, non-confrontational approach encouraged obstruction by local elites. In both Kosovo (Visoka 2017) and Bosnia-Herzegovina (Belloni 2008) local institutions came to be co-opted by local actors. In Kosovo, local ownership of both the central administration and the judiciary did not make these bureaucracies more effective (Skendaj 2014: 61–96).

With regard to the EU enlargement process, the incentive structure put in place by EU institutions did not work as intended because incentives were not always clearly defined, the reforms demanded by the EU threatened the position of domestic elites, and citizens were not involved in the enlargement process (Keil and Arkan 2015a). Frequently domestic leaders engaged in 'faked compliance' (Noutcheva 2009), whereby they formally adopted reforms and rule changes but without ever allowing for deep-rooted transformations. According to Mendelski (2016), the EU's transformative power ultimately metamorphosed into a 'pathological power'. Not only did domestic elites block the implementation of liberal reforms, but EU policies had the unintended effect of reinforcing the power of incumbent authoritarian and corrupt elites. Overall, the EU member state-building resulted in the creation of 'minimalist states', that is, states with 'limited legitimacy and a weak scope and strength of the state' (Bieber 2011: 1786).

In sum, EU member statebuilding, with its depoliticized and technocratic approach largely focused on domestic political elites, conflicted with liberal peacebuilding goals (Juncos 2012). Above all, the elite-driven and top-down features of member state-building clashed with the need to build consensus within society on the new institutions, especially in Bosnia-Herzegovina and Kosovo (Van Willigen 2013: 140–165). Despite the EU's efforts, opinion polls repeatedly registered a 'major dissatisfaction' throughout the region with regard to governance performance. In particular, the perception of corruption corroborated 'the overwhelming sentiment that the rule of law remains a problem' (Regional Cooperation Council 2017: 115–135). Ever more frequently since the early 2010s, citizens in the region either left (Derens and Geslin 2018) or protested against the emerging political and economic order. Many citizens disapproved of both the EU, seen as distant and technocratic, and local politicians, who are considered as profoundly inadequate. It was a just a matter of time before a new awareness among both scholars and policy-makers of the importance for peacebuilding of citizens' views and actions would emerge.

2.2.3   Phase 3: Tuzla, or the Local Turn

Liberal peacebuilding, both in its assertive and more participatory versions discussed above, has been criticized as a discourse that produces states 'failed by design' (Richmond 2014a). International interveners rely on problematic elites and their often chauvinistic, nationalistic or personal interests, failing to consider the population whose needs are left unaddressed. Rather than constructing local authority and developing state–society relations, the liberal peacebuilding framework does not foster either institutions' legitimacy or direct links with citizens. Characterized by strong top-down dynamics, peacebuilding often circumvents citizens' rights to determine their own peace. As a result, the main outcome of peacebuilding interventions is a condition of negative peace which perpetuates 'local power relations and unmitigated conflict structures' and leads to 'exclusion, discrimination, inequality and other forms of structural violence' (Richmond 2014a: 12). This outcome both reflects the conceptual limitations of the liberal peacebuilding paradigm, which is obsessively focused on the architecture of the state, and the shortcomings of its standard operating procedures, which prioritize local elites vis-à-vis the population, the centre vis-à-vis the periphery, and international/expert knowledge vis-à-vis domestic experience.

The problems with the liberal framework implemented by the EU in the Balkans, and more generally by the international community in weak and fragile states in the Global South, have paved the way for the so-called 'local turn' in peacebuilding. While some critics have explained the crisis of the liberal peace by focusing on the contradictions within liberalism (Jahn 2013), the 'post-liberal' or 'hybrid peace' literature characterizing the local turn in peacebuilding studies highlights the dynamic relations between interveners and intervened upon. In particular, one of the defining features of the local turn is the importance of local resistance to international peacebuilding interventions. It is precisely resistance and contentious politics that opens the opportunity to create a space for the development of contextualized, everyday versions of peace (Richmond 2016). For some scholars, a coherent approach to the local demands the use of non-linear reasoning. While previous paradigms followed a linear causal methodology, these approaches are informed by primarily constructivist, post-structural and neo-materialist methods, focus on complexity and systems theory and do not aim at generating cause and effect explanations (Chandler 2013; Körppen et al. 2013).

The local turn underscores the limits of liberal epistemologies and provides an overdue attention to local agency, ordinary people and the dynamic, multi-level dimensions of peace processes (Kappler 2015). It takes stock of the failures of liberal frameworks in building sustainable peace in weak and fragile states by highlighting the role of local actors and their agency, and striving to close the gap between the aspirations of conflict societies and the kind of peace generated by international intervention. The importance of the local turn lies primarily in the increasing awareness of the hiatus between the promises of liberal peacebuilding and the realities on the ground.

The introduction of the 'local' in peacebuilding debates is mostly attributed to Jean Paul Lederach, who identified the middle level of society, including civil society organizations, community leaders and so on, as best placed to work with both the national and the grassroots levels of society to further peace (Lederach 1997). In the early phase of peacebuilding, his work stimulated a generation of civil society support projects through capacity building. By contrast, the newer local turn emerged in the 2000s as a critique of the liberal peacebuilding paradigm and largely rested on the simplistic binary distinction between the 'international' and the 'local'. It identified the former with post-colonial and neo-imperialist attitudes and the latter with authenticity and the right to express resistance to the liberal peacebuilding project (Paffenholz 2014).

At the methodological level, this turn involves the attempt to decolonize knowledge from western and Eurocentric conceptions to more pluralist modes of knowledge. The dominance of the liberal peace paradigm is criticized in favour of an understanding and even acceptance of pre-liberal, nonliberal, and post-liberal forms of political and social practice. The multiple dimensions of peace require questioning standardized blueprints, performance indicators, the obsession with institution-building and elites, while focusing the attention on multiple forms of agency, including the perceptions, ideas, needs and strategies of ordinary people largely neglected by grand peacebuilding narratives.

There are two main intellectual and policy dimensions involved in this turn (Leonardsson and Rudd 2015). The first dimension underscores the importance of local ownership of peace processes. Both as a result of the critique of the liberal peace and of mounting resistance on the ground, international peacebuilding organizations and state donors have adapted in response (Richmond and MacGinty 2015). The endorsement of policies that call for more local knowledge and engagement with pre-existing peace structures has become commonplace in peacebuilding interventions. The need to provide domestic anchoring and legitimacy to the liberal peacebuilding agenda, and thus to improve the effectiveness of peacebuilding efforts, suggests the value in involving local actors. In this framework, the local remains essentially a tool, understood as indispensable in achieving peacebuilding goals in partnership and collaboration with the international.

In practice, however, similarly to the EU's understanding of the term discussed above, local ownership has been more rhetorical than real. The rhetoric of local ownership never fully materialized, since external interveners worry they could lose their legitimacy if local solutions prevailed (Miklian et al. 2011). Ownership did not translate into self-determination or self-government but turned into a long-term process in which autonomy is enhanced and supervised, and the equality between supervised populations and the rest of the sovereign nations is permanently deferred (Bargués-Pedreny 2018). This is unsurprising since, as Timothy Donais (2012: 4) argues, 'the strong version of local ownership relegates the donor community to the role of writing checks and hoping for the best'.

The second dimension of the local turn criticizes the neo-colonial, undemocratic and arrogant attitude of international actors and focuses on the emancipatory, everyday elements of peace. The significance of the local lies in its open and hidden agency revealing the contestation of the liberal peacebuilding approach and the attempt to shape the peace process in order to meet those everyday needs frequently marginalized by international projects. Here the local involves practices and traditions, as well as the intricacies of everyday life, as the essential sources for opposing, mitigating, or hybridizing the liberal peace (Belloni 2012; Björkdahl and Höglund 2013; Richmond 2014b; MacGinty 2011). In particular the notion of 'everyday' emerges as an authentic field of agency, as opposed to liberal, western-based frameworks (Randazzo 2017: 63–64; Richmond 2016).

Both dimensions of the local turn question the prevailing liberal framework and approach, and aim at understanding and problematizing agency, the power dynamics between internationals and locals and the outcome of their interaction. While critical analyses of peacebuilding have stressed the undemocratic, disciplinary and even panoptic character of external involvement in weak and fragile states (e.g. Chandler 2010; Richmond 2014a), the local turn underscores the interplay of the 'international' and the 'local' during the peacebuilding process (e.g. Autesserre 2014). It draws attention to the importance of bottom-up approaches to peacebuilding, the everyday life of ordinary people and the agency of sub-national actors in shaping the peace process during the encounter with the 'international' (Hughes et al. 2015; Leonardsson and Rudd 2015; MacGinty and Richmond 2013).

Despite its critical, emancipatory ethos, the local turn involves several conceptual and practical problems which may undermine its progressive potential. To begin with, the local turn risks romanticizing the local and even forgiving illiberal behaviours of local actors (Richmond 2009). In addition, there is little evidence to suggest that informal channels of resistance provide more opportunity for emancipation or participation as a whole (Randazzo 2017). Second, it may perpetuate artificial binaries between international and local actors, between liberal and nonliberal, and between indigenous and exogenous elements of peacebuilding. In particular, the identification of the international as the liberal and the local as the indigenous is both misleading and reductive. Not only does this dichotomy underestimate the diversity of views, interests and approaches within both the international and the local, but also it ignores that the international has always been involved in the formation of those subjectivities and practices that later are understood as self-evident problems for the liberal peace (Jahn 2013: 191). Accordingly, the local and the international are not naturally oppositional and the spatial and cultural boundaries between the international and the local are not fixed. The international and the local, the liberal and the illiberal, are not necessarily in a competitive relationship, but are mutually constituted (Rampton and Nadarajah 2017). Through their co-habitation, political authority is constantly refashioned across multiple political and geographical scales (Hameiri and Jones 2017).

Third, analyses inspired by the 'local turn' tend to underestimate the power structures and their constraining and/or enabling nature where local actors operate (Peterson 2012). By failing to address the tensions resulting from international-local encounters, they may reify oppressive political, economic and social structures (Debiel and Rinck 2016). In addition, the dismissal of formal expressions of agency and organized forms of representation obscures other, equally legitimate, expressions of local needs, such as joining NGOs (Randazzo 2017: 140). Finally, as mentioned above, peacebuilding practice continues to be poorly equipped to deliver on the local turn's normative promise. In particular, peacebuilding actors engage insufficiently with local agency and the normative ideal of local ownership never fully materializes in practice (Hirblinger and Simons 2015; Schierenbeck 2016).

While these critical aspects represent a serious risk for any research agenda aiming at investigating the local, nonetheless they do not detract from the major methodological and epistemological innovation in the local turn, that is, the placing of local, everyday views, needs, norms, expectations and practices at the centre of peacebuilding research. By refocusing the peacebuilding agenda on individuals, the local turn stresses the importance of essential principles of liberalism, such as individual rights, equality and personal autonomy.

With few exceptions (i.e. Pickering 2007; Kappler 2014; Randazzo 2017; Visoka 2011), in the context of the Balkans academic analysis has rarely investigated the local—even though citizens have increasingly voiced their dissatisfaction with the type of peace supported by external interveners and implemented locally by nationalist elites. Particularly since the early 2010s citizens have vociferously protested against poor governance, widespread corruption, economic inequalities, declining living conditions, lack of opportunities, and in general against the glaring gap between the promises of liberal peacebuilding and the realities of the endless post-war transition. The slow pace of change in the region has also led to disillusionment and resentment towards both local power-holders and international peacebuilders, both implicated in a 'broken promises' (Talentino 2007) syndrome whereby persisting political, social and economic woes are attributed to their failure to promote positive change.

This local level attitude has been expressed in a variety of different instances, including disengagement from the political process, various forms of violent and non-violent protest, the defence of the 'commons', the adoption of passive resistance, the articulation of alternative social platforms and the demand for more equality, inclusion, and social justice. Two noteworthy empirical instances of local, bottom-up engagement with international liberal intervention, discussed, respectively, in Chapters 7 and 8, involve the growing region-wide Euroscepticism, and the development of social movements both contesting the existing political and economic order and advancing alternative ideas on how to move beyond the current stalemate. While the support to local civil society development during the first phase of intervention, which was steered primarily by international donors, has led to superficial and mostly inconsequential local involvement, the mounting protest against the unpalatable status quo represents the expression, occasionally even violent, of bottom-up views, needs, and aspirations (Richmond 2016).

The outburst of local discontent has prompted international interveners to re-evaluate their approach to the region. International actors involved in the dynamics of experimentalist governance reassessed their intervention strategy in light of the widespread local dissatisfaction with the outcome of liberal peacebuilding. This dissatisfaction has paved the way for the growing influence of regional actors, such as Turkey, and global ones, including China and, above all, Russia. In order to counter political and socio-economic difficulties and growing geopolitical competition, the European Commission renewed its plans for the accession of the Western Balkans into the EU. In February 2018, the Commission released 'A credible enlargement perspective for an enhanced EU engagement with the Western Balkans', which put forward the ambitious goal of achieving EU accession for Montenegro and Serbia by 2025, and supporting the opening of negotiations with the other states in the region. While the burden of advancing the process of meeting EU requirements remains on the shoulders of local elites, the EU promised renewed financial and technical support. Thus, for the EU the 'local turn' does not refer so much to domestic ownership, democratic representation and institutional legitimacy, but rather to the attempt to reduce local resistance through the reconfiguration of intervention to make it more locally acceptable, in particular vis-à-vis ordinary citizens. European officials understand EU intervention in the region as so commonsensical that there is no need to consider its substance matter. Rather, the EU simply aims at being more effective in its modus operandi, since what it does is axiomatically correct.

2.3   Conclusions

Since the mid-1990s, liberal peacebuilding in the Balkans has evolved significantly. In the first phase, international actors optimistically believed that liberal democratic norms and institutions could be transplanted from the outside in. In order to remove what they considered as domestic obstacles for the peacebuilding agenda, they assumed vast executive powers. In both Bosnia-Herzegovina and Kosovo, international actors assertively intervened to reform political, economic and social institutions. By the early 2000s, however, it became increasingly clear that domestic institutions lacked local legitimacy. As a result, political, economic and social life frequently developed outside of the formal democratic framework.

From the early 2000s, the EU hoped to set into motion a domestically driven reformist dynamic through its member state-building strategy. This involved an approach of 'reinforcement by reward' that relied on the possibility to provide incentives in order to stimulate local compliance with the requirements of the EU integration process. However, frequently, domestic elites formally accepted and adopted the requirements of integration, but implemented changes only superficially, failing to affect the deeper political, economic, and social structures. In general, during the first two phases of peacebuilding intervention in the Balkans, external actors relied extensively on local elites, and engaged only partially, if at all, with society.

By the early 2010s, popular dissatisfaction with liberal peacebuilding, and with the EU in particular, gradually increased. Continuing socio-economic stagnation, widespread corruption, and growing ethno-nationalist rhetoric revealed the limits of international ambitions to remake the region according to liberal democratic values and principles. Everywhere in the region citizens put forward various strategies to challenge, contest and shape the peacebuilding process, sometimes even violently. As a result, external actors began to reconsider the meaning of liberal peacebuilding, and the strategy to implement it. As Chapter 9 will argue, despite the attempt to re-launch the European integration process, the EU has moved away from previous conceptions of peacebuilding involving grand schemes aimed at transferring liberal institutions and 'good governance' to fragile states in favour of a more humble approach. Western aspiration is no longer that of transforming society, but rather of managing or regulating it. The transformative ambition has been set aside in favour of a pragmatic approach. The new policy consensus is that state institutions cannot be imposed from the outside but depend on the conditions in the subject society. This revised understanding of peacebuilding emerged after the failure of the liberal hubris of the first phase of intervention in the Balkans—discussed in the next two chapters.

NOTE

1. Kosovo statehood is contested. UN Security Council Resolution 1244 adopted on 10 June 1999 recognized both the sovereignty and territorial integrity of the Federal Republic of Yugoslavia and the need to establish meaningful autonomy and self-determination for Kosovo. In February 2008 Kosovo unilaterally declared independence and in the following years a growing number of states recognized Kosovo. For stylistic reasons I will always refer to Kosovo as a state, keeping in mind its status was and remains contested, above all by Serbia.

REFERENCES

Anastasakis, O. (2005). The Europeanisation of the Balkans. *The Brown Journal of World Affairs, 12*(1), 77–88.

Anastasakis, O., & Bechev, D. (2003, April). *EU conditionality in South Eastern Europe: Bringing commitment to the process.* Oxford: South Eastern European Studies Programme.

Ashdown, P. (2004, May 12). From Dayton to Brussels. *Reporter.* http://www.ohr.int/ohr-dept/presso/pressa/default.asp?content_id=32492. Accessed 12 March 2012.

Autesserre, S. (2014). *Peaceland: Conflict resolution and the everyday politics of international intervention.* New York: Cambridge University Press.

Bargués-Pedreny, P. (2018). *Deferring peace in international statebuilding: Difference, resilience and critique.* London and New York: Routledge.

Belloni, R. (2001). Civil society and peacebuilding in Bosnia-Herzegovina. *Journal of Peace Research, 38*(2), 163–180.

Belloni, R. (2008). *Statebuilding and international intervention in Bosnia.* London and New York: Routledge.

Belloni, R. (2012). Hybrid peace governance: Its emergence and significance. *Global Governance, 18*(1), 21–38.

Bieber, F. (2011). Building impossible states? State-building strategies and EU membership in the Western Balkans. *Europe-Asia Studies, 63*(10), 337–360.

Björkdahl, A., & Höglund, K. (2013). Precarious peacebuilding: Friction in global-local encounters. *Peacebuilding, 1*(3), 289–299.

Blockmans, S. (2010). EU enlargement as a peacebuilding tool. In S. Blockmans, J. Wouters, & T. Tuys (Eds.), *The European Union and peacebuilding* (pp. 77–106). The Hague: T.M.C. Asser Press.

Caplan, R. (2005). Who guards the guardians? International accountability in Bosnia. *International Peacekeeping, 12*(3), 463–476.

Capussela, A. (2015). *State-building in Kosovo: Democracy, corruption and the EU in the Balkans.* London: I.B. Tauris.

Chandler, D. (2007). European Union statebuilding: Securing the liberal peace through EU enlargement. *Global Society, 21*(4), 593–607.

Chandler, D. (2010). *International statebuilding: The rise of post-liberal governance*. London: Routledge.

Chandler, D. (2013). Peacebuilding and the politics of non-linearity: Rethinking 'hidden' agency and 'resistance'. *Peacebuilding, 1*(1), 17–32.

Chandler, D. (2017). *Peacebuilding: The twenty years' crisis, 1997–2017*. Houndmills: Palgrave.

Chivvis, C. (2010). The Dayton dilemma. *Survival, 52*(5), 47–74.

Debiel, T., & Rinck, P. (2016). Rethinking the local in peacebuilding: Moving away from the liberal/post-liberal divide. In T. Debiel, T. Held, & U. Schneckener (Eds.), *Peacebuilding in crisis: Rethinking paradigms and practices of transnational cooperation* (pp. 275–293). New York: Routledge.

Denti, D. (2018). *The European Union and member state building in Bosnia and Herzegovina*. Trento: School of International Studies, University of Trento, Thesis submitted in partial fulfilment of the requirements for the degree of Doctor of Philosophy in International Studies.

Derens, J.-A., & Geslin, L. (2018, June). Cet exode qui dépeuple les Balkans. *Le Monde Diplomatique*, pp. 5–6.

Dijkstra, H. (2011). The planning and implementation of the rule of law mission of the European Union in Kosovo. *Journal of Intervention and Statebuilding, 5*(2), 192–210.

Donais, T. (2012). *Peacebuilding and local ownership: Post-conflict consensus-building*. Abingdon: Routledge.

Džankić, J. (2015). The role of the EU in the statehood and democratization of Montenegro. In S. Keil & Z. Arkan (Eds.), *The EU and member state building: European foreign policy in the Western Balkans* (pp. 83–101). London and New York: Routledge.

Ejdus, F. (2017). 'Here is your mission, now own it!' The rhetoric and practice of local ownership in EU interventions. *European Security, 26*(4), 461–484.

ESI (European Stability Initiative). (2005, February 1). *The Helsinki moment: European member state building in the Balkans*. Berlin.

Fukuyama, F. (2004). *State-building: Governance and world order in the twenty-first century*. London: Profile Books.

Grabbe, H. (2005). *The EU's transformative power: Europeanization through conditionality in Central and Eastern Europe*. Basingstoke: Palgrave.

Grindle, M. (2017). Good governance, R.I.P.: A critique and an alternative. *Governance, 30*(1), 17–22.

Hameiri, S., & Jones, L. (2017). Beyond hybridity to the politics of scale: International intervention and 'local' politics. *Development and Change, 48*(1), 54–77.

Hirblinger, A. T., & Simons, C. (2015). The good, the bad, and the powerful: Representations of the local in peacebuilding. *Security Dialogue, 46*(2), 422–439.

Hughes, C., Öjendal, J., & Schierenbeck, I. (2015). The struggle versus the song—The local turn in peacebuilding: An introduction. *Third World Quarterly, 36*(5), 817–824.

ICB (International Commission on the Balkans). (2005). *The Balkans in Europe's future*. Sofia: Centre for Liberal Strategy.

Ignatieff, M. (2003). *Empire light: Nation-building in Bosnia, Kosovo and Afghanistan*. London: Vintage.

Jahn, B. (2007a). The tragedy of liberal diplomacy: Part one. *Journal of Intervention and Statebuilding, 1*(1), 87–106.

Jahn, B. (2007b). The tragedy of liberal diplomacy: Part two. *Journal of Intervention and Statebuilding, 1*(2), 211–229.

Jahn, B. (2013). *Liberal internationalism: Theory, history, practice*. Houndmills: Palgrave.

Jeffrey, A. (2008). Contesting Europe: The politics of Bosnian integration into European structures. *Environment and Planning D: Society and Space, 26*(3), 428–443.

Juncos, A. (2012). Member state-building versus peacebuilding: The contradictions of EU state-building in Bosnia and Herzegovina. *East European Politics, 28*(1), 58–75.

Juncos, A. (2018). EU security sector reform in Bosnia and Herzegovina: Reform or resist? *Contemporary Security Policy, 39*(1), 95–118.

Kacarska, S. (2015). The EU in Macedonia: From inter-ethnic to intra-ethnic political mediator in an accession deadlock. In S. Keil & Z. Arkan (Eds.), *The EU and member state building: European foreign policy in the Western Balkans* (pp. 102–121). London and New York: Routledge.

Kappler, S. (2014). *Local agency and peacebuilding: EU and international engagement in Bosnia-Herzegovina, Cyprus, and South Africa*. Houndmills: Palgrave.

Kappler, S. (2015). The dynamic local: Delocalisation and (re)localisation in the search for peacebuilding identity. *Third World Quarterly, 36*(5), 875–889.

Keil, S., & Arkan, Z. (Eds.). (2015a). *The EU and member state building: European foreign policy in the Western Balkans*. London and New York: Routledge.

Keil, S., & Arkan, Z. (2015b). Theory and practice of EU member state building in the Western Balkans. In S. Keil & Z. Arkan (Eds.), *The EU and member state building: European foreign policy in the Western Balkans* (pp. 235–239). London and New York: Routledge.

Knaus, G., & Martin, F. (2003). Travails of the European Raj. *Journal of Democracy, 14*(3), 60–74.

Körppen, D., Ropers, N., & Giessmann, H. J. (Eds.). (2013). *The non-linearity of peace processes: Theory and practice of systemic conflict transformation*. Opladen and Farmington Hills, MI: Barbara Budrich.

Kurki, M. (2015). Political economy perspective: Fuzzy liberalism and EU democracy promotion: Why concepts matter. In A. Wetzel & J. Orbie (Eds.), *The substance of EU democracy promotion: Concepts and cases* (pp. 35–46). London: Palgrave.

Lederach, J. P. (1997). *Building peace: Sustainable reconciliation in divided societies*. Washington, DC: United States Institute of Peace Press.

Lemay-Hébert, N. (2009). Statebuilding without nation-building? Legitimacy, state failure and the limits of the institutionalist approach. *Journal of Intervention and Statebuilding, 3*(1), 21–45.

Lemay-Hébert, N. (2013). Everyday legitimacy and international administration: Global governance and local legitimacy in Kosovo. *Journal of Intervention and Statebuilding, 7*(1), 87–104.

Leonardsson, H., & Rudd, G. (2015). The 'local turn' in peacebuilding: A literature review of effective and emancipatory local peacebuilding. *Third World Quarterly, 36*(5), 825–839.

MacGinty, R. (2011). *International peacebuilding and local resistance: Hybrid forms of peace*. Houndmills: Palgrave.

MacGinty, R., & Richmond, O. P. (2013). The local turn in peacebuilding: A critical agenda for peace. *Third World Quarterly, 34*(5), 763–783.

Mendelski, M. (2016). Europeanization and the rule of law: Towards a pathological turn. *Southeastern Europe, 40*(3), 346–384.

Miklian, J., Lidén, K., & Kolås, Å. (2011). The perils of 'going local': Liberal peace-building agendas in Nepal. *Conflict, Security & Development, 11*(3), 285–308.

NATO (North Atlantic Treaty Organization). (2005, February). *Bringing peace and stability to the Balkans*. Brussels: NATO Briefing.

Noutcheva, G. (2009). Fake, partial and imposed compliance: The limits of the EU's normative power in the Western Balkans. *Journal of European Public Policy, 16*(7), 1065–1084.

Paffenholz, T. (2014). International peacebuilding goes local: Analysing Lederach's conflict transformation theory and its ambivalent encounter with 20 years of practice. *Peacebuilding, 2*(1), 11–27.

Peterson, J. H. (2012). A conceptual unpacking of hybridity: Accounting for notions of power, politics, and progress in analysis of aid-driven interfaces. *Journal of Peacebuilding and Development, 7*(2), 9–22.

Pickering, P. M. (2007). *Peacebuilding in the Balkans: The view from the ground floor*. Ithaca: Cornell University Press.

Pospisil, J. (2019). *Peace in political unsettlement: Beyond solving conflict*. Houndmills: Palgrave.

Pugh, M. (2001). Elections and 'protectorate democracy' in South-East Europe. In E. Newman & O. P. Richmond (Eds.), *The United Nations and human security* (pp. 190–207). Basingstoke: Palgrave.

Rampton, D., & Nadarajah, S. (2017). A long view of liberal peace and its crisis. *European Journal of International Relations, 23*(2), 441–465.

Randazzo, E. (2017). *Beyond liberal peacebuilding: A critical exploration of the local turn.* London and New York: Routledge.

RCC (Regional Cooperation Council). (2017). *Balkan barometer 2017: Public opinion survey.* Sarajevo: Regional Cooperation Council.

Richmond, O. P. (2009). The romanticisation of the local: Welfare, culture and peacebuilding. *The International Spectator, 44*(1), 149–169.

Richmond, O. P. (2014a). *Failed by design: Intervention, the state and the dynamics of peace formation.* New Haven and London: Yale University Press.

Richmond, O. P. (2014b). The dilemmas of a hybrid peace: Negative or positive? *Cooperation and Conflict, 50*(1), 50–68.

Richmond, O. P. (2016). *Peace formation and political order in conflict affected societies.* New York: Oxford University Press.

Richmond, O. P., & MacGinty, R. (2015). Where not for the critique of the liberal peace? *Cooperation & Conflict, 50*(2), 171–189.

Sabel, C. F., & Zeitlin, J. (2010). Learning from difference: The new architecture of experimentalist governance in the European Union. In C. F. Sabel & J. Zeitlin (Eds.), *Experimentalist governance in the European Union: Towards a new architecture* (pp. 1–28). Oxford: Oxford University Press.

Schierenbeck, I. (2016). Beyond the local turn divide: Lessons learnt, relearnt and unlearnt. *Third World Quarterly, 36*(6), 1023–1032.

Schimmelfennig, F., & Sedelmeier, U. (2004). Governance by conditionality: EU rule transfer to the candidate countries of central and Eastern Europe. *Journal of European Public Policy, 11*(4), 669–687.

Sebastian Aparicio, S. (2014). *Post-war statebuilding and constitutional reform: Beyond Dayton in Bosnia-Herzegovina.* Houndmills: Palgrave.

Sisk, T. D. (2013). *Statebuilding.* Cambridge: Polity.

Skendaj, E. (2014). *Creating Kosovo: International oversight and the making of ethical institutions.* Ithaca: Cornell University Press.

Sørensen, G. (2011). *A liberal world order in crisis: Choosing between imposition and restraint.* Ithaca and London: Cornell University Press.

Talentino, A. K. (2007). Perceptions of peacebuilding: The dynamic of imposer and imposed upon. *International Studies Perspectives, 8*(2), 152–171.

Tuerkes, M., & Goegoez, G. (2006). The European Union's strategy towards the Western Balkans: Exclusion or integration? *East European Politics and Society, 20*(4), 659–690.

Van Willigen, N. (2013). *Peacebuilding and international administration: The cases of Bosnia and Herzegovina and Kosovo.* London and New York: Routledge.

Venice Commission. (2005, March 12). *Opinion on the constitutional situation in Bosnia and Herzegovina and the powers of the high representative.* Venice: Venice Commission.

Venneri, G. (2010). Beyond the sovereignty paradox: The EU 'hands-up' statebuilding in Bosnia-Herzegovina. *Journal of Intervention and Statebuilding, 4*(2), 147–171.

Visoka, G. (2011). International governance and local resistance in Kosovo: The thin line between ethical, emancipatory and exclusionary politics. *Irish Studies in International Affairs, 22*(1), 99–125.

Visoka, G. (2017). *Shaping peace in Kosovo: The politics of peacebuilding and statehood.* Houndmills: Palgrave.

Wolfgram, M. A. (2008). When the men with guns rule: Explaining human rights failures in Kosovo since 1999. *Political Science Quarterly, 123*(3), 461–484.

Woodward, S. L. (2011). Varieties of state-building in the Balkans: A case for shifting focus. In M. Fischer, B. Austin, H. J. Giessmann (Eds.), *Advancing conflict transformation. The Berghof handbook* (pp. 315–333). Opladen and Framington: Barbara Budrich.

Woodward, S. L. (2017). *The ideology of failed states: Why intervention fails.* Cambridge: Cambridge University Press.

World Bank. (2011). *World development report: Conflict, security and development.* Washington, DC: World Bank.

PART I

Dayton, or Liberal Imposition

CHAPTER 3

Stability and the Anti-corruption Agenda

3.1 INTRODUCTION

With the end of the war in Bosnia-Herzegovina in 1995 and in Kosovo in 1999, international peacebuilders engaged in the first phase of peace-building intervention and deployed large missions to help stabilize the region. The magnitude of the international effort to assist the post-conflict and post-communist transition in these countries has few precedents in contemporary peacebuilding. Both Bosnia-Herzegovina and Kosovo received enormous amounts of money which, combined with the presence of a lenient legal framework, created the condition for the consolidation of 'rentier states', that is, entities dependant on sources of income based on external inflows, above all reconstruction and official development assistance (Lemay-Hébert and Murshed 2016). Although pledged aid for reconstruction and development was sometimes slow to arrive, it found a lax regulatory environment where the old rules had been discredited, while new ones were at best still embryonic. Old and new actors bent norms of social conduct to reflect new power configurations. Behaviour normally seen as deviant was tolerated on grounds of the post-war 'exceptional circumstances'.

Not only external inflows contributed to the creation of rents, which were then used to sustain the patronage network underpinning the new post-war order, but also they were often misappropriated for criminal activities and illegal and corruption deals (Center for the Study of

© The Author(s) 2020   55
R. Belloni, *The Rise and Fall of Peacebuilding
in the Balkans*, Rethinking Peace and Conflict Studies,
https://doi.org/10.1007/978-3-030-14424-1_3

Democracy 2010). By the early 2000s, the World Bank and the OECD began to soften their shock-therapy recipes, shifting towards promotion of good governance and anti-corruption; other international organizations followed. Above all, since the 2003 Thessaloniki summit the European Union (EU) developed an enlargement strategy, which will be discussed in Chapters 5 and 6, featuring the fight against corruption as a requirement in the Western Balkans' path towards membership. However, far from being transitory phenomena, practices against or beyond the law became (or remained) the norm, despite the peacebuilding and state-strengthening efforts of the international community.

The externally driven double transition from war to peace and from communism to democracy created conditions favourable to the growth of corruption. Corruption constituted the cost international actors were ready to accept in the name of stability, at least in the first post-conflict phase. Later, with corruption already engrained in the social fabric, governance reforms were devised by international officials and more or less openly accepted by local ones, but corruption continued to prosper under the surface of formal institutions. Because the neo-liberal approach has always been beyond questioning, international peacebuilders have explained corruption through the culture dependant behaviour of local people, thus re-enacting an orientalist tradition imposed upon the region with the use of the term 'Balkan' in derogatory or patronizing ways (Capussela 2015: 219–223; Horvat and Štiks 2015).

After a brief discussion of the meaning of corruption and how power relations sustain it, this chapter examines the politics of transition that contributed to make corruption endemic, and identifies corruption dynamics in Bosnia-Herzegovina and Kosovo. In the second section, it shows how international actors have contributed directly and indirectly to the phenomenon. The concluding part suggests that, rather than being a pathological manifestation of the peacebuilding process, corruption is the hallmark of a distinctive form of state where informal/illegal rules and norms coexist with formal ones, often trumping them.

3.2   Rents and Patronage

The analysis of corruption in post-conflict peacebuilding settings should take into account domestic political, economic and social structures, and how international actors affect them. These structures contribute to elucidate both perceptions and practices of corruption (Xenakis 2010), as well as the deep transformations that constitute the conflict legacy, with contested statehood and political authority changes. Unlike narrowly conceived neo-Weberian perspectives, a focus on the structuring of local power relations makes it possible to overcome the dichotomy between state capacity and lack of will that characterizes much of the thinking about peacebuilding (Bojičić-Dželilović and Kostovicova 2013). This approach requires including in the analysis those broader political, economic and social structures within which institutions develop—thereby seeing the state and its administrative capacity as products of these structures and underlying relationships (Jayasuriya 2005: 382).

In Bosnia-Herzegovina and Kosovo, the war facilitated the initial process of capital accumulation, which later allowed the new elites to take advantage from the peace process (Andreas 2008: 123–124). Armed conflict expanded the space for criminal groups to operate, often in close cooperation with sections of the political leadership, from the local to the state level. The lack, or extreme weakness, of formal institutional structures during the war facilitated the emergence of political leaders whose legitimacy was not based on democratic mechanisms but derived from sources like violence and patronage.

After the war, nationalist rhetoric and fear dominated each round of elections, allowing the wartime political leadership to achieve forms of legitimation via democratic means. Frequent nationalist rhetoric has been indispensable for galvanizing electoral constituencies. Ethnic competition served the fundamental purpose of legitimizing each nationalist leadership. However, despite the use of inflammatory rhetoric elites have been able to accommodate each other's interests across national lines. Political leaders of all ethnic groups adjusted well to the new post-war relations of power (domestic and international) allowing them ample room for manoeuvre. Ethnic rivalry evolved within shared strategies, arising from the common resolve to preserve inter-group tensions in order to present each nationalist leadership as the solution to the problems actually caused by the nationalists themselves. While containing violence, the political elites stirred social tensions instrumentally to preserve their power.

Legitimized by fear-dominated post-war elections, this nationalist leadership accessed political and administrative positions and through an unscrupulous use of economic resources cultivated relationships with clients and supporters. The post-conflict setting involved an unspoken pact of security and patronage, between nationalist parties and their followers and between government and provincial elites. At the local level, power structures formed around wartime leaders who capitalized on wartime economic activities and, after the signing of the peace agreement, on access to international assistance programmes (ESI 1999). In this politico-economic system, corruption was not an aberration caused by the presence of a few dishonest public officials: it was structural, and became standard operating procedure.

In both Kosovo and Bosnia-Herzegovina, an unwritten pact involved the political leadership of each national group with the main goal of freezing the political status quo, maintaining the control over each respective community and (mis)managing economic resources to the advantage of a relatively small clique of people. This pact allowed for the development of two syndromes of corruption, defined by Michael Johnston (2005) as 'oligarchs and clans' and 'elite cartels'. 'Oligarchs and clans' emerge in the first peacebuilding phase when both the political and economic spheres liberalize and power and wealth are up for grabs in a context of weak institutions and rules. 'Elite cartels' are networks of individuals (including politicians, military officers, businesses people and others) who share benefits among themselves and thus have a common interest in maintaining the status quo (Johnston 2005; see also, more generally, Cama and Coticchia 2018).

Oligarchs and clans in both countries organized society through patronage networks ensuring the protection of those individuals holding power, either formally in local institutions or informally through extralegal relationships. Indeed, post-war power structures have involved various 'informal actors' (Cheng 2012) whose power is sometimes in competition with formal state institutions but more often is 'complementary' and 'accommodating' towards the state (Helmke and Levitsky 2004). Informal actors emerged from the war with enormous political influence which they could exploit to manipulate the rules of the game—for example by taking advantage of economic liberalization and the distribution of international aid. For actors holding public office in both countries, the presence of such players in their power networks has been advantageous because of their contribution in extraction and protection. Ultimately, the institutions which emerged from the war were weak, with formal liberal structures intertwined with informal, illegal and frequently criminal norms and actors and characterized by high levels of corruption (Belloni and Jarstad 2012). Since its inception, this system has guaranteed the control of violence, which is the primary function of each social order (North et al. 2009).

Networks involving both formal and informal actors extended to society. In both Bosnia-Herzegovina and Kosovo, as well as in much of the so-called Global South, civil society and the state intertwine (Migdal 2001). While in ideal-typical Weberian states, civil society organizations (CSOs) represent bottom-up concerns and even contribute to hold institutions accountable, in states emerging from war governmental authorities and CSOs and networks are frequently linked by a clientelistic and patronage system. Contrary to the expectation that civil society is the key arena that supports democratic development (as discussed in Chapter 4), in fact civil society tends to strengthen existing political institutions and regimes—which in post-conflict states are often dysfunctional, corrupt and scarcely accountable (Belloni 2008b). Patronage politics undermines the autonomy of civil society groups who, rather than holding political authorities accountable, may become a reservoir of political support for the ruling party (or parties). As the next chapter will argue, in such cases many organizations, including sport and youth clubs, religious associations, veteran groups and associations of displaced persons refrain from criticism of the political establishment in exchange for access to resources (Paffenholz et al. 2010).

What makes this politico-economic structure viable and self-enforcing is the availability of rents. Rentier economies can be successful in reducing violence, since the distribution of rents motivates elite loyalty to the existing political and economic system, which in turn protects rents, and prevents violence and disorder (North et al. 2009: 5). In addition, limited political and economic competition guarantees patrons' preservation of privileges and the distribution of economic assets and resources to clients (Pugh 2017). Assets and resources, as well as services and public goods, are not distributed on the basis of objective and/or efficiency criteria, but according to the identity of the recipients and their connections. Accordingly, this structure creates incentives for citizens to join patron–client networks, limit political competition and foster a condition of social apathy. In sum, rather than depending on culture or tradition, clientelism and corruption are rational responses to the prevailing politico-economic system. This system has negative consequences for peacebuilding, which includes among its primary goals that of restoring trust levels to what they were before the conflict began (Cheng and Zaum 2012). Indeed, both patronage and clientelism undermine the legitimacy and efficiency of institutions, strengthen mistrust and undemocratic norms and values, and damage generalized trust in society.

3.3   PEACEBUILDING AND THE SEARCH FOR STABILITY

Needless to say, any efforts to improve the efficiency of institutions through expanded political and economic competition has been resisted by the elites (Capussela 2015: 27). Faced by predictable opposition, international peacebuilders have failed to effectively counter this power structure marked by strong criminal, illegal, corrupt and clientelistic activities. Peacebuilders have mostly interpreted this structure as reflecting the weakness of formal state institutions requiring a more concerted international effort to further build and shape local capacities, rather than a political, economic and social configuration with its own ordering logic. Thus, while assertively intervening to mould local institutions, peacebuilders have guaranteed the existing configuration of power, becoming deeply implicated in the disconnection between formal institutional rules and the ways in which these rules have been bent to preserve the political and economic order which emerged from the war.

The heavy emphasis on stability in the immediate post-conflict phase explains the reluctance of external actors to take prompt action against intermediaries, strongmen and leaders whose criminal links and corruption channels were often known. Despite all the invectives against corruption, peacebuilders in both Bosnia-Herzegovina and Kosovo have had a clear understanding of how corruption, along with clientelism, can play an important function in stabilization. This is not necessarily to say that the international community has literally been 'bribing the peace' (Zabyelina and Arsovska 2013) but it recognizes the existence of 'paying for peace' (Le Billon 2003) by creating direct or permissive conditions for malpractice, and by condoning illegal and unethical behaviour because of instrumental reasons. For example, in the case of Kosovo international peacebuilders had detailed information about cases of corruption and organized crime committed by both Albanians and Serbs but they did not initially act on this information. Instead, they used criminal evidence for disciplining and controlling local actors when needed (Visoka 2017: 96).

Overall, rent-seeking and corruption have been central ingredients of these systems. Because of their stabilizing characteristics, even peacebuilders subscribed and acquiesced to the consolidation of routines based on the exploitation of patronage and access to both domestic and international resources (Belloni and Ramović 2019; Capussela 2015: 53). In Kosovo, the post-war United Nations mission (UNMIK) has followed the 'line of least resistance' and adopted a 'disconcertingly passive, compromising approach' (Capussela 2015: 35 and 60). In Bosnia-Herzegovina, despite the fact that international actors have frequently clashed with local nationalists, they have guaranteed the ethnically based political order which emerged in the aftermath of the war and they have been willing to back down from their own liberal principles and conditions when facing elite resistance to change (Belloni 2003).

In both cases, international officials' behaviour resulted from very realist concerns for stability. Because any outbreak of violence would have contradicted the international rhetoric about progress, international peacebuilders have been ready to appease elites, rather than confronting them (Capussela 2015; Leroux-Martin 2014). Particularly in the very first phases of international intervention, when uncertainty offered a wide range of choices, international peacebuilders understood how a heavy-handed emphasis on rule-of-law issues and law enforcement could have had more of a destabilizing impact than the recognition of the complex bargaining patterns between elites and economic entrepreneurs emerging from the war (Cheng and Zaum 2012).

When, by the late 1990s in Bosnia-Herzegovina and the early 2000s in Kosovo, rule of law and corruption started to be a priority of international assistance, this unfolded very cautiously, with implementation of anti-corruption programmes postponed until institutions were deemed sufficiently consolidated to withstand scandals and traumas. In Bosnia-Herzegovina, in February 1999 the Office of the High Representative (OHR) announced the first 'Comprehensive Anti-Corruption Strategy for Bosnia and Herzegovina', which was followed by many more subsequent strategies. The outcome of these efforts was the creation of a 'Potemkin village of reform without many lasting and tangible results' (Perry 2015: 14). International interveners even tried to break the nationalists' hold on power by supporting less-compromised elites through the allocation of significant reconstruction aid. However, when the new international darlings—the Bosnian Serb Milorad Dodik and the Bosniak-dominated but formally multi-ethnic Social Democratic Party— used aid to consolidate their clientelist and authoritarian power structures, they generically cited lack of political will on the part of elites, and citizens' apathetic post-war attitude, to explain why corruption remained pervasive in sectors ranging from the health system to customs. In sum, rather than attempting to tackle those power structures feeding malpractice, peacebuilders remained focused on the symptoms.

3.4   Peacebuilding Transitions and Corruption

Bosnia-Herzegovina and Kosovo have undergone a double transition—from war to peace and from a communist to a formally democratic system—and much of the explanation for continuing malpractice is found in how their mutual interaction has evolved. A first issue concerns the transition from war to peace, or rather—the idea that war would remove the economic rubble of the past. In the 1990s many external observers saw the Balkan wars as the final implosion of unsustainable politico-economic structures—highly destructive events that, by clearing the ground of rent-seeking positions, could provide the opportunity for an externally supported 'fresh start', a way to 'reboot the country' (Strazzari and Kamphuis 2012).

In the reconstruction of Bosnia-Herzegovina during the 1990s and Kosovo in the ensuing years, peacebuilders applied prototypical neoliberal policy packages premised on deregulation and government retreat from economic control, at least in formal terms. Informal, extra-legal arrangements and selective inducements played a role in minimizing the cost of achieving a new market-based system promoting efficiency, without losing sight of stability questions connected to political legitimacy and consent. This tacit understanding was central in the strategic calculus, constituting a large area of don't-ask-don't-tell policies that proved resilient even when other priorities, like economic efficiency, kicked in.

There is a second problem with how international peacebuilders failed to understand the intricacies of previous property regimes (Mungiu-Pippidi 2012). In particular, the institution of social ownership, whereby the Yugoslav legal system identified society as a whole as the owner of a wide range of assets, was ignored, thus paving the way for manipulation during the privatization process (Knudsen 2013). This attitude facilitated, or at least did not hinder, asset-stripping in the immediate aftermath of hostilities, as well as a plethora of accommodation practices to 'get the right document fix' by realigning property and entitlement rights to the ensuing new power configuration. Even though domestic oligarchy took advantage of the persistence of pre-modern social order (Mujanović 2018), international policies actually underpinned the system. Contrary to common mis-characterization, employee or management buy-outs were not encouraged: the main goal was to settle workers' patrimonial claims and open the way to a western governance model (Medjad 2004: 317). In the absence of a functioning domestic market for corporate control, politically loyal managers and entrepreneurs preserved their control, now as new majority stakeholders. In practice, the development of a 'national' economy in both Bosnia-Herzegovina and Kosovo, as well as all other post-Yugoslav states, meant the creation of a national economic elite able to concentrate in its hands the country's wealth.

The second transition from a communist to a formally liberal-democratic but substantively hybrid state intertwined with the first, in favouring the emergence and consolidation of a collusive politico-economic system bent on spoiling state resources and feeding patronage networks. In particular, the vicious 1992–1995 war in Bosnia-Herzegovina, and the 1998–1999 violent escalation in Kosovo contributed to the preservation of authoritarian methods of political control which had characterized the previous regime, and fostered at least three more corruption-conducive conditions.

First, state structures developed symbiotic relations with criminal structures (Strazzari 2007). Some analysts even described the case of Bosnia-Herzegovina as one of 'state capture' by a political-economic criminal elite which emerged from the war: 'a situation in which the ruling oligarchy has complete control over the institutions of the system and manipulates the legal framework and policies to suit their own narrow individual interests' (Transparency International 2013: 23). In the case of Kosovo, virtually all intelligence reports of the post-war period have warned of the threat represented by organized crime, highlighting the role played by extra-legal intelligence structures managed by the main political parties (Capussela 2015: 48–51). The accusations of involvement in human organ smuggling, launched by the Council of Europe against no less than Kosovo's prime minister and ex-KLA commander, Hashim Thaci, further worsened the country's image abroad (Council of Europe 2010).

Second, the heavily decentralized governance structure emerging from the war, including the existence of separate 'entities' and 'quasi-entities' in Bosnia-Herzegovina and Kosovo may be seen as an additional corruption-conducive circumstance.[1] In Bosnia-Herzegovina, this means a central state internally divided into two 'entities' (the Bosniak-Croat Federation and the Serb Republic of Bosnia), a separate Brčko District, in addition to 10 cantons and 143 municipalities. Such a baroque system, in addition to which come the governance powers of the international administration, complicates accountability and provides ample opportunities for rent-seeking behaviour (Andreas 2008: 120). Furthermore, the existence of four semi-independent judicial systems—at the state level, at the level of the two entities, and Brčko District—makes prosecution highly inefficient. Unsurprisingly, 'the judiciary is completely inert and ineffective in the fight against corruption' (Transparency International 2013: 70). Only very few low-ranking officials are prosecuted. Not only excessive backlog cases and long court proceedings make the road to justice expensive and time-consuming, but also nominally independent judges are de facto reliant on political support for their appointments and career advancements, with obvious negative consequences for the fight against corruption involving the political class.[2] In Kosovo, the judiciary is equally ineffective (Skendaj 2014). In addition, the parallel institutions of Kosovo Serbs, backed by Serbia via the Coordination Centre for Kosovo and Metohija, have given rise to an opaque mechanism of territorial self-governance in the Serb-dominated North, with widespread patronage, clientelism and corruption. In both Bosnia-Herzegovina and Kosovo, politically loyal bureaucrats who wrapped themselves patriotically in new nationalist flags could benefit from 'facilitation fees' collected from private business in exchange for authorizations and permits, thereby funding party structures.

Third, nationalism and clientelist politics brought disproportionate growth in the public sector, since nationalist political parties used public institutions to secure political support through patronage and clientelism (Nenadović 2010). In order to get a job in the public administration or government sector, in the first peacebuilding phase it was indispensable, and remains so, to be politically networked and/or to pay a bribe. In Bosnia-Herzegovina it is widely believed, and frequently related to foreign researchers, that even a cleaning job at the University has become a political appointment. Needless to say, well-connected employees have few or no incentives to do their jobs professionally. Used as a pool of votes, the costs of the bloated public sector increased exponentially: over 60% of the RS and Federation Entity budgets are spent to finance public sector salaries and the social safety network (Blagovcanin and Divjak 2015: 12), with particular attention to groups constituting an electoral reservoir such as war veterans (as further discussed below). Similarly, in Kosovo the elites used the public administration as an instrument for patronage (Tadić and Elbasani 2018).

The perverse impact of the lack of accountability and transparency of post-war institutions fostered an environment wherein political leaders could both misappropriate public funds and use state resources to strengthen their clienteles. Political parties have been central in the management of this corruption system (Briscoe and Price 2011). In Bosnia-Herzegovina political parties have captured institutions, which are used for political appointments and fiscal blackmail, thus transforming the political system into a 'partitocracy' (Blagovcanin and Divjak 2015: 6). Political parties have become the vehicles through which former bitter enemies frequently collude to guarantee the smooth operation of their illegal activities. In other words, they embody what Johnston (2005) described as 'elite cartels'. Collaboration among former enemies has been convenient and necessary for safeguarding common interests from external threats posed by domestic and international investigations. Suffice it to mention how the amnesty for crimes committed during the 1992–1995 war did not simply include the war period, but dated back to January 1991, when the three main nationalist parties were first voted into office, and tellingly included economic crimes.

Ruling political parties de facto control public companies which, through public tenders have been 'cash cows' (Perry 2015: 55) for the political elite and a major source of patronage. For example, in the Bosnia-Herzegovina Federation large public companies such as *Elektroproveda* in practice operate as a private company in the hands of the main ruling Bosniak party. Politically affiliated managers regularly hire new employees not on the basis of merit or need, but discretionally to reward supporters. In addition, while the law on public procurement prescribes public tenders, the majority of public procurement is carried out privately while different forms of embezzlement are permitted, including the addition of annexes changing the values of contracts after they are signed, the failure to respect the contract terms, and so on.[3]

Similarly, in Kosovo the management of tenders for major public procurements became big business shortly after the end of hostilities: as powers were delegated from international to local authorities, irregularity, arbitrariness, bribery and, more generally, politicization became increasingly evident, revealing the salience of informal connections (Danielsson 2014; Skendaj 2014). Debates focused on the draining of public budgets for monumental works like the construction of the 'patriotic highway' connecting Pristina to Tirana, an initiative bristling with administrative irregularities and anomalies, eventually resulting in a huge tender won by a US–Turkish consortium (Capussela 2015: 189–192). While monies were spent for questionable infrastructural projects, salaries remained low compared to rising post-war prices, inflated by war-time legacies, by the influx of international aid and by remittances from abroad. In a 2004 survey, 60% of respondents agreed that low salaries for public-sector officials were the main cause of corruption (Hajredini and Ponzio 2004). Electoral pledges of higher salaries clashed with the strict dictates of the IMF: the move was criticized as populism and contributed to creating a serious debt problem. Salary increases for civil servants were never linked to efforts to improve the performance of the civil sector, but functioned as a way to maintain patronage networks and the loyalty of key sectors of the public administration (Capussela 2015: 192–195; Skendaj 2014: 86–88; for a region-wide analysis of the phenomenon, see Bartlett and Prica 2018).

In sum, the transition from a state to a market economy and from a communist to a formally democratic system led to the emergence of a political-economic structure prey to nationalist manipulation, asset-stripping and rent-seeking behaviour. Rather than an aberration, corruption developed as intrinsic to the new power configuration. The proliferation of similar practices deterred foreign investors from the post-war reconstruction machine, while selectively attracting only those who would be politically protected. In short, the post-war/post-communist conditions entailed a sharp increase in the demand for protection, beginning with the protection of contracts and property. As the nature of political authority was contested, and laws were considered obsolete with respect to nascent power configurations, side-payments and extra-legal settlements became the norm.

3.5   CORRUPTION PRACTICES

Considering the politico-economic set of relationships and interests emerging from the double, intersecting transition from a state to a market economy and from war to peace, it is no surprise that since the beginning of the peacebuilding process, both Bosnia-Herzegovina and Kosovo have regularly ranked poorly in Transparency International's Corruption Perception Index. Citizens perceive corruption as endemic.

Within the broader phenomenon as recorded and analysed by corruption surveys, two main categories with different logics and implications can be identified: 'greed' or grand corruption is considered detrimental to public trust; petty or 'need' corruption tends to be condoned, seen as part of informal ways of accommodating things to allow societal life to flow. This can explain why Bosnians remain apparently intolerant of corrupt practices, while these attitudes do not prevent them from participating in informal and illegal behaviour in daily interactions within schools, industries, associations, etc. (UNDP 2009). Likewise, some 55% of Kosovo respondents condemn grand corruption, but say they are willing to pay bribes if there are no alternatives. Thus, if it is necessary to achieve their ends and 'everyone does so', people feel it would be insane to behave otherwise: they compromise their principles and pay the bribe (Center for the Study of Democracy 2010). This kind of conduct shows how corruption in Bosnia-Herzegovina and Kosovo is primarily a collective action problem where, if paying the bribe is the expected behaviour, the benefits are likely to outweigh the costs (Persson et al. 2013).

Involvement in petty or need corruption should be interpreted against a background of traumatic changes in people's lives. Everyday experience was disrupted by the emergence of war and post-war economies, with all related consequences—including massive migration to the cities, swelling the ranks of the economically marginalized and downtrodden. A household that had not fled abroad by the early days of peacebuilding was likely to have an unemployed father, and possibly a daughter who would earn much more than her father's lost salary by knowing some English and working as an interpreter for an international organization (Baker 2012). The salary disparity between locals working for international organizations and others employed by domestic public and private enterprises was considerable, with the former earning four to five times more than the latter (Skendaj 2014: 15). Furthermore, the arrival *en masse* of international organizations often challenged existing cognitive schemes: international assistance meant the presence of officials from former Warsaw Pact 'enemies' such as Romania or Bulgaria, whose transition during the 1990s was not particularly encouraging despite wholehearted international realignment. Such officials were dispatched to monitor economic liberalization and democratization, triggering perplexed and sceptical reactions among local officials and the general population. These foreign officials often admitted the context in which they were working in Bosnia-Herzegovina was frequently less dysfunctional than the one they left back home.[4]

Transformation followed the refrain that corruption was the legacy of the old system, and that liberalization and privatization would do away with it (Knudsen 2013). But that was not what people experienced on the ground, where favouritism was blossoming and new clientelist relations were established towards the international peacebuilding presence. Entering the international circle would typically mean status and privileges, like gaining prominent customers for restaurants or inheriting a car once the mission withdrew. At the same time, international demands for liberalization were accompanied by little effort to rekindle industrial production interrupted by the war, or attempts to build a service economy that could absorb unemployment.

Post-conflict rebuilding in Bosnia-Herzegovina and Kosovo saw survival economies as well as reservoirs of wealth creation in those areas where legality had become evanescent, and where bribes and corruption were increasingly common. By 'areas' it should be understood not only sectors of activity, but also portions of territory: borderlands and customs, for example. Moreover, corruption has been most frequently witnessed in those public sectors producing services to the people (like health care and higher education), or as a form of facilitation in activities concerning the *économie de permis*, where public regulation takes the form of licences and patents (Pugh 2002).

While people have experienced routine dealings with petty corruption, the political and economic leadership has been actively involved in sustaining high-level, or grand, corruption. As mentioned, central to the Bosnian corruption system has been the role played by political parties and high-level politicians. In the summer of 1999, political leaders were accused of embezzling up to $1 billion of reconstruction aid (Hedges 1999). Although this accusation later proved exaggerated, political parties do provide ample opportunities for personal enrichment. There is no state law on organizing and funding political parties, which are established and registered separately in each Entity, where the legal framework does not offer efficient mechanisms for preventing irregularities and abuses. For example, that anonymous donations are allowed permits concealment of both donors and donations. Moreover, since political parties are not public bodies, they are not subject to laws on freedom of access to information enabling public scrutiny. The lack of transparency and the opportunities for abuse combine with sanctions that are mild and rarely applied (Transparency International 2010). Indeed, 'legislation is not implemented sufficiently, appropriately and consistently' (Perry 2015: 20). Bosnian politicians are well aware of the situation in neighbouring Croatia, where in 2012 the former Prime Minister Ivo Sanader was condemned to 10 years in jail on corruption charges, and thus operate to water down legislation and hinder its implementation.[5]

As a result, high-ranking officials suspected of involvement in bribery have generally not been removed from office. The Prime Minister of the Serb Republic of Bosnia, Milorad Dodik, came under investigation for several corruption scandals. In denying the charges, he accused 'Muslim judges' of political bias against him, thus deflecting criticism and effectively consolidating his political status as a champion of the Serb cause—and a patron of the Serb people. Even when trials ended with a conviction, they were overturned. In the most well-known case, Ante Jelavić (Croat member of the Bosnian Presidency between June 1999 and February 2000) was charged with corruption in 2004, found guilty in 2005 and sentenced to 10 years imprisonment. His conviction was overturned a year later, when Jelavić fled to Croatia.

3.6   THE RISE OF THE ANTI-CORRUPTION AGENDA

Since the early peacebuilding days rooting out corruption has been an extremely complicated affair. To begin with, colluding elites have a stake in the status quo, which has served them well by facilitating their access to state's spoils, thus appropriating the means to ensure the perpetuation of their influence in public policy (Bassuener 2017). In Bosnia-Herzegovina, since the government must come to a consensus to deliberate, each party can effectively veto a decision, including those that introduce effective anti-corruption measures. Moreover, because consociational institutions allow each faction to assert control over its own turf, they hinder both transparency and accountability. Voters, CSOs and opposition parties all face considerable monitoring difficulties under consociational institutions elected through proportional representation (Kunikova and Rose-Ackerman 2005).

While the presence of domestic institutions easily prey to ethno-nationalists' interests are important contextual factors, such a presence is not enough to explain the incidence of corruptive behaviour. To understand how peacebuilding organizations have contributed to feeding corruption—at least indirectly—we need to see how the policies they have promoted have had contradictory effects. In theory, such policies were aimed at reducing sleaze, for example by favouring less government involvement in the economy, consequently lessening the opportunities for abuse of public office (Gerring and Thacker 2005). In practice, neo-liberal precepts have given the post-war political-economic elites many opportunities to abuse public office—as explained below—while leaving the citizenry to their own devices, with little access to social insurance or the rule of law. Neo-liberal policies have both encouraged self-help and undermined social cohesion and the establishment of a liberal social contract based on the rule of law (Pugh and Divjak 2012).

In Bosnia-Herzegovina and Kosovo, privatization, perhaps more than any other neo-liberal policy, has helped to create vast opportunities for manipulation and abuse. In Bosnia-Herzegovina, many public assets have been sold off without public bidding, or through dubious deals. The existence of 13 different privatization laws for 13 different constituencies (in addition to the 2 entities, the laws apply to the 10 Federation Cantons, and to the Brčko District) have led to different privatization models easily prey to political parties, who have indirectly managed and guided the process to their advantage by appointing officials in privatization agencies and the management boards of public companies (Transparency International 2013: 183).

In Bosnia-Herzegovina the process of privatization of state-owned assets provided a golden opportunity for quick enrichment for politically well-connected businessmen (Sunj 2013). The most well-known case was perhaps that of *Aluminij* Mostar—Bosnia's most profitable industry (Belloni 2008a: 105). In this instance, a dubious process of privatization transferred ownership from institutions controlled by the local Croat nationalist leadership, to managers affiliated to the main Croat nationalist party. Despite the fact that *Aluminij* suffered little damage during the war, its management board devalued the company from $US 620 million to $US 84 million. As with the vast majority of other Croat-run industries, *Aluminij* did not employ non-Croat workers, effectively preserving a major obstacle to the post-war sustainable return of ethnic minorities.

In Kosovo, endless controversies have surrounded the privatization process, largely due to problems with cutting the double knot of the legal status of the country and social ownership. For years, fundamental questions such as who controls the assets and benefits from the revenues were settled outside the legal system, in power struggles over enterprise management between KLA clienteles and the rival circles of the Democratic League of Kosovo, while the UN Interim Administration did not dare to intervene and challenge emerging power structures (Capussela 2015; ESI 2002: 6). The arrest in 2002, on charges of corruption, of the former director of Kosovo Energy Corporation, the German Jo Trutschler, cast a long shadow on the international lead. After the riots that swept the country in 2004 (King and Mason 2006), a Kosovo Trust Agency (KTA) was established under EU control: its activities have been guided by the concern not to be held accountable for selling off assets too cheaply through dubious tenders marred by corruption allegations (Knudsen 2008: 298–299). Before the handover to local authorities, KTA records were destroyed in a mysterious fire. Overall, the privatization in Kosovo did not lead to an improvement of citizens' economic situation but provided government officials and political parties with the opportunity to favour those groups and companies affiliated with their party (Visoka 2017: 101–102).

While the controversial international role in the privatization process in Bosnia-Herzegovina and Kosovo is frequently commented on, less known is the international indirect support to patronage through civil society development programmes. As part of their goal of developing sustainable domestic governance structures, international peacebuilders have exerted pressure on CSOs and local authorities at all levels to establish partnerships, often conditioning the provision of funding on such a linkage. This pressure has provided the political cover for domestic authorities to distribute resources to their own clientele. In Croat areas of Bosnia-Herzegovina, some of the organizations such as, for example, the veterans' association HVIDRA, have been key components of the local power structure. Likewise, in Serb- and Bosniak-dominated areas, many CSOs are embedded in the existing hybrid governance. Thus, as the next chapter will argue, a major element in effective anti-corruption campaigns—an active and independent civil society playing a watchdog role—has been absent (Belloni 2012). The situation in Kosovo does not differ significantly. Its CSOs have generally reflected existing cleavages within political society and have been embedded in clientelist networks.

After an initial period when the nexus between reforms, clientelism and corruption was avoided in public debate, peacebuilding organizations have begun to place heavy emphasis, in Bosnia-Herzegovina and in Kosovo, on good governance, supporting initiatives to fight malpractice. As a result, anti-corruption work has often responded more to international demands than to local sensitivities and needs. As in the other southeast European countries, anti-corruption programmes have been linked with the commitment to getting closer to the EU, and eventually becoming a member (as further discussed in Chapter 6). This internationally driven process has stressed the ratification of international conventions as the main approach, at least initially, to fighting corruption (Center for the Study of Democracy and Center for Investigative

Reporting 2012). However, although peacebuilding officials were rhetorically committed to the battle against sleaze, they held a keen awareness of the importance of not undermining stability.[6]

The fact that corrupt behaviour has been de facto de-criminalized has facilitated the goal of not upsetting domestic power-holders. Law enforcement activities in Bosnia-Herzegovina involve a range of actors, including police agencies at two entity levels, ministries at the level of the entities and of the 10 cantons, and the Prosecutor's Office. Even when law enforcement officials are free from political interference, which is rarely the case, the baroque institutional system has resulted in difficult obstacles for investigation and prosecution. As a result, in Bosnia-Herzegovina, less than a third of the reported acts of corruption has led to an investigation (Transparency International 2013: 27). About a third of corruption proceedings result in a pardon for the defendants, while the remaining cases result have ended with paroles or fines. Cases brought against high-level politicians or key organized crime actors have been very few and generally ended with release from custody (Center for Investigative Reporting 2011).

Also in Kosovo corruption came into the spotlight a few years after the region was put under interim administration under UNMIK (Capussela 2015). The appearance of various alarming intelligence reports, media articles and survey studies paved the way for the adoption of a national strategy (2003) and for the establishment of an Anti-Corruption Agency (2006). In Kosovo too, officially due to IMF-imposed draconian cuts on public expenditure, the Agency for a long time had no office facilities, no staff other than the director, and no budget. Despite widespread complaints about corruption, no high-profile prosecutions went on record during the first years of international administration. UNMIK generally avoided conducting investigations on high-level corruption, organized crime or war crimes. Combined with the limited independence of the judiciary, which was exposed to heavy interference, this created a corruption-permissive environment which made corruption 'endemic in most sectors' (Capussela 2015: 44). Only later, when Kosovo's CSOs became more differentiated and influential, with some of them (such as *Fol '08* and *Çohu!*) avoiding clientelistic relationships with political parties and beginning to play a watchdog role systematically, did high-level indictments begin to reveal the nature of the problem. Still, doubts remained about whether anti-corruption action was in fact instrumentally bowing to political manipulation and selective targeting (Karadaku 2013).

Overall, since the early peacebuilding phase corruption and clientelism became endemic to political and economic life in both Bosnia-Herzegovina and Kosovo, and remained so in subsequent years. Those structural components for effective anti-corruption action, such as the presence of transparent public institutions, an independent judiciary, free media and an active civil society, have always been either weak or absent. Formally democratic institutions have been put in place, but these are often empty shells, flanked by extra-legal governance structures that exert substantial control over political, economic and social life.

3.7   Conclusions

Rents, corruption and clientelism have been crucial to maintain stability and avoid a relapse into violence in Bosnia-Herzegovina and Kosovo. The architecture of anti-corruption laws, commissions and agencies set up under international pressure did not deter individuals from engaging in bribery. In order to be effective, anti-corruption activities should have been based on a political reading of power relations able to influence the cost–benefit calculus and the expectations of the actors involved, while also promoting the consolidation of new public standards of appropriateness and social legitimacy. However, international peacebuilders have not been willing to accept the risks for stability involved in any activity that could have served to undermine the social, political, and economic conditions upon which the post-war elites have built their power structures.

While international efforts to counter corruption in these new states have been evident, the idea that the international community sat on part of the solution to what is a deeply rooted, indigenous problem is misleading. As regards with the intervening actors, especially in the early post-conflict years, ideological belief in neo-liberal transplant and the existence of an embedded 'ok reporting culture', together with the need to demonstrate that results can be achieved without becoming too deeply involved, played a significant role in the search for stabilization shortcuts. Little effort was made to understand existing continuities with the political past and the war economy.

With regard to those local actors who have emerged from the war to become key stakeholders in the peacebuilding process, Bosnia-Herzegovina and Kosovo show how violent dominance or the elimination of internal competitors has become less and less of an available option, given the watchful eye of an increasingly intrusive international community. While violent competition has often taken the form of organized crime, inter-ethnic accommodation and collusion, including the expectation that each national leadership will (mis)manage its own economic resources itself, has become the norm. Likewise, formal economic policy has never been something that could be decided by victorious elites at the state level: new states came into existence with their hands tied by international financial institutions and various forms of aid conditionality.

Especially in contexts deeply imbued with nationalism and (supposedly non-negotiable) identity issues, therefore, the area that stretches below the level of formal transactions and official service provision has been where negotiable interests could be traded, where accommodation could be sought, and where under-the-table deals could be struck. Corruption has worked as a 'compensation chamber' enabling power relations to be reproduced despite formal constraints and rules: it successfully accelerated the achievement of formalized deals, endowing them with an informal substantial dimension. The latter sometimes bordered on criminal collusion, and were typically regulated by other forms of trust and protection than those of a formal contract.

New states such as Bosnia-Herzegovina and Kosovo have come into being under external protection in a phase in which international peacebuilding organizations were pushing for strong macroeconomic discipline, with public budgets and public spending under tight control. With public spending constrained and international aid as the main resource, corruption allowed consensus to be maintained and loyalty mechanisms oiled according to prevailing power configurations—thus reproducing them, while formally complying with external injunctions and keeping foreign donors happy. However, corruption diverted resources from the public and discouraged new investments, while smoothing the mechanics of the client–state system (local clients for international patrons), and those of the local clientele (notables vs. *peones*). This system of social and political cohesion has been compatible with the survival of the many (who were made docile by war) and with social mobility (read: enrichment) for the very few.

The persistence of corruption, therefore, has to do not so much with a temporary pathological gap characterizing the incomplete business of building a Weberian state, but rather with the emergence of different power constellations and of a distinctive form of the state, characterized by hybrid systems of accountability, discontinuous forms of regulation and control, and pervasive extra-legal governance structures. This system works as long as the rents from reconstruction aid can be guaranteed, but shows cracks, signs of growing discontent and possible anti-corruption and anti-elite popular outbursts when external assistance dwindles. Large-scale violent protests erupting in February 2014 in Bosnia-Herzegovina, discussed in Chapter 8, testified to the long-term difficulties with maintaining social peace when resource allocation is skewed in favour of a relatively small group of politically connected people, and international aid constantly decreases. As the next chapter will show, in order to improve the functioning of state institutions international peacebuilders turned their energies towards building domestic civil society, seen as an alternative to corrupt public officials. However, in so doing, they addressed only the symptoms of the post-war economic system.

NOTES

1. Interview with Azhar Kalamujić, journalist, Center for Investigative Reporting, Sarajevo, July 2015. Similar corruption-conducive tendencies are visible in Serbia and Croatia (Kleibrink 2015).
2. Interview with Srdjan Blagovcanin, Executive Director of Transparency International Bosnia Herzegovina, Sarajevo, July 2015; see also, Blagovcanin and Divjak (2015).
3. Interview with Eldin Karić, ACCOUNT, Sarajevo, July 2015. See also, Voloder (2015).
4. Private conversations with OSCE officials in Sarajevo, August 1996.
5. Interview with Srdjan Blagovcanin, Transparency International, Sarajevo, July 2015.
6. Interview with Brigitte Kuchar, Programme Manager for Home Affairs, Delegation of the European Union to Bosnia and Herzegovina, Sarajevo, July 2015.

REFERENCES

Andreas, P. (2008). *Blue helmets and black markets: The business of survival in the siege of Sarajevo.* Ithaca: Cornell University Press.

Baker, C. (2012). Prosperity without security: The precarity of interpreters in postsocialist, postconflict Bosnia-Herzegovina. *Slavic Review, 71*(4), 849–872.

Bartlett, W., & Prica, I. (2018). *Debt in the super-periphery: The case of the Western Balkans* (Unpublished paper), on file with author.

Bassuener, K. (2017). A durable oligarchy: Bosnia and Herzegovina's false post-war democratic transition. In S. P. Ramet, C. M. Hassenstab, & O. Listhaug

(Eds.), *Building democracy in the Yugoslav successor states: Accomplishments, setbacks, and challenges since 1990* (pp. 216–255). Cambridge: Cambridge University Press.

Belloni, R. (2003). *A dubious democracy by fiat.* Transitions Online. https://www.tol.org/client/article/10465-dubious-democracy-by-fiat.html?print.

Belloni, R. (2008a). *Statebuilding and international intervention in Bosnia.* London and New York: Routledge.

Belloni, R. (2008b). Civil society in war-to-democracy transitions. In A. K. Jarstad & T. D. Sisk (Eds.), *From war to democracy: Dilemmas of peacebuilding* (pp. 182–210). Cambridge: Cambridge University Press.

Belloni, R. (2012). Part of the problem or part of the solution? Civil society and corruption in post-conflict states. In C. Cheng & D. Zaum (Eds.), *Corruption and post-conflict peacebuilding: Selling the peace?* (pp. 136–218). London: Routledge.

Belloni, R., & Jarstad, A. (Eds.). (2012). Hybrid peace governance [special issue]. *Global Governance: Review of Multilateralism and International Organization, 18*(1).

Belloni, R., & Ramović, J. (2019, forthcoming). Elite and everyday social contracts in Bosnia-Herzegovina: Pathways to forging to a national social contract? *Journal of Intervention and Statebuilding.*

Blagovcanin, S., & Divjak, B. (2015). *How Bosnia's political economy holds it back and what to do about it.* Washington, DC: Center for Transatlantic Studies, Johns Hopkins University.

Bojičić-Dželilović, V., & Kostovicova, D. (2013). Europeanisation and conflict networks: Private sector development in post-conflict Bosnia-Herzegovina. *East European Politics, 29*(1), 19–35.

Briscoe, I., & Price, M. (2011). *Kosovo new map of power: Governance and crime in the wake of independence* (Resource document). The Clingendael Institute. http://www.clingendael.nl/publication/kosovos-new-map-power-governance-and-crime-wake-independence. Accessed 5 December 2013.

Cama, G., & Coticchia, F. (2018, November 30). Political parties matter: A research agenda on interactions among elites in post-conflict democracies. *Contemporary Politics*, online first. https://doi.org/10.1080/13569775.2018.1552236.

Capussela, A. L. (2015). *State-building in Kosovo: Democracy, corruption and the EU in the Balkans.* London and New York: I.B. Tauris.

Center for Investigative Reporting. (2011, March). *Camping around fire instead of going to prison* (Resource document). http://www.cin.ba. Accessed 5 December 2013.

Center for the Study of Democracy. (2010). *Examining the links between organized crime and corruption.* Sofia: Center for the Study of Democracy.

Center for the Study of Democracy and Center for Investigative Reporting. (2012). *Countering corruption in Bosnia and Herzegovina: 2001–2011.* Sofia and Sarajevo: Center for the Study of Democracy and Center for Investigative Reporting.

Cheng, C. (2012). Private and public interests: Informal actors, informal influence, and economic order after war. In M. Berdal & D. Zaum (Eds.), *The political economy of post-conflict statebuilding* (pp. 63–78). London: Routledge.

Cheng, C., & Zaum, D. (Eds.). (2012). *Corruption and post-conflict peacebuilding: Selling the peace?* London: Routledge.

Council of Europe. (2010, December 12). *Inhuman treatment of people and illicit trafficking of human organs in Kosovo.* Brussels, S/Jur (2010) 46.

Danielsson, A. (2014). *On the power of informal economies and the informal economies of power: Rethinking informality, resilience and violence in Kosovo.* Uppsala: Acta Universitatis Upsaliensis.

ESI (European Stability Initiative). (2002). *The Ottoman dilemma: Power and property relations under the UNMIK.* Pristina: ESI.

ESI (European Stability Initiatives). (1999, October 14). *Reshaping international priorities in Bosnia and Herzegovina: Bosnian power structures, Part I.* Berlin, Brussels, and Sarajevo: ESI.

Gerring, J., & Thacker, S. C. (2005). Do neoliberal policies deter corruption? *International Organization, 59*(Winter), 233–254.

Hajredini, H., & Ponzio, R. (2004). *Combating corruption in Kosovo citizens survey: A citizens' perceptions survey in support of the Kosovo's anti-corruption strategy.* Pristina: Office of the Prime Minister and UNDP Kosovo.

Hedges, C. (1999, August 17). Leaders in Bosnia are said to steal up to $1 billion. *The New York Times*, p. A1.

Helmke, G., & Levitsky, S. (2004). Informal institutions and comparative politics: A research agenda. *Perspectives on Politics, 2*(4), 725–740.

Horvat, S., & Štiks, I. (Eds.). (2015). *Welcome to the desert of post-socialism: Radical politics after Yugoslavia.* London and New York: Verso.

Jayasuriya, K. (2005). Beyond institutional fetishism: From the developmental to the regulatory state. *New Political Economy, 10*(4), 381–387.

Johnston, M. (2005). *Syndromes of corruption: Wealth, power and democracy.* Cambridge: Cambridge University Press.

Karadaku, L. (2013, March 2). High-level corruption still a problem in Kosovo, some say. *Southeast European Times*, p. 1.

King, I., & Mason, W. (2006). *Peace at any price: How the world failed Kosovo.* Ithaca, NY: Cornell University Press.

Kleibrink, A. (2015). *Political elites and decentralization reforms in the post-socialist Balkans: Regional patronage networks in Serbia and Croatia.* Houndmills: Palgrave.

Knudsen, R. A. (2008). *Privatisation in Kosovo: The international project 1999–2008.* Oslo: NUPI Report.

Knudsen, R. A. (2013). Privatization in Kosovo: 'Liberal peace' in practice. *Journal of Intervention and Statebuilding, 7*(3), 287–307.

Kunikova, J., & Rose-Ackerman, S. (2005). Electoral rules and constitutional structures as constraints on corruption. *British Journal of Political Science, 35*(4), 573–606.

Le Billon, P. (2003). Buying peace or fuelling war: The role of corruption in armed conflicts. *Journal of International Development, 15*(4), 413–426.

Lemay-Hébert, N., & Murshed, S. M. (2016). Rentier statebuilding in a post-conflict economy: The case of Kosovo. *Development and Change, 47*(3), 517–541.

Leroux-Martin, P. (2014). *Diplomatic counterinsurgency: Lessons from Bosnia and Herzegovina.* Cambridge: Cambridge University Press.

Medjad, K. (2004). The fate of the Yugoslav model: A case against legal conformity. *American Journal of Comparative Law, 52*(1), 287–319.

Migdal, J. (2001). *State in society: Studying how states and societies transform and constitute one another.* Cambridge: Cambridge University Press.

Mujanović, J. (2018). *Hunger and fury: The crisis of democracy in the Balkans.* London: Hurst & Co.

Mungiu-Pippidi, A. (2012). Perpetual transitions: Contentious property and Europeanization in south-eastern Europe. *East European Politics and Society, 26*(2), 340–361.

Nenadović, M. (2010). An uneasy symbiosis: The impact of international administrations on political parties in postconflict countries. *Democratization, 17*(6), 1153–1175.

North, D. C., Wallis, J. J., Webb, S. B., & Weingast, B. R. (2009). *Limited access orders: Rethinking the problems of development and violence* (Unpublished working paper).

Paffenholz, T., Belloni, R., Spurk, C., Kurtenbach, S., & Orjuela, C. (2010). Enabling and disabling factors for civil society peacebuilding. In T. Paffenholz (Ed.), *Civil society and peacebuilding: A critical assessment* (pp. 405–424). Boulder, CO: Lynne Rienner.

Perry, V. (2015). Constitutional reform in Bosnia and Herzegovina: Does the road to confederation go through the EU? *International Peacekeeping, 22*(5), 490–510.

Persson, A., Rothstein, B., & Teorell, J. (2013). Why anticorruption reforms fail—Systemic corruption as collective action problem. *Governance: An International Journal of Policy, Administration, and Institutions, 26*(3), 449–471.

Pugh, M. (2002). Postwar political economy in Bosnia and Herzegovina: The spoils of peace. *Global Governance, 8*(4), 467–482.

Pugh, M. (2017). Oligarchy and economic legacy in Bosnia and Herzegovina. *Peacebuilding, 5*(3), 223–238.

Pugh, M., & Divjak, B. (2012). The political economy of corruption in Bosnia and Herzegovina. In C. S. Cheng & D. Zaum (Eds.), *Corruption and post-conflict peacebuilding: Selling the peace?* (pp. 99–113). London: Routledge.

Skendaj, E. (2014). *Creating Kosovo: International oversight and the making of ethical institutions.* Ithaca: Cornell University Press.

Strazzari, F. (2007). The decade horribilis: Organized crime and organized violence along the Balkan peripheries, 1991–2001. *Mediterranean Politics, 12*(2), 185–209.

Strazzari, F., & Kamphuis, B. (2012). Hybrid economies and statebuilding: On the resilience of the extralegal. *Global Governance, 18*(1), 57–72.

Sunj, N. (2013, May). Top ten privatization plunders in Bosnia and Herzegovina: A root cause of the rebellion. *Europe Solidaire Sans Frontières* (Resource document). https://www.europe-solidaire.org/spip.php?article31614. Accessed 8 December 2013.

Tadić, K., & Elbasani, A. (2018). State-building and patronage networks: How political parties embezzled the bureaucracy in post-war Kosovo. *Southeast European and Black Sea Studies, 18*(2), 149–164.

Transparency International. (2010). *CRINIS study: Study of the transparency of political party financing in Bosnia-Herzegovina.* Sarajevo: TI.

Transparency International. (2013). *National integrity system assessment: Bosnia and Herzegovina 2013.* Banja Luka and Sarajevo: TI.

UNDP (United Nations Development Programme). (2009). *The ties that bind: Social capital in Bosnia-Herzegovina.* Sarajevo: UNDP.

Visoka, G. (2017). *Shaping peace in Kosovo: The politics of peacebuilding and statehood.* Houndmills: Palgrave.

Voloder, N. (2015, August). *Transparent public procurement in Bosnia and Herzegovina: New solutions for an old problem.* Sarajevo: Analitika Center for Social Research.

Xenakis, S. (2010). Pride and prejudice: Comparative corruption research and the British case. *Crime, Law and Social Change, 54*(1), 39–61.

Zabyelina, Y., & Arsovska, J. (2013). Rediscovering corruption's other side: Bribing for peace in post-conflict Kosovo and Chechnya. *Crime, Law and Social Change, 60*(1), 1–24.

CHAPTER 4

Addressing the Symptoms Through Civil Society Building

4.1 Introduction

The initial peacebuilding phase in both Bosnia-Herzegovina and Kosovo allowed ethno-nationalists with dubious democratic credentials to occupy political and managerial positions and to manage public resources to the advantage of a small clique of people. International peacebuilding agencies oversaw the post-war transition while ensuring the preservation of stability, or negative peace, at all costs. Their approach paved the way to the further consolidation of political elites through patronage and clientelism. The subsequent rise and affirmation of intransigent ethno-national leaders further complicated the peacebuilding process, and induced external interveners to consider alternative avenues to influence domestic political dynamics. International actors attempted to exit from a political cul-de-sac essentially through two main means: the assertive use of executive, legislative and judicial powers to remove domestic obstacles to the peacebuilding agenda, and the strengthening of civil society, which was identified as the arena able to mediate and possibly solve the contradictions inherent in a political process hijacked by intransigent elites.

Neither one of these two strategies proved particularly successful. The imposition of legislation, policy framework, and even institutions both allowed domestic elites to free ride on international initiatives and fostered a culture of dependency. Meanwhile, while praising bottom-up

© The Author(s) 2020
R. Belloni, *The Rise and Fall of Peacebuilding
in the Balkans*, Rethinking Peace and Conflict Studies,
https://doi.org/10.1007/978-3-030-14424-1_4

participation as an essential democratization component, the effort aimed at sustaining the development of domestic civil society was driven from the top-down, with international agencies providing the resources and often the blueprint for the process to take place. As a result, rather than providing the space for a new social contract, civil society became an arena for the implementation of a technocratic governance agenda. The gradual phasing out of bilateral donors, and the related growing role of the European Union (EU) in the country since the early 2000s, did not significantly change this pattern of intervention.

In discussing the internationally-led civil society building agenda, this chapter focuses on the case of Bosnia-Herzegovina where the civil society strategy was initially implemented. Later international engagement in Kosovo reflected a 'copy, paste and delete strategy' (McMahon 2017: 125) which was essentially modelled on its neighbour to the north. In both Bosnia-Herzegovina and Kosovo (in addition to FYROM, Croatia, Serbia, and Montenegro) peacebuilding agencies funded, trained, evaluated, advised and, eventually, de-funded local civil society organizations. A dependency trap involved domestic organizations everywhere in the region. Aid distortion, a short-term project-based obsession, the focus on service delivery, and the privilege given to urban-based organizations all testify to the limits and flaws involved in attempting to develop civil society organizations from the outside. The unequal power dynamics between outsiders and insiders discouraged empowerment and capacity building, and ultimately had a limited impact in advancing peace. When the NGO boom was followed by a bust as a result of declining international assistance, the disembeddedness of local civil society organizations from local structures became increasingly apparent (McMahon 2017).

This chapter is structured as follows. First, it briefly reviews the structural contradictions of the 1995 DPA and the international community's attempt to overcompensate for these contradictions by creating a de facto protectorate. Second, it shows how this interventionist approach went hand in hand with an exploration of alternative peacebuilding avenues, and in particular with an increasing focus on civil society development. Third, the chapter discusses the top-down, NGO-focused, technocratic nature of civil society building and its limitations. In particular, because the Bosnian political system was both prey to poor governance and unable to produce a constituency for reform, international actors attempted to support the 'demand side' of reform through their backing and funding of civil society's anti-corruption activities.

Bottom-up pressures and demands for better governance were expected to dissuade officials from engaging in corrupt practices for fear of electoral and/or social consequences (Perry 2015: 87). Finally, the chapter introduces the increasing EU role in the country, which is further discussed in Chapters 5 and 6. The EU supported an approach to peacebuilding placing less emphasis on external imposition and more on the domestic ownership of reforms and on local agency. However, despite the rhetoric on participation, inclusion and ownership, the EU furthered a narrow vision of civil society, instrumentally focused on NGOs.

4.2   Peace Troubles and the Rise of the Civil Society Agenda

The DPA created a byzantine institutional structure composed of two federal units, or 'entities': the Federation of Bosnia-Herzegovina, dominated by Croats and Bosniaks (Muslims) and the Republika Srpska (RS), controlled by the Serbs. At Dayton, it was decided that the Federation would be internally divided into ten cantons, each with their own constitution, an assembly elected by the Federation voters, a prime minister and ministries. By contrast, the RS constitutional structure was conceived in a much more centralized way. The central government, standing above the two entities, was granted only limited powers: only three ministries were created (Foreign Affairs, Foreign Trade, and Civil Affairs and Communications)—a number which increased overtime to the current nine ministries. Despite this growth, the Bosnian state remains rather weak, leaving much political power at the level of the entities, which maintain wide legislative prerogatives. The post-Dayton increase in the number of state ministries and the related transfer of competences from the entities to the state has not removed real power from the sub-state level (FPI BH 2008). The most significant indicator of the weakness of central institutions lies in their budget, which is not only significantly smaller than that of the entities, but also largely dependent upon transfers from them (see Belloni 2008a: Chapter 3; Bieber 2005: Chapter 3).

This decentralized political structure was supposed to facilitate the achievement of some key liberal peacebuilding objectives identified by the agreement's international midwives. Not unlike other post-conflict states, Bosnia-Herzegovina was expected to benefit from the key tenets of the liberal peace, including democratic institutions and a market economy. Accordingly, the Constitution, which is included in the DPA as Annex 4, affirmed that 'Bosnia and Herzegovina shall be a democratic state', operating 'under the rule of law and with free and democratic elections', ensuring the 'highest level of internationally recognized human rights and fundamental freedoms' and promoting, among other things, 'the general welfare and economic growth through the protection of private property and the promotion of a market economy'. From the beginning of the peace process, however, progress towards these ambitious liberal-democratic goals and market principles was hindered by at least three major structural weaknesses underpinning the agreement (for further analysis of the DPA's contradictions see Caplan 2000).

First, the DPA established political institutions which were not intended to create the conditions for effective government but to prevent each group from imposing its own views on the others (FPI BH 2008). The nationalist leadership of each ethnic group obtained almost exclusive control over its own national constituency, as well as the possibility of vetoing decisions affecting its own 'national interest'. In practice, central institutions were constantly deadlocked. In the first post-war years political parties did not even need to formally exercise their veto rights, since law-making bodies rarely met and contentious issues did not make any progress in the legislative process. Opportunities for obstructing the process increased with the slow improvement in the functionality of institutions. Overall, between 1996 and 2010 the veto was placed on over 160 legal acts and proposals (Džihić and Wieser 2011: 1812). Together with the central institutions all other institutional levels, from the entities to the municipalities, came to be dominated by wartime leaders—who skilfully ensured their political survival by depicting the other groups as an existential threat while simultaneously proposing themselves as the solution to that threat. As discussed in Chapter 3, the use of patronage and access to post-war reconstruction funds further consolidated their grip on power. As a result, the peace process moved forward at a glacial pace, and sometimes not even that. Since the mid-2000s, in particular, nationalist rhetoric has been increasing, while the working of democratic institutions has 'deteriorated significantly' (BTI 2009: 3).

Second, not only did Bosnia-Herzegovina's constitution create inefficient institutions prey to nationalist manipulation, but also it elevated ethnic discrimination as a principle of law, with important consequences for individual human rights. By granting each of the three main ethnic groups a special status as a 'constituent people' of Bosnia-Herzegovina, the constitution created the conditions for the ethnicization of state institutions (Mujkić 2007). The three-member Presidency consists of one Croat, one Bosniak and one Serb. Membership to the Upper House of the state parliament is also restricted to representatives of the same three constituent peoples. In practice, the DPA prohibits members of ethnic minorities (identified in the constitution as 'others')—about half a million Bosnians, out of a total of about 4 million—from holding major state posts.

In addition to openly discriminating against individuals who do not belong to the three main ethnic groups, the DPA's prioritization of group rights created an obstacle to the pursuit of other goals of the peace agreement, in particular the commitment to support the conditions for the post-war re-establishment of a degree of multi-ethnicity. As Annex 7 of the DPA stated, Bosnian refugees and displaced persons (DPs) have 'the right freely to return to their home of origin'. However, the simultaneous presence of a collective right to exclusive self-government for the three main ethnic groups and the right of individuals to return to the places from which they were expelled during the war through multiple campaigns of ethnic cleansing, proved hard to reconcile. While pushing for return, prominent international officials had to recognize how the re-creation of the celebrated multi-ethnic character of the country was wishful thinking (see, for example, Petritsch 2001: 331–333).

The DPA's third, main structural weakness involves the role assigned to international actors in peace implementation. The civilian head of the peace operation, the High Representative of the International Community and its Office (OHR), was given the task to supervise the implementation of the DPA but was not granted any authority over the military component. Local ethno-nationalists exploited this enforcement gap in order to hinder or delay the implementation of various terms of the agreement. After little progress in peace implementation, the OHR's limited powers were increased in late 1997, when the institution was granted extensive executive prerogatives such as the possibility of imposing legislation and removing elected officials. These new powers were used extensively and have led to the establishment of a de facto protectorate. In economic, financial and social policy, Bosnia-Herzegovina's numerous governments have generally been keen to receive from international agencies a set of pre-packaged policies, which they could implement (or not) while blaming foreign peacebuilders for the consequences of their actions. At least in some cases, international assertiveness has been fundamental in advancing peacebuilding goals. For example, the imposition of a set of property laws created favourable conditions for refugees and DPs to reclaim their properties. However, while tens of thousands took advantage of this possibility, the majority of them did so only to sell their properties and leave again for those areas where their group constituted a numerical majority (Toal and Dahlman 2011).

According to Sumantra Bose (2002), in the first few peacebuilding years most positive results in the implementation of the DPA were achieved primarily through the presence, assistance, pressure and, above all, the assertiveness of the international community. On the down side, however, peacebuilding agencies increasingly focused their attention on the symptoms of dysfunctional politics, rather than its causes. International officials imposed legislation, removed elected officials, vetted police officers, created new ministries and state agencies—while continuing to guarantee the political (dis)order established by the DPA. Extensive international intervention stimulated the development of a 'dependency syndrome' (Ashdown 2007: 238)—as local actors often refused to implement significant political, economic and social reforms on the expectation that the OHR would intervene and assume the political costs of change. In addition to undermining domestic political responsibilities, the external imposition of policy created the superficial impression that the system was 'working', thus alleviating pressures for structural reforms (FPI BH 2008: 42; Belloni 2008a: 32).

In sum, while the DPA proved successful in ending the war, it failed to create the foundations for a functioning polity, and the conditions for successful peacebuilding. The DPA did not create ethnic and religious divisions in the country, but cemented their existence, severely hindering the possibility that civic, non-nationalist identities could emerge and affirm themselves. An 'apartheid cartography' (Campbell 1999) enforced a nationalist spatial framework upon citizens. Thus, the constitutional structure both reflected and reinforced the deep divisions existing within Bosnian society.

At the societal level, division remained the fundamental characteristic of the country, with considerable levels of mutual mistrust and suspicion (O'Loughlin 2010; Hakånsson and Sjöholm 2007). After a decade of peacebuilding activities, a major UNDP study on social attitudes concluded that trust between people was 'virtually non-existent' (UNDP 2007). Especially in the countryside, ethnic homogenization was apparent and divisions were rife in all sectors of life (BTI 2009). Everything from greetings to soccer shirts was utilized to identify one's ethnic belonging and religious persuasion. Religious divisions were frequently carried over to the political sphere, with each group claiming the superiority of its own worldviews and practices and religious leaders repeatedly sought to influence election results in favour of the main nationalist parties. Education policy perpetuated ethnic separation through the adoption of separate curricula, teaching languages and religious education. Crucially, education policy also failed to provide young people with practical skills to improve their employability. Between 1995 and 2006, youth unemployment increased from 50 to 62%. Unsurprisingly, tens of thousands of young people, frequently the most skilled ones, left the country in droves during the first post-war decade (UNDP 2007), and many more continued to do so in later years.

Confronted by an unworkable political system, dominated by wartime ethnic leaders, and a deeply divided citizenry, from 1998 onwards international actors increasingly began to rethink their peacebuilding strategy. Rather than addressing the structural conditions that favoured the affirmation of dysfunctional, nationalist, and corrupt domestic politics, the international community circumvented the problem by turning to the development of civil society. All actors involved in the peacebuilding experimentalist governance (see Chapter 1) found in the enhancement of civil society the best option to address the limits of implementation of the DPA. The international community used civil society as a subcontractor for implementing its peacebuilding agenda. Local elites understood civil society as either a reservoir of political support or a toothless sphere with no significant local grounding—and thus endorsed the effort. Finally, domestic English-speaking entrepreneurs, particularly in bigger towns, hoped to capitalize on the international community's strategy and rushed to set up civil society organizations.

This civil society building enthusiasm emerged as a result of the difficulties with the implementation of the DPA. Although the civil society realm is undoubtedly a key component of the liberal peace, such a realm was ignored by the DPA. Rather, the agreement relied on the post-war cooperation of wartime ethnic leaders, in progressing towards ambitious democratization and marketization goals. However, the structural contradictions of the agreement, with the related Sisyphean difficulties in peace implementation, led donors to revise their intervention strategy to include an important civil society element. Civil society building came to be interpreted as a way to address, and possibly resolve, the weaknesses embedded in the deal which ended the war (Belloni 2001).

Rather than directing their attention exclusively to the building of state institutions, international actors increasingly focused on cultivating and promoting the 'right' kind of democratic culture from the bottom-up. Research emerging during the first post-Cold War years on civil society's contribution to both democracy and peace seemed to confirm the possibility that civil society could bring important practical benefits to post-war transitions. In particular, the presence of a robust civil society was thought to be strongly correlated to that of a functioning democracy, leading some scholars to claim that civil society and democracy reinforced each other (Putnam 1993; Edwards 2003). In addition, civil society was frequently credited for its positive contribution to the development of peaceful, non-violent relationships among citizens and groups (Varshney 2002). In sum, as Birte Vogel (2016: 14) argues, 'to donors, peace-oriented civil society *is* the liberal peace' (italics in the original).

Needless to say, civil society's positive impact on both democracy and peace could require a long time to take root, and could not be taken for granted (Belloni 2008b; Paffenholz 2010). Civil society organizations could also have a negative influence on post-war political transitions since, as explained in the previous chapter, some of these organizations perpetuate societal divisions, breed sectarianism and, in the most extreme cases, even participate in violence. Nonetheless, international donors held a generally positive view of civil society organizations and their role in advancing a democratization agenda. To begin with, by directing resources to civil society organizations, international donors could sidestep, at least in part, unpalatable domestic nationalist elites. Moreover, donors widely believed that the non-governmental sector provided a cheaper and more efficient alternative to government service provision, thus removing the responsibility of the state (and more broadly of international organizations) from such a task. At the same time, civil society organizations were perceived as closely connected to the grassroots and therefore able to reach the most marginalized and disadvantaged. Thus, civil society organizations could provide a channel for both expressing and meeting citizens' needs, and a means to favour local 'ownership' of the peace process, at least on paper. Finally, as further discussed below, civil society organizations were also thought to be an antidote against widespread corruption (Belloni 2012).

Overall, by re-focusing their intervention on civil society development, international organizations hoped to turn complex political, social and economic processes into manageable issues of governance and policy. The emphasis on civil society development implicitly allowed international actors to set aside the structural contradictions embedded in the peace agreement and to focus on local conditions as matters requiring technical and mechanistic approaches rather than political solutions. Crucially, by re-focusing intervention on civil society, the international community located the difficulties in peace implementation at the level of domestic factors (such as underdevelopment, post-war trauma, lack of democratic traditions, scarce technical capacities and so forth). The Bosnian people themselves were thought to lack the capacities to fully gain from the benefits offered by the presence and work of peacebuilding organizations and thus they also became targets of international attention.

International organizations' understanding of Bosnians' electoral behaviour, and ways to change it, provides an example of the technocratic approach adopted by peacebuilding actors. For international policymakers it was puzzling that, despite their record, nationalist parties were regularly voted into power (Hulsey 2010). Peacebuilders' confusion about Bosnians' choices at the polls reflected a limited understanding of the political and social context of intervention. To begin with, setting aside the first few post-war electoral rounds when participation at the polls was high (in one instance, voter turnout was actually more than 100%) about half of the population does not participate into the elections, since institutions are captured by corrupt and inept leaders and the consociational system makes political accountability very difficult to achieve. Those who do choose to participate fall within three broad categories: first, there are die-hard nationalists, who consistently support their respective political parties. Second, members of political parties' patronage networks pragmatically support those leaders who guarantee them access to state jobs and other perks, such as pensions. Patronage makes many Bosnians invested in the existing system, and thus helps discipline dissent at the polls—and more generally in the public sphere. Finally, some citizens may recognize the limits of the existing political and economic order, but choose to vote for their nationalist leadership in the expectation that voters of other groups will choose the most extremist option available to them, thus being trapped in what could be described as the 'dilemma of the ethno-political prisoner' (Mujkić and Hulsey 2010).

International peacebuilders rarely grasped the complex set of motivations behind electoral behaviour. Rather, they judged Bosnians as apathetic and/or lacking civic virtues because of the influence of a supposed 'Bosnian mentality.' Decades of totalitarianism and war presumably required local authorities to initiate and/or approve change. Furthermore, citizens were supposedly prevented from opposing nationalism by the fear of the social consequences resulting from being singled out as a 'troublemaker' (Nansen Dialogue Centre Sarajevo and Saferworld 2012: 41–42). Accordingly, by the late 1990s the reform of Bosnians' mentality in the direction of greater political moderation and civic activism was considered as necessary to foster the emergence of a democratic ethos, convince Bosnians to vote for moderate political parties, and thus to ground the building of democratic institutions on better foundations (Belloni 2001). Voter education programmes, typically provided by NGOs, provided the supposed technical solution to the political conundrum presented by Bosnians' electoral behaviour.

Needless to say, such a solution failed to take into proper account the complexity of Bosnian political life. It downplayed the responsibilities of both domestic elites, who built political consensus by exploiting ethnic divisions, and those of international organizations, who frequently failed to present a workable strategy to further the liberal peacebuilding goals of the DPA.

4.3   The Ambiguities of Civil Society Building

From these assumptions, international donors provided considerable resources to civil society building projects (McMahon 2017: 97). This international support led to important quantitative achievements (Belloni and Hemmer 2010). By 2010, more than 12,000 organizations were registered in the country, although it was estimated that only about 55% of them (around 6600) were active. More than 70% of active organizations were member benefit organizations (MBOs), established to work in the interests of their members, while the remaining ones were so-called public benefit organizations (PBOs), whose purpose was to work in the general public interest (TACSO 2010: 17–18). While MBOs were generally small and financially dependent on local authorities, which tended to direct the bulk of their economic support towards sports clubs and veterans associations, PBOs were professional, well-developed organizations, located in Bosnia-Herzegovina's major towns, with more or less regular access to international donors.

Despite the significant numerical presence of civil society organizations, their overall impact was rather modest. There are two sets of reasons for this. The first was the domination of ethnic affiliation over civic consciousness. Because political representation depended on ethnic belonging, bottom-up, citizens-based, ethnic-blind initiatives were discouraged. Rather than aggregating and expressing citizens' interests, the public space tended to be channelled via ethnic representation (Mujkić 2007). The legal framework, which reflected the divided nature of the Bosnian state, further hindered civil society activities. The 2002 state level Law on Associations and Foundations coexisted with three other different laws, one for the Federation, one for the RS, and one for the Brcko District in the north-east corner of the country. The place of registration of an association made immediately apparent its ethnic character, thus hindering the possibility of conducting activities in areas controlled by another ethnic group (Žeravčić and Biščević 2009: 9). In this context, civil society organizations were unsuccessful in their efforts to aggregate across ethnic lines, to engage with the general public and to influence domestic political processes. The second reason for civil society's modest impact had to do with international policy-making. Rather than engaging with the complexities of the social, political and economic context and the constraints and opportunities it could offer to civil society development, international donors adopted a rather technical approach based on the focus, and sometimes even the obsession, with the quantifiable, numerical growth of NGOs.

The international approach to civil society building has been criticized on several grounds. To begin with, the attempt to 'export' civil society in the shape of NGOs has been described as a benevolent form of colonialism (Sampson 2002). Rather than supporting the development of indigenous, locally rooted resources, the civil sector was colonized by international actors and 'their frameworks, assumptions, meanings and practices' (Stubbs 2001: 24). Frequently, peacebuilding intervention led to the creation of organizations which were virtual clones of their western counterparts and which contributed to the imposition of exogenous agendas on local communities. These agendas, in turn, had only a limited connection with local needs. Among the many possible examples, suffice it to mention international donors' focus on projects aimed at post-war 'reconciliation' between former warring parties, which were particularly popular among international donors in the second half of the

1990s and early 2000s. While this focus was intuitively understandable in a post-civil war context, in reality one was hard pressed to find any genuine interest among Bosnians of different ethnic backgrounds for this theme (Belloni and Hemmer 2010: 147).

Second, and consequently, peacebuilding organizations boosted an artificial non-state sector with little or no connection with the local reality, thus contributing to the creation of a credibility gap with citizens. Bosnian organizations, and above all PBOs, were largely dependent on the desires and interests of their donors (Žeravčić and Biščević 2009: 93). As David Chandler (1999: 151–152) put it: 'the unintended consequence of creating civil society NGOs which are reliant on external support has been that they are never forced into building their own base or popular support or take on the arguments or political programmes of the nationalists'. Unsurprisingly, this lack of connection with the local reality had significant negative repercussions. Local organizations were frequently seen by the population at large as either opportunistic or as rent-seeking—or both (TACSO 2010: 16). At the same time, local, donor-driven organizations were perceived by domestic authorities as either a nuisance or as a potential threat and they therefore acted to discredit them and keep them at the margins of political life.

Third, international donor agencies did not devise a proper civil society development programme, but proceeded without ever engaging in a proper impact assessment, preferring instead to use domestic organizations instrumentally as alibis for international failures.[1] This externally-driven process focused on the development of 'projects' rather than 'programmes', that is, of well-defined, short-term initiatives (usually lasting between six months and one year) with a clear beginning, implementation and completion, rather than broader and more ambitious schemes with greater potential to make a difference (TACSO 2010: 23). A syndrome described as 'projectomania' (Sejfija 2006: 135–136) or 'projectitis' (Yakinthou 2018: 74–75) overwhelmed local organizations, which became obsessed with the goal of developing 'projects', meeting donor criteria and expectations rather than the needs of the communities where the projects were implemented. Project-obsessed organizations, in Bosnia-Herzegovina as elsewhere, were easily caught in an endless, self-referential process of proposal writing, tenders and reports, until a project was completed, and a new proposal was written. Missing in this process was a clear sense of the organization's mission in the community.

Fourth, the beneficiaries of western monies typically were individuals and PBOs based in bigger towns and cities and embodying the middle-class values, interests and objects which best resonated with the priorities of international donors. Smaller and more recently established organizations received only limited attention from donors. Perhaps more importantly, international support overlooked organizations which did not fit the liberal parameters established by international actors. These organizations included a wide range of groups, such as those linked to the country's communist past (including cultural and sports organizations) and non-liberal groups (such as religious communities, veterans' groups and even labour organizations), some of which occasionally undertook initiatives against aspects of the liberal peace. For their part, these organizations showed a remarkable ability to simply ignore, adapt to or subvert international initiatives (Kappler and Richmond 2011). By neglecting groups such as these, international peacebuilding both failed to take into account the articulation and expression of significant local needs and promoted an artificial civil society with limited connections with the local reality.

Because organizations of demobilized soldiers, religious organizations, community groups and even sports leagues provide an important electoral basis for ethno-national political parties, they received funding, support and privileges by state authorities. Sport groups and veteran associations together received about 50% of total civil society funding (Perry 2015: 83). For example, between 2007 and 2011, the authorities at various levels allocated at least €150 million to veterans, sport organizations, humanitarian and other associations, without any clear criteria or adequate monitoring afterwards (Center for Investigative Reporting 2012). As a result, these organizations became part of the clientelistic networks supported by political patrons wishing to preserve and/or extend their influence into society. Locally funded organizations were predicated upon exclusionist values and norms that fitted uncomfortably with democratic practices, including transparency and accountability. Their contribution to building generalized trust, that is, the belief that you should treat strangers as if they were trustworthy (Putnam 1993: 163–164), was limited. These organizations strengthened in-group ties but at the cost of undermining cross-community links and generalized trust. This state of affairs had important implications for corruption, discussed in Chapter 3. Indeed, there is an inverse relationship between generalized trust and corruption. States with low levels of trust have high levels of corruption and vice versa (Uslaner 2004).

The relationship between state and society challenges the ideal-typical Weberian understanding of the state promoted by peacebuilding agencies. In Bosnia-Herzegovina the state does not stand above society but is embedded in it, that is, it possesses the capacity 'to penetrate society, regulate social relationships, extract resources, and appropriate and use resources in determined ways' (Migdal 2001: 4–5). Under these circumstances favourable conditions for patronage, clientelism and corruption are set in place. Not only do political authorities effectively extract resources from society, but they also use some of those resources to gain political support. Patron–client networks are used by incumbent elites to secure the support of clients who would otherwise threaten the political stability of the system. Accordingly, patronage and corruption are used as tools to maintain stability and political control. State officials bolster key supporters with the distribution of resources while, in turn, formal and informal civil society groups and organizations champion their ethnic and national patrons. As a result, 'civil society organizations in Bosnia-Herzegovina are to some extent part of the problem, and not simply the solution to corruption, mismanagement, and poor governance'.[2]

Among these organizations, veterans' groups stood out for both their representativeness and political importance. By the early 2000s, veterans' groups enjoyed a membership estimated at 4.4% of the entire Bosnian population (Živanović 2006: 39). Many of them were linked to nationalist groups or political parties and took a stand against the internationally-driven liberal peacebuilding agenda. Rather than being supporters of the peace process, they were frequently considered to be 'spoilers', blocking the possibility of cooperation between the three main national groups. In the RS, for example, the Serb Movement of Independent Associations (SPONA), a diverse group composed of eleven nationalist NGOs and war veteran groups, were very vocal in opposing internationally-led reforms while, from 2000s onwards, supporting calls for a referendum on the RS's secession from Bosnia-Herzegovina (Belloni and Hemmer 2010: 145).

In sum, through their civil society building programmes international organizations supported and reinforced a distinction between 'two Bosnias', separated by their relation to liberal, civic values and norms. While a 'first Bosnia' was made up of educated professionals who spoke foreign languages, lived in the major urban areas and received the lion's share of international attention and funding, the 'second Bosnia' did not necessarily endorse donor discourses, or agree with all the tenets of the liberal peace, and thus was largely neglected by the western aid system. As Chapter 7 will argue, this 'second Bosnia' involving marginalized citizens whose life prospects often remained unchanged, or even deteriorated, in the course of the peace process, became increasingly exasperated and, particularly from the early 2010s onwards, began to challenge the status quo from below. As of the 'first Bosnia', there is an inverse relationship between the ability of Bosnian organizations to attract foreign donor support and their ability to mobilize local constituencies around an agenda close to the needs of the local population. To put it another way, rather than strengthening civil society, international support widened the gap between domestic organizations and their social constituencies, in particular by making civil society agendas irrelevant for the majority of the population.

4.4   Civil Society and the Fight Against Corruption

In the context where generalized trust is low and where some organizations and groups are involved in patronage relations and have no will to engage in any activity which could be seen as critical of established authorities, few organizations engage in anti-corruption work. Those who do are exposed to public pressure, intimidation and even violence (Blagovcanin and Divjak 2015: 23). While national organizations are generally quite vulnerable to governmental retaliation, international NGOs such as Transparency International have access to foreign funding and are relatively protected from domestic pressures (and threats), making them more outspoken than local associations.

   In general, like most policy issues entering the public agenda, even anti-corruption activities have been stimulated by external donors. As Chapter 3 argued, until the mid-2000s international peacebuilders considered domestic political leaders as partners, and were willing to turn a blind eye to poor governance and malpractice. However, from 2006 onwards when the peace process began increasingly to stall, peacebuilding agencies recalibrated their priorities, and those of their local civil society partners, to address the corruption problem. In doing so, they took care of avoiding confronting the roots of the problem for fear of antagonizing local counterparts. For example, in 2011 corruption charges against RS President Milorad Dodik were dropped when Dodik agreed to tone down his secession rhetoric (as further explained in

Chapter 5). Having compromised on their own anti-corruption stance, peacebuilders turned to civil society organizations in the paradoxical attempt to bring corruption under control.

For peacebuilding agencies in general, and for the EU in particular, anti-corruption activities had to be carried out 'below the political radar screen'[3] in order to make it more acceptable to all stakeholders. Rather than supporting a few developed NGOs, European officials and their partners decided to involve a large number of organizations in order to increase the 'demand side' of anti-corruption work, that is, the domestic constituency insisting on the need for good governance, transparency and accountability. Demand-driven approaches are based upon 'the premise that creating demand for a cleaner, less corrupt system through bottom-up, grassroots pressure will (in time) dissuade officials from engaging in corrupt... practices' (Perry 2015: 87). Accordingly, in 2009–2010 the EU created a small grant programme to support NGOs fighting corruption. However, to the surprise of European officials the response from domestic civil society organizations was very modest.

In the early 2010s USAID took the lead in putting civil society at the forefront of the anti-corruption struggle. In June 2012, USAID allocated $1,050,000 to establish an umbrella network of NGOs and other stakeholders under the name Anti-Corruption Civic Organizations Unified Network (ACCOUNT). In June 2014, ACCOUNT II was established and additional $450,000 were allocated. More than 140 NGOs signed up to the ACCOUNT network. The few established anti-corruption organizations, such as Transparency International and the Center for Investigative Reporting, did not join it. In addition, despite the overall encouraging number of organizations involved, only a limited number were active (Perry 2015: 95). Most worryingly, ACCOUNT members did not share a clear sense of what the specific focus of their work should have been beyond a generic commitment on networking and strengthening organizations interested in anti-corruption activities (Perry 2015: 100). In other words, as with other previous instances, the corruption issue and the anti-corruption strategy emerged under the impulse of international peacebuilding agencies, and its impact on the quality of local involvement was limited.

Although USAID denied that the initiative was 'donor-driven' by arguing that funding supported existing efforts at countering corruption,[4] nonetheless the USAID grant was instrumental in establishing the NGO consortium. The scheme's externally-driven character was confirmed by the expectation that the initiative would last as long as external financial support would ensure its survival, and would cease to exist with the end of funding.[5] Most significantly, despite the efforts the domestic impact of anti-corruption activities remained modest. To begin with, the lack of transparency and accountability and the shortage of good governance and the rule of law made public scrutiny a chimera. In addition, while in the initial post-war period political parties and their members barely hid their dubious practices, their methods have become more subtle and sophisticated overtime. As a result, it became increasingly more difficult for watchdog organizations to document malpractice.[6] More generally, anti-corruption members of the ACCOUNT network did not possess either the leverage or the political resources to perform the tasks handed over by peacebuilding agencies.

Even the public reception of watchdog activities was discouraging for anti-corruption organizations. Most citizens have been well aware of the presence and corrosive influence of corruption since the beginning of the peacebuilding process and consequently do not react when they receive additional information about corrupt activities (Scharbatke-Church and Reiling 2009). Rather, they succumb to a condition of learned resignation further undermining their trust in domestic institutions, ending up relying more on patronage networks than on public institutions. In the process, public awareness of corruption turns into cynicism. In sum, the most striking and disheartening aspect of anti-corruption activities lies in their limited impact. Despite the proliferation of conventions, commissions, programmes and projects, corruption seems to be as widespread as ever. As confirmed by the experience of Bosnia-Herzegovina and the other post-Yugoslav states, those countries with the largest number of good governance anti-corruption programmes in Europe tend to be the most corrupt (Tisne and Smilov 2004).

4.5   THE EUROPEAN UNION AND CIVIL SOCIETY

Since 2002, OHR has been 'double hatted' and also performs the role of the EU Special Representative—signalling the increasing presence and importance of European institutions in the country. From roughly the same time, many bilateral donors began to phase out their civil society activities. The international spotlight, and financial resources, gradually moved to Kosovo and later to Afghanistan and Iraq. As a result of the decreasing availability of funding, competition among local organizations increased, leading to the closure of some organizations or their de facto disappearance even though they may continue to exist on paper (McMahon 2017). The decreasing presence of bilateral donors went hand in hand with a growing EU influence over Bosnian affairs. As discussed in Chapters 5 and 6, the EU furthered the peacebuilding agenda with less blatantly top-down means as compared with previous international practices. While the OHR intervened directly in state construction, the EU recognized that external imposition is in contradiction with the rule of law and democratic governance (Venice Commission 2005). It has adopted a softer approach based on a set of procedural measures grounded on contractual relationships, asymmetrical conditionalities and the need to enhance the domestic ownership and democratic participation of Bosnian citizens in the EU integration process. The emerging 'EU peacebuilding framework' (Richmond et al. 2011) is based on the 1993 Copenhagen criteria involving 'traditional' liberal peacebuilding concerns such as the promotion of democratic governance, a market economy and respect for human rights.

While attempting to foster the adoption of a set of institutional reforms compatible with liberal-democratic principles, in Bosnia-Herzegovina as in other candidate and acceding states, the EU has also placed great emphasis on assisting the development and strengthening of civil society organizations (Fagan 2010: 9). For the EU, a vibrant civil society is a central pillar of liberal democracies (European Commission 2012) and a key component of the EU's enlargement agenda (Rehn 2008). Similar to the approach adopted by other bilateral donors discussed above, the EU privileged support to NGOs rather than other civil society actors such as community groups, grassroots organizations, religious groups, veterans associations and trade unions. NGOs were deemed as important for a number of reasons. Not only could they provide a link with grassroots and community-based groups but also, and more importantly, they could support the EU's access to first-hand information on democratization processes in Bosnia-Herzegovina, they could act as multipliers in circulating information about EU policies, and they could advocate in favour of reforms required by the process of EU accession (TACSO 2010: 10).

In 2005, the European Commission explained how a comprehensive and sustained dialogue between societies from EU member states and EU candidate states represented an essential component of the EU involvement in neighbouring states. In addition, it affirmed that civil society must play a fundamental role in developing mutual understanding and integration between different peoples and in favouring the harmonization of different policies and economic systems (European Commission 2005). In order to turn this vision into reality, the EU attempted to enhance the coherence and effectiveness of its aid programme. In 2006, it rationalized its pre-accession financial support into a single framework, through the establishment of an Instrument for Pre-Accession Assistance (IPA). IPA funds for the entire south-eastern European area for the 2007–2013 period amounted to €11.46 billion and included a significant civil society building component. Armed with such a considerable financial leverage, the EU developed country-specific assistance papers for both candidate and potential candidate states.

In the Bosnian case, the EU stressed the need to develop the relationship between civil society organizations and state authorities, in particular foreseeing the possibility that local organizations would 'become better "watchdogs" and also stronger partners of the Government' (European Commission 2007: 14). It welcomed the signing, in May 2007, of a Memorandum of Understanding between the Council of Ministers and representatives of Bosnian NGOs. However, little progress towards implementing the agreement was made (TACSO 2010: 13). Civil society continued to not be consulted by Bosnian authorities and its input and views were not taken into account in the policy-making process. The ability of civil society organizations to participate in the formulation and implementation of public policies was 'almost negligible' (Žeravčić and Biščević 2009: 145). The Parliament ignored the demands coming from citizens and their associations, thus providing additional grounds for citizens' apathy and dissatisfaction (Džihić and Wieser 2011: 1818). Overall, despite the EU's efforts, cooperation between the governmental and non-governmental sectors in Bosnia-Herzegovina remained 'in its infancy' (Žeravčić 2008: 8). Perhaps the main problem with the EU approach lied in its attempt to pursue both cooperation between public institutions and NGOs, and to support politically sensitive NGO monitoring activities. According to Srdjan Blagovcanin, Executive Director of the Bosnia-Herzegovina office of Transparency International, 'it is difficult both to be partners of state institutions and to criticize them'.[7]

Overall, despite the rhetoric on domestic ownership of reforms and citizens' democratic participation, in engaging with Bosnian civil society the EU did not put forward an agenda genuinely open to domestic inputs, but rather it conceived of civil society development instrumentally. In particular, the focus on developing civil society actors, and above all NGOs, was rationalized as a way to prepare aspiring members, such as Bosnia-Herzegovina, for integration into EU governance structures. Indeed, the EU managed civil society building with a functional, output-oriented approach, which values civil society because of its contribution to political problem-solving. In this context, citizens' opportunities to participate depended on the resources they introduced into the political process (Finke 2007: 6) and not, despite EU rhetoric, on a democratic right deriving from membership in a political community. For some critics, the EU approach was post-liberal in that, rather than supporting individual and collective self-government, it reflected the desire to directly regulate Bosnian governance (Chandler 2010).

The EU's instrumental expectations in supporting civil society organizations proved to be misplaced. While the EU expected local organizations to disseminate information about the EU itself, its policies and enlargement mechanisms, the vast majority of domestic organizations continued to have scant knowledge of the process of EU integration and its significance (TACSO 2010: 21). Moreover, rather than broadening the reach of international assistance beyond a relatively small number of organizations based in the Bosnia-Herzegovina's bigger cities, EU assistance confirmed an approach based on top-down, project-based intervention focused on more developed organizations (O'Brennan 2013). European institutions were not even able to provide resources and support for local civil society in an efficient way. Bureaucratic inefficiencies remained, often leading local civil society organizations to apply for European funds only when no other realistic alternative existed (Partners Limited 2005). Indeed, only a small portion of organizations possessed the technical capacity to apply for IPA or other European funding (Fagan 2010: 98). These more developed organizations were easily caught in a version of the project-obsession described above with reference to other bilateral donors. The adoption of the logical framework (log frame) project management system for EU projects encouraged NGOs to focus on activity-based initiatives leading to quantifiable and isolatable effects. These service-oriented activities were implemented at the expense of the promotion of more explicitly political and structural types of change (Kurki 2011: 361).

4.6 Conclusion

By the end of the 2000s, after many years of internationally-led peace-building efforts, Bosnia-Herzegovina continued to suffer from 'an acute case of virtual statehood' (FPI BH 2008: 9). Political institutions designed at Dayton were both discriminatory and dysfunctional, and were frequently deadlocked; many citizens did not recognize state institutions as legitimate and, if given a choice, preferred stronger ties with neighbouring Croatia and Serbia; a lack of educational and economic opportunities encouraged many citizens, especially the young and skilled ones, to leave; there was little sense of common belonging and mutual trust between members of the three main ethnic communities.

In order to address the Bosnian conundrum, international organizations placed great emphasis on civil society building but with limited results. Instead of supporting the development of indigenous democratic and peaceful resources, international support ultimately reinforced the existence of 'two Bosnias': while a 'first Bosnia' was primarily located in bigger cities and enjoyed international donor support but lacked a connection with the grassroots, a 'second Bosnia' was largely excluded from the international aid system but remained much more representative of domestic needs and expectations than internationally-supported civil society.

The EU's growing presence in Bosnia-Herzegovina did not fundamentally changed this pattern of intervention. In the civil society realm, the EU substantially followed in the steps of other international donors, investing instrumentally in civil society rather than broadening the opportunities for citizen participation. On balance, the results were disappointing. As the European Commission acknowledged, the 'overall pace of reform has been very limited' (European Commission 2011: 1). Next two chapters will discuss how the EU grew to become the most important peacebuilding actor, and how it attempted to address those unresolved political, economic and social problems affecting the region.

Notes

1. Interview with Kurt Bassuener, Democratization Policy Council, Sarajevo, July 2015.
2. Interview with Srdjan Blagovcanin, Executive Director, Transparency International Bosnia-Herzegovina Herzegovina, Sarajevo, July 2015.

3. Interview with Brigitte Kuchar, Programme Manager for Home Affairs, Delegation of the European Union to Bosnia-Herzegovina and Herzegovina, Sarajevo, July 2016.
4. Interview with Jasna Kilalić, USAID, Deputy Democracy Officer Director, Sarajevo, July 2016.
5. Interview with Valery Perry, policy-analyst, Sarajevo, July 2015.
6. Interview with Azhar Kalamujić, journal, Center for Investigative Reporting, Sarajevo, July 2015.
7. Interview with Srdjan Blagovcanin, Executive Director, Transparency International Bosnia-Herzegovina Herzegovina, Sarajevo, July 2015.

References

Ashdown, P. (2007). *Swords and ploughshares: Bringing peace to the 21st century.* London: Weidenfeld & Nicolson.

Belloni, R. (2001). Civil society and peacebuilding in Bosnia-Herzegovina. *Journal of Peace Research, 38*(2), 163–180.

Belloni, R. (2008a). *State building and international intervention in Bosnia-Herzegovina.* London: Routledge.

Belloni, R. (2008b). Civil society in war-to-democracy transitions. In A. Jarstad & T. Sisk (Eds.), *From war to democracy: Dilemmas of peacebuilding* (pp. 182–210). Cambridge: Cambridge University Press.

Belloni, R. (2012). Part of the problem or part of the solution? Civil society and corruption in post-conflict states. In D. Zaum & C. Cheng (Eds.), *Selling the peace: Post-conflict peacebuilding and corruption* (pp. 220–238). London: Routledge.

Belloni, R., & Hemmer, B. (2010). Bosnia-Herzegovina: Building civil society under a semiprotectorate. In T. Paffenholz (Ed.), *Civil society and peacebuilding: A critical assessment* (pp. 129–152). Boulder: Lynne Rienner.

Bieber, F. (2005). *Post-war Bosnia-Herzegovina: Ethnicity, equality and public sector governance.* Basingstoke: Palgrave.

Blagovcanin, S., & Divjak, B. (2015). *How Bosnia-Herzegovina's political economy holds it back and what to do about it.* Washington, DC: Johns Hopkins University Centre for Transatlantic Studies.

Bose, S. (2002). *Bosnia-Herzegovina after Dayton: Nationalist partition and international intervention.* Oxford: Oxford University Press.

BTI (Bertelsmann Stiftung). (2009). *BTI 2010—Bosnia-Herzegovina country report.* Gütersloh: Bertelsmann Stiftung.

Campbell, D. (1999). Apartheid cartography: The political anthropology and spatial effects of international diplomacy in Bosnia-Herzegovina. *Political Geography, 18*(4), 395–435.

Caplan, R. (2000). Assessing Dayton: The structural weaknesses of the general framework agreement for peace in Bosnia-Herzegovina. *Diplomacy & Statecraft, 11*(2), 213–232.

Center for Investigative Reporting. (2012). *Non-profits collect millions from government budgets* (Resource document). http://www.cin.ba. Accessed 5 December 2013.

Chandler, D. (1999). *Bosnia-Herzegovina: Faking democracy after Dayton.* London: Pluto Press.

Chandler, D. (2010). The EU and southeastern Europe: The rise of post-liberal governance. *Third World Quarterly, 31*(1), 69–85.

Džihić, V., & Wieser, A. (2011). Incentives for democratisation? Effects of EU conditionality on democracy in Bosnia-Herzegovina. *Europe-Asia Studies, 63*(10), 1803–1825.

Edwards, M. (2003). *Civil society.* Cambridge: Polity Press.

European Commission. (2005, June 29). *Civil society dialogue between the EU and candidate countries.* http://europa.eu/legislation_summaries/enlargement/ongoing_enlargement/e50022_en.htm.

European Commission. (2007). *Multi-annual indicative planning document 2007–2009 for Bosnia-Herzegovina.* http://ec.europa.eu/enlargement/pdf/mipd_Bosnia-Herzegovina_herzegovina_2007_2009_en.pdf.

European Commission. (2011, October 12). *Bosnia-Herzegovina 2011 progress report.* SEC (2011) 1206 final. http://ec.europa.eu/enlargement/pdf/key_documents/2011/package/ba_rapport_2011_en.pdf.

European Commission. (2012, September 12). *The roots of democracy and sustainable development: Europe's engagement with civil society in external relations.* Communication from the commission to the European Parliament, the council, the European Economic and Social Committee and the Committee of the Regions, Brussels. http://eur-lex.europa.eu/LexUriServ/LexUriServ.do?uri=COM:2012:0492:FIN:EN:PDF.

Fagan, A. (2010). *Europe's Balkan dilemma: Paths to civil society or state-building?* London: I.B. Tauris.

Finke, B. (2007). Civil society participation in EU governance. *Living Review in European Governance, 2*(2). www.livingreviews.org/lreg-2007-2. Accessed 5 February 2012.

FPI BH (Foreign Policy Initiative Bosnia-Herzegovina Herzegovina). (2008). *Governance structures in BiH: Capacity, ownership, EU integration, functioning state.* Sarajevo: FPI BH.

Hakånsson, P., & Sjöholm, F. (2007). Who do you trust? Ethnicity and trust in Bosnia-Herzegovina. *Europe–Asia Studies, 59*(6), 961–976.

Hulsey, J. (2010). 'Why did they vote for those guys again?' Challenges and contradictions in the promotion of political moderation in post-war Bosnia-Herzegovina. *Democratization, 17*(6), 1132–1152.

Kappler, S., & Richmond, O. P. (2011). Peacebuilding in Bosnia and Herzegovina: Resistance or emancipation? *Security Dialogue, 42*(3), 261–278.

Kurki, M. (2011). Governmentality and EU democracy promotion: The European instrument for democracy and human rights and the construction of democratic civil societies. *International Political Sociology, 5*(4), 349–366.

McMahon, P. C. (2017). *The NGO game: Post-conflict peacebuilding in the Balkans and beyond.* Ithaca and London: Cornell University Press.

Migdal, J. (2001). *State in society: Studying how states and societies transform and constitute one another.* Cambridge: Cambridge University Press.

Mujkić, A. (2007). We, the citizens of ethnopolitics. *Constellations, 14*(1), 112–128.

Mujkić, A., & Hulsey, J. (2010). Explaining the success of nationalist parties in Bosnia and Herzegovina. *Croatian Political Science Review, 47*(2), 143–158.

Nansen Dialogue Centre Sarajevo and Saferworld. (2012, March). *Leaving the past behind: The perceptions of youth in Bosnia and Herzegovina.* Sarajevo: Saferworld.

O'Brennan, J. (2013). The European Commission, enlargement policy and civil society in the Western Balkans. In V. Bojicic-Dzelilovic, J. Ker-Lindsay, & D. Kostovicova (Eds.), *Civil society and transitions in the Western Balkans* (pp. 29–46). London: Palgrave.

O'Loughlin, J. (2010). Inter-ethnic friendships in post-war Bosnia-Herzegovina. *Ethnicities, 10*(1), 26–54.

Paffenholz, T. (Ed.). (2010). *Civil society and peacebuilding: A critical assessment.* Boulder, CO: Lynne Rienner.

Partners Limited. (2005, April). *Striking a balance—Efficiency, effectiveness and accountability: The impact of the EU financial regulation on the relationship between the European Commission and NGOs.* Brussels.

Perry, V. (2015). *A cross-cutting survey of corruption and anti-corruption issues in Bosnia and Herzegovina: Overview, challenges and recommendations.* Sarajevo: USAID.

Petritsch, W. (2001). *Bosna i Hercegovina: od Daytona do Evrope.* Sarajevo: Svjetlost.

Putnam, R. (1993). *Making democracy work: Civic traditions in modern Italy.* Princeton: Princeton University Press.

Rehn, O. (2008, April 17). *Civil society at the heart of the EU's enlargement agenda.* Speech by the EU Commissioner Olli Rehn, conference on civil society development in Southeast Europe: Building Europe together, Brussels. SPEECH/08/201. http://europa.eu/rapid/press-release_SPEECH-08-201_en.htm.

Richmond, O., Björkdahl, A., & Kappler, S. (2011). The emerging EU peacebuilding framework: Confirming or transcending liberal peacebuilding? *Cambridge Review of International Affairs, 24*(3), 449–469.

Sampson, S. (2002). Weak states, uncivil societies and thousands of NGOs: Western democracy export as benevolent colonialism in the Balkans. In S. Resić & B. Tornquist-Pewa (Eds.), *Cultural boundaries of the Balkans* (pp. 27–44). Lund: Lund University Press.

Scharbatke-Church, C., & Reiling, K. (2009). Lillies that fester: Seeds of corruption and peacebuilding. *New Routes: A Journal of Peace Research and Action, 14*(3–4), 4–9.

Sejfija, I. (2006). From the civil sector to civil society? Progress and prospects. In M. Fischer (Ed.), *10 years after Dayton: Peacebuilding and civil society in Bosnia and Herzegovina* (pp. 125–140). Berlin: Lit.

Stubbs, P. (2001). 'Social sector' or the diminution of social policy? Regulating welfare regimes in contemporary Bosnia-Herzegovina. In Open Society Fund BiH (Ed.), *International support policies to SEE-countries—Lessons (not) learned in Bosnia-Herzegovina* (pp. 95–107). Sarajevo: Open Society Fund.

TACSO (Technical Assistance for Civil Society Organizations). (2010, January 4). *Bosnia & Herzegovina: Needs assessment report*. Sarajevo: TACSO.

Tisne, M., & Smilov, D. (2004). *From the ground up: Assessing the record of anticorruption assistance in southeastern Europe*. Budapest: Center for Policy Studies/Central European University.

Toal, G., & Dahlman, C. T. (2011). *Bosnia-Herzegovina remade: Ethnic cleansing and its reversal*. Oxford: Oxford University Press.

UNDP (United Nations Development Programme). (2007). *The silent majority speaks: Snapshots of today and visions of the future of Bosnia-Herzegovina*. Sarajevo: UNDP.

Uslaner, E. M. (2004). Trust and corruption. In J. Graf, M. Taube, & M. Schramm (Eds.), *Corruption and the new institutional economics* (pp. 76–92). London: Routledge.

Varshney, A. (2002). *Ethnic conflict and civic life: Hindus and Muslims in India*. New Heaven and London: Yale University Press.

Venice Commission. (2005, March 11). *Opinion on the constitutional situation in Bosnia and Herzegovina and the powers of the high representative*. CDL-AD (2005) 004. www.venice.coe.int/docs/2005/CDL-AD(2005)004-e.pdf.

Vogel, B. (2016). Civil society capture: Top-down interventions from below? *Journal of Intervention and Statebuilding, 10*(4), 472–489.

Yakinthou, C. (2018). Fighting windmills, ignoring dragons: International assistance to civil society in post-conflict Bosnia-Herzegovina. In P. Arthur & C. Yakinthou (Eds.), *Transitional justice, international assistance, and civil society* (pp. 52–85). Cambridge: Cambridge University Press.

Žeravčić, G. (2008). *Analysis of institutional cooperation between governmental and non-governmental sectors in BiH*. Sarajevo: Kronauer Consulting.

Žeravčić, G., & Biščević, E. (2009). *Analysis of the civil society situation in Bosnia and Herzegovina*. Sarjevo: HTSPE Ltd. UK & Kronauer Consulting.

Živanović, M. (2006). Civil society in Bosnia and Herzegovina: Lost in transition. In W. Benedek (Ed.), *Civil society and good governance in societies in transition* (pp. 23–53). Belgrade: Centre for Human Rights.

PART II

Brussels, or the Power of Attraction

CHAPTER 5

EUtopia and the Pull of Integration

5.1   INTRODUCTION

European institutions were unprepared for the end of communist
regimes in Eastern Europe and the Yugoslav tragedy of the 1990s.
Integration had advanced considerably since the 1950s, but not enough
to develop effective foreign policy tools able to deal with systemic issues
of this scale. Yet, after little more than a decade, European leaders
launched a series of reforms to respond to the new international environment. Europe grew noticeably both in size (to the current 28 members)
and in the scope, breadth and depth of its political, economic, military
and humanitarian agenda. The first ever European Security Strategy, *A
Secure Europe in a Better World*, 2003, reflected the widely held optimism of the early 2000s, when officials both in Brussels and throughout the Balkans believed that the Union could play an important role in
ensuring a future of peace and prosperity in European peripheries, and
beyond.

The EU's strategy paper declared the building of a 'ring of well-gov-
erned countries' in the neighbourhood as a key strategic objective and
elevated 'good governance' as a guiding principle of its foreign policy.
Geographically, it singled out the Balkans as the 'best illustration' of the
benefits of enlargement in supporting the democratic transformation of
aspiring new EU members. Both policy-makers and several scholars recognized enlargement as the key policy instrument in order to achieve

© The Author(s) 2020   109
R. Belloni, *The Rise and Fall of Peacebuilding
in the Balkans*, Rethinking Peace and Conflict Studies,
https://doi.org/10.1007/978-3-030-14424-1_5

political stability and support the process of democratic transformation in the region. The accession process entails the application of a number of conditionalities, identified by the 1993 Copenhagen criteria, which have been progressively tightened and made more stringent in the course of several enlargement rounds. This inherently top-down and material process, whereby the stronger actor (the EU) sets out the conditions, while the weaker actors (Western Balkan states) have to accept and apply them with relatively minor leverage to negotiate particular issues, was premised upon the EU's normative power of attraction (Manners 2002). EU soft power was exercised through the gravitational force it projected towards its neighbouring states, in particular through its promise of association, and potentially accession, to European institutions (Schimmelfenning and Sedelmeier 2005; Vachudova 2005).

The EU believed that only in extreme cases, if at all, conditions should have been imposed through arm twisting, sanctions and the like. Rather, because these conditions were expected to benefit aspiring new EU members by bringing them closer to universal values of democracy and human rights, they were inherently appealing and should have been subscribed to more or less voluntarily. Thus, the EU's own narrative highlighted its attractiveness as a beacon of universal values and principles (Rehn 2005) Needless to say, understanding the EU as the key representative of European/universal values was profoundly Eurocentric and predictably put the local people with their own values, history and traditions in a subordinated position vis-à-vis the western part of the continent (Diez 2005). From the point of view of policy-makers in Brussels, it was precisely this disadvantaged position that demanded the leadership and direction of European institutions.

By the time the European Security Strategy was published, European integration was almost universally recognized as the key strategy for achieving the twin goals of peace and prosperity in the Balkans (see, for example, International Commission on the Balkans 2005). The European Commission (2006) identified the prospect of EU membership as 'the ultimate conflict prevention strategy' and committed itself to maintain and increase its pro-active presence in the region. The academic near-consensus was that the Balkans' greater involvement in European institutions was the necessary condition for stabilization and rising levels of prosperity and democratic accountability (see, for example, Batt 2004; Diez et al. 2008). Whether the focus was placed on Europe's entry into the Balkans, or the Balkans' entry into Europe, most observers agreed on the positive effects of increased links between these two still quite distinct areas. Perhaps most importantly, these views were also shared by many politicians and citizens in the region, who were for once united in considering access to European political, economic and financial institutions as the long-term answer to fragmentation, conflict and economic backwardness. Opinion polls regularly showed levels of popular support for European integration ranging between 75 and 85%.

This chapter examines this optimistic view of the EU's peacebuilding and developmental role. This view, as Part III will argue, proved to be relatively short-lived. However, before discussing the decline of the EU's attractiveness and impact on the region, this chapter considers why expectations were so high in the early 2000s. The focus is not on the details of the various programmes of EU assistance to the region but on the 'big picture', that is, the comparative advantages and disadvantages of the increasing European role in the Balkans. First, Europe's role is discussed within the political context where it originated. Widespread agreement on the need for European integration stemmed from disillusionment with the failures of managing the violent process of Yugoslav dissolution throughout the 1990s, and then with the difficulties faced by post-conflict international peacebuilding missions—particularly the one to Bosnia-Herzegovina. Accordingly, the section starts with a brief overview of the lessons learned in this process, followed by the reforms adopted in light of these lessons. Second, the chapter examines the advantages and opportunities that European integration presented when compared to previous involvement. Only when contrasted with the limits of the earlier ad hoc, short-term, and un-coordinated approach did European integration emerge as the potentially most effective strategy. Finally, the chapter concludes with a brief discussion of how the EU's 2003 promise of enlargement to the Balkans was soon sidelined by the EU member states' own disagreements about the future shape of the Union.

5.2   Lessons Learned

The track record of international involvement in the region is decidedly mixed, and the aim of this section is to highlight the troubling lessons learned from multilateral involvement during the 1990s, with special reference to the role played by European institutions.

European Institutions Lacked the Military Capability for Conflict Intervention. European institutions failed to address the evolving crisis of the 1990s. In part, this failure was of a military nature, and in part it reflected the lack of political cohesion among key international/ European actors (see below). Militarily, European institutions did not possess the capabilities to deploy credible force to prevent or stop the escalation of war. Moreover, multiple chains of command made it very difficult to fill the gap between the threat of intervention and the actual use of force. The 'dual key' command structure, requiring the approval of both the UN and NATO to use air power, guaranteed almost continuous inaction in face of civilian suffering in Bosnia-Herzegovina (Mulchinock 2017: Chapter 2)—until the United States took the lead, bombed Bosnian Serb positions and negotiated an end to the war.[1]

European Institutions Lacked Political Unity to Address the Crisis. Jacques de Poos, Foreign Minister of tiny Luxembourg and Council of Ministers President at the outset of the crisis in June 1991, optimistically announced Europe's readiness to tackle the Yugoslav problem. Europe, however, lacked the necessary unity and resolve to follow through on this. The most striking political divisions among European allies involved Germany on the one hand and the United Kingdom on the other. While Lord Carrington, the former British Foreign Secretary, attempted to find a comprehensive political solution to the evolving political crisis at the Yugoslav conference in the Hague, Germany broke ranks with her European (and transatlantic) allies, advocating full recognition of Croatia in the name of the right of self-determination and as a deterrent to Serb aggression (Crawford 1996). A further, similar row among European allies involved the issue of the recognition of the Former Yugoslav Republic of Macedonia (FYROM). Greece objected vigorously, causing severe embarrassment to its partners in the European Community and making a coherent approach to the Yugoslav crisis very difficult. As a whole, Europe displayed deep divisions and the inability to act effectively (Caplan 2005). Perhaps unsurprisingly given these internal divisions, Europe's main political strategy throughout the 1990s was to contain the conflict while preventing cross-border consequences.

European Institutions Lacked Experience and Expertise to Address the Crisis. Europe's lack of a strategy also depended, at least in part, on its limited foreign policy experience. When Yugoslavia began to dissolve in the early 1990s European institutions did not have any experience in dealing with armed conflict, nor did they consider enlargement to be a useful stabilizing tool. To put it another way, the European toolbox was relatively empty. By contrast, at the time of the Kosovo crisis in 1999 the EU recognized enlargement as a valuable tool to bring about political change, and responded with the creation of the Stability Pact (see below) and the perspective of full integration of the Western Balkans into Europe (Friis and Murphy 2000).

Post-war, Multilateral Intervention Displayed Similar Divisions Among Third Parties. Once the guns fell silent, the task of post-war political, economic and social reconstruction presented international interveners with a tremendous challenge. Unfortunately, the conflicting assessments and different priorities of international actors complicated the effectiveness of intervention. In Bosnia-Herzegovina, international divisions were reflected in the architecture of the post-Dayton peace operation, with a sharp separation between the military component led by the Americans and the civilian one controlled by the Europeans (Belloni 2008). In Kosovo, third parties created a more coherent international structure (the four-pillar UNMIK) following the 1999 war, but never quite comprehended the long-term character and nature of the dispute and acted too slowly, particularly in providing effective policing (King and Mason 2006). By contrast, international actors in FYROM learned from the failures of Bosnia-Herzegovina and Kosovo (Cooley 2019: 117). Strategic coordination among international interveners is often credited with the overall stability and democratic development of this country after it found itself on the verge of bloodshed in 2001 (Latifi 2007). Overall, post-war international involvement reflected the growing influence of the respective national interests of the intervening states at the expense of a common European strategy/policy.

Top-Down International Imposition Created Domestic Dependency. In the attempt to further the various peace processes in the region external actors have frequently imposed decisions and policies on reluctant domestic ones. As noted in Chapter 3, this strategy led to a significant free-riding phenomenon. In Bosnia-Herzegovina, which since 1998 was run as a semi-protectorate, local politicians regularly maintained an intransigent attitude, avoided inter-ethnic cooperation and accommodation and then blamed international organizations for their own failure to make good on their electoral promises (Belloni 2008: 176–177). In Kosovo, international interveners imposed a set of 'standards' to be achieved before any meaningful discussion of the final status of the province could begin. Serbs reacted by boycotting local institutions, while Albanians for the most part paid lip service to international priorities (King and Mason 2006: 234–239). Following Kosovo's independence, declared in February 2008, an International Civilian Representative was deployed under the aegis of the EU and was granted executive powers similar to those held by the High Representative in Bosnia-Herzegovina. As in Bosnia-Herzegovina, these powers led to forms of domestic dependency (Capussela 2015). Only in FYROM were international powers not blatantly used. Both Slav Macedonian and Albanian elites recognized the dangers of inter-ethnic confrontation and accepted the need to compromise, although they later dragged their feet in the implementation of the reform agenda (Latifi 2007).

Top-Down International Intervention Prevented Meaningful Partnerships with Local Actors. Post-war international peacebuilding was modelled after a general template, including economic and political liberalization and support for civil society programmes, the return of refugees, demobilization and reconstruction projects (see Chapter 1). Despite the size of the task, which suggested the need for a comprehensive and long-term approach, short-term priorities shaped international intervention. In the post-colonial age the pressure to demonstrate quick and visible positive results to legitimate international involvement was strong (Jarstad and Sisk 2008). Due to the brevity of projects, international agencies had little scope to develop significant local partnerships and include local actors in a process of joint planning, implementation and assessment. As explained in Chapter 4, despite the rhetoric of fostering 'domestic ownership', international intervention was largely a top-down, frequently short-term and ad hoc enterprise, moving from crisis to crisis and unable to develop a coherent, shared and effective conflict management strategy (Sampson 2002).

5.3   Reforming Europe's Ways

These lessons, arising from more than a decade of external involvement in the region, were gradually learned—at least to an extent. Perhaps counter-intuitively, the Balkans changed Europe and the EU as much as the EU has been trying to change its South-eastern neighbours (Woodward 2017: 88).[2] The European failure to address the crisis throughout the 1990s contributed to a process of reform aimed at strengthening European political and military capabilities. In a 2005 influential report the International Commission on the Balkans (ICB) described the options available to the EU as between 'empire and enlargement'. In dealing with the Western Balkan region the strategic choices were essentially reduced to two: either the EU imposed a number of semi-protectorates and ran them in a quasi-colonial fashion, thus imposing the law of the stronger while violating basic principles of self-determination and human rights, or it provided the region with an enlargement perspective to support a process of domestically driven political, economic and governance reforms. The Commission's own choice was stated explicitly: while the EU possessed the power to impose its own views (and institutions) on Western Balkan states, such an imposition would have amounted to a short-term (and short-sighted) superficial change. By contrast, the ICB believed that an enlargement perspective would have unleashed the EU's attractiveness, supported the domestic ownership of reforms, and thus led to more profound and lasting restructuring of domestic institutions.

The EU chose the path of enlargement and offered the entire Western Balkans area the prospect of membership. The 2000 Feira European Council affirmed that Western Balkan countries were 'potential candidates for EU membership' (Council of the European Union 2000: para. 40). Normatively, the EU's offer required a transformation of the European perception of its Other. Despite its reputation for divisiveness, war and carnage (Todorova 1997), the Balkans is not external to European civilization, and should not be kept at arm's length. Europe's main Other is not identified by geography, but by Europe's own history (Weaver 1998). Symbolically, the Balkans embodies Europe's own recent, bloody past, not its Other, and should be included in the European mainstream. Thus, the key change in the European approach involved a shift from a view of the region as violent and irremediably alien, leading to a policy of containment, to a view that stressed the common heritage and interlocked future between the two areas. Ultimately, this led to a policy of inclusion/integration.

The 1999 Kosovo war was waged by NATO against the remnants of Yugoslavia, with no formal UN endorsement, and was in practice planned and executed by the United States (Mulchinock 2017). This war contributed decisively to a new consciousness about the role the EU could and should play in the region. Through a slow, step-by-step approach, both military and political means were built, until the EU emerged as the central player in the region in the areas of peacebuilding and conflict prevention. In late 1998, France and the United Kingdom had already agreed at St. Malo that the acquisition of military means and the introduction of a more effective common defence policy was necessary in order to make European foreign policy more credible. Following the Kosovo war, European Heads of State and Government met in Cologne and decided to speed up the development of capabilities and assets for conflict management. They agreed to make available by 2003 a 50,000–60,000 military personnel deployable within two months, to better coordinate political and military tasks within the Common Security and Defence Policy, and to develop a framework for cooperation with NATO and third states. The creation of a Rapid Reaction Mechanism in February 2001 also enhanced the EU's ability to respond to short-term crises, and proved to be a useful tool for crisis management before, during and after the 2001 Macedonian crisis (Wolff and Peen Rodt 2007: 14).

Later meetings of the European Council contributed further to developing European military, civilian and political capabilities and to deepening coordination and cooperation with other institutions. A Framework Agreement signed by the EU's High Representative for the Common Foreign and Security Policy (CFSP) Javier Solana and NATO's Secretary General Lord Robertson in March 2003 regulated the EU's access to NATO assets. Cooperation between these two institutions flowed from common security concerns and shared membership, with nineteen EU states at that time also members of NATO. As a result of these activities, a division of responsibilities took place. The EU focused increasingly on police reform and internal security, while NATO dealt with military issues (NATO 2005: 3; Pond 2006).

New European civilian and military capabilities were soon put to the test (Wolff and Peen Rodt 2007). The EU Police Mission in Bosnia-Herzegovina and Herzegovina, launched on 1 January 2003, was the first operation of its kind deployed as part of the CFSP. Operation Concordia, established on 31 March 2003, aimed at guaranteeing security and stability in FYROM as part of the implementation of the 2001 Ohrid Agreement and saw the first EU-NATO cooperation on the ground, with the former using the capabilities of the latter (Yusufi 2004). This positive experience convinced NATO's Heads of State and Government to attempt a similar arrangement in Bosnia-Herzegovina-Herzegovina. In July 2004, Operation Althea was deployed to smooth the transition from the NATO-led Stabilization Force (SFOR) to an EU Force (EUFOR). Finally, Operation Proxima was the second police operation in the region after the Bosnian one, and launched in December 2003 to monitor and mentor FYROM's police and to promote 'European policing standards'.

Increasing EU military responsibilities in the Western Balkans represented a partial departure from its traditional emphasis on 'soft power', which gave prominence to confidence-building activities, support for judicial/police reform, and commitment to multilateral action and cooperation with other organizations such as the UN, NATO and the OSCE (Solana 2003).

Through the Stabilisation and Association Process (SAP), launched in 1999 in response to the war in Kosovo, the EU stated that countries in the Western Balkans (including Bosnia-Herzegovina, FYROM, Serbia, Montenegro and Kosovo) were 'potential candidates' for membership (European Commission 1999). The promise of association and eventual membership changed the relationship between the Western Balkans and the EU since it provided the region with a set of yardsticks to use and measure their advance towards Europe, and the Union with the opportunity to deploy the full strength of political conditionality (Van Meurs 2003; for an assessment, see Noutcheva 2012).

The SAP conditionality policy is a process involving several steps, and including the establishment of a Consultative Taskforce, the drafting of a Feasibility Study on a Stabilisation and Association Agreement (SAA), and the negotiation and ratification of the Agreement—which in turn opened the way for an application for EU membership. All agreements follow the same format and are divided into ten titles. Rules and procedures to establish a free trade area are legally binding and laid out in some detail, while the remaining titles on democratic principles, justice and home affairs and so on are broader declarations of intent expected to be specified during the accession negotiations. As a 'process', the SAP is designed to give interim rewards to those local politicians willing to embrace necessary but politically sensitive reforms (Gordon 2009; Lehne 2004; Reljić 2007).

The SAP constitutes the primary tool of the EU's 'member statebuilding' strategy put forward by the ICB. With this strategy, the EU aimed at building functional states able to assume the responsibilities of EU integration. While attempting to regulate and shape each country's journey towards joining the EU, European institutions also began addressing the Western Balkans as a region with common problems and prospects. The Stability Pact for Southeast Europe, launched in June 1999 on the EU's initiative, attempted to replace a reactive intervention policy with a comprehensive long-term approach consciously modelled on the post-1945 Marshall Plan (European Commission).[3] The Pact was structured as an internationally coordinating body for civilian aid. It aimed at developing a partnership between international and local actors and at creating the conditions for effective local ownership of the post-Yugoslav/post-war transition process (Busek 2004).[4]

The Thessaloniki European Council in July 2003 removed any doubt about the rationale and direction of this transition when it declared unambiguously that 'the future of the Balkans is in the European Union' (Council of the European Union 2003: para. 40). The Council affirmed that accession to the EU would be dependent upon fulfilling the same requirements applied to Central and Eastern European (CEE) states. Significantly, in late 2004 responsibility for the Western Balkans was transferred to the new EU Enlargement Commissioner, Olli Rehn. The shift from post-war stabilization to an agenda of enlargement provided two important advantages compared to previous peacebuilding policies. First, addressing the situation in the Western Balkans as an enlargement issue rather than a foreign policy one allowed European institutions and EU member states to reduce ambiguities and divergent preferences (CEPS 2005: ii). Second, the promise of association and eventual membership provided the EU with the opportunity to deploy the full strength of political conditionality (Van Meurs 2003).

Thus, since the end of the Kosovo war the goal of international intervention shifted gradually from one of managing the consequences of the Yugoslav Succession Wars to that of integrating the Balkans into Europe. Since 2002 the High Representative in Bosnia-Herzegovina has also represented European institutions and in 2005 his office formally became that of the EU Special Representative (EUSR) and was tasked with monitoring and assisting Bosnia-Herzegovina in her progress towards EU integration. Likewise, Kosovo's future lies in EU integration. In 2003 the European Commission adopted a Tracking Mechanism for Kosovo to monitor its development in a variety of policy areas, followed in January 2006 by a European Partnership policy (not being a state, Kosovo could not have a SAA). FYROM made the most progress towards European integration, with the exception of Croatia. In April 2001, in the midst of this country's crisis, the EU signed an SAA with FYROM and, few weeks later, it nominated an EUSR. In early 2004 FYROM submitted its application for EU membership. However, as discussed below, the country experienced a deteriorating internal political climate and also it was caught in the European soul-searching process that followed the 2005 French and Dutch rejection of a proposed new EU Constitution (ESI 2005c). Overall, the EU policy in the region was effectively described as one of 'conditional support for reforms in the direction of Europeanization' (CEPS 2005: 7). As European officials were fond of saying, the EU's exit strategy for Bosnia-Herzegovina, FYROM and Kosovo was expected to be their entry into the Union.

5.4   THE PROMISES OF THE INTEGRATION PROCESS

At last, after more than a decade of ineffective, crisis-driven and reactive conflict intervention, the prospect of integrating the Western Balkans into European political, economic and military institutions appeared to provide a long-term perspective to international involvement and a valuable peacebuilding tool. Conditionality (based on the short-term cost/benefit calculations in which EU aspiring members respond to the material incentives offered by European institutions) and social learning (the long-term redefinition of interests and identities of domestic players) were singled out as the two main pathways of EU influence in the region (Coppitiers et al. 2004; Diez et al. 2008). These mechanisms constituted important peacebuilding tools and provided a clear improvement vis-à-vis the limits of previous international intervention. Whether because of a process of 'reinforcement by reward' (Schimmelfennig and Sedelmeier 2005) or as a result of the internalization and 'appropriation' of European norms (Subotić 2011), the region was supposedly destined to modernize and increasingly integrate into Europe. Not all EU member states were equally enthusiastic about the prospect of integrating the region into the EU, but in the optimistic mood of the 2000s, they endorsed the policy strategy strongly promoted by the Commission. For its proponents, the prospect of European integration offered a long-term and coherent perspective, encouraged domestic ownership and institutional development, supported stability and regional cooperation, and softened nationalist identities. Each of these promises and expectations deserves a short analysis.

Sustaining a Long-term and Coherent Perspective. To being with, the idea of integrating the Western Balkans into the EU constituted a long-term vision that aimed at articulating and sustaining a coherent international peacebuilding approach towards the region. Integration was the alternative to conflicting and contradictory objectives pursued through short-term, discrete interventions and projects. According to Solana (2003), the European states' capacity to overcome their own narrow national self-interest gave the EU a unique advantage in its ability to export freedom, democracy and good governance. To turn this vision into a reality, substantial financial resources were made available. The Stability Pact was able to direct a considerable amount of funds towards the region. Under its stewardship, more than €25 billion arrived in the Western Balkans from some fifty donor countries (Pond 2006: 242). Between 1991 and 2007 the EU alone spent some €10 billion (EU/ World Bank Joint Office for South East Europe 2008). Perhaps more importantly, the EU budget covers a span of seven years, allowing for a long-term approach to post-war stabilization and peacebuilding.

Favouring Domestic Ownership. Europe's attractiveness for non-EU states was expected to exert a positive reforming influence without embarking on civilizational missions and the blatant neo-colonial imposition of western institutions and policies (Manners 2006: 175). As argued above, not only was external imposition of this kind a doubtful strategy reminiscent of a recent imperial past, but also it created domestic dependency and prevented the development of effective partnerships between international and domestic actors. By contrast, the European perspective should have provided aspiring members with the necessary incentives to set into motion a virtuous cycle of political, social and economic reforms. The EU's experience with CEE states suggested the EU integration process was crucial in order to commit all major political forces to the goal of EU membership (Knaus and Cox 2005).

In particular, the EU hoped to strengthen supporters of reform, while at the same time weakening opposition to integration, thus tipping the balance in favour of change (ESI 2005a). In problematic states such as Bosnia-Herzegovina, the neo-colonial powers granted to the High Representative of the International Community in his effort to implement the 1995 DPA, involving the authority of imposing legislation and removing elected local officials from office, were expected to be gradually replaced by the commitment of all major political forces to the goal of EU membership. As international officials in Sarajevo and Brussels used to say, 'the push of Dayton will be replaced by the pull of Brussels' (Ashdown 2004; see also Ashdown 2007). Political elites in all other Western Balkan states were projected to embrace analogous reformist zeal.

The EU's engagement in the Western Balkans involved techniques of liberal governmentality, that is, a form of government that takes population as its main target and seeks to govern through consent,

self-regulation and individual responsibilization rather than direct imposition (Juncos 2018). Indeed, the EU's enterprise was both highly
asymmetrical and unaccountable (Chandler 2006), but not imposed.
Accordingly, the EU has been reluctant to openly force decisions to solve
domestic problems, as for example in the case of the unsuccessful attempt
at constitutional reform in Bosnia-Herzegovina (Sebastian Aparicio 2014).

Overall, the EU resembled a neo-medieval empire characterized by
overlapping authorities and divided sovereignty, multiple identities, fuzzy
borders and various forms of external power projection. The relationship
between members and non-members involved both imperial and cooper-
ative aspects, with Europe's centres and peripheries constantly (re)nego-
tiating the terms of their relationship (Zielonka 2006). It is this process
of negotiation that should have opened Western Balkan societies to
alternative worldviews and prospects, encouraging much needed domestic debate.

At its best, this process could embolden reformers within government
and society and, perhaps more importantly, support a change in nationalists' priorities. For example, in late 2007 Bosnia-Herzegovina faced its
most profound political crisis since the signing of the 1995 DPA. The crisis was triggered by the Bosnian Serbs' refusal to accept both procedural
rules limiting ethnic vetoes and a plan to create a single police force in the
country (Leroux-Martin 2014). Bosnian Serbs feared that the first proposal would have marginalized them in state institutions, while the second one would have led to a loss of autonomy for their self-governing RS.
The crisis was solved when the EU agreed to initial an SAA in exchange
for acceptance of procedural changes and of an action plan phasing in
the implementation of police reform (B92 News 2007). In FYROM, the
European perspective emboldened reformers and engaged society as a
whole. The EU made fulfilment of the Ohrid Agreement a precondition
for elevating the country from 'potential candidate' to 'candidate' status.
Macedonian and Albanian politicians for the most part supported the
implementation of the Agreement, and the Macedonian public subscribed
to it as the necessary stepping-stone towards admission into the EU and
NATO (Petruseva 2004). Similar dynamics were visible in Kosovo. Prime
Minister Agim Ceku startled the audience in 2005 when he addressed
Kosovo Serbs in fluent Serbian, promised to protect them and endorsed
the much-contested 'standards'. Although Kosovo remained the most
volatile area in the region, these developments testified to the moderating
effects of the lure of European membership (Pond 2006: 265–266).

As these examples suggest, domestic reformers could seize 'local own-ership' to prepare the ground and push through the difficult changes required to join European institutions. In the process, not only was international imposition of policy attenuated or prevented but also part-nerships and coalitions between international and domestic actors could be created and nurtured. Thus, the European perspective showed the potential to achieve further reforms without the blatant top-down, social engineering tools frequently adopted by international actors (Bechev and Andreev 2005). The stimulus to the further development of good gov-ernance and peacebuilding, the EU claimed with some reason, was one of the areas of its real 'comparative advantage' vis-à-vis other institutions, and was part of a 'coherent international community response' to the region's needs (European Commission 2001: 8–9).

Supporting Institutional Development. European governance princi-ples were expected to contribute to improve policy-making and strengthen local institutions. The EU itself is a multi-layered polity that regularly 'shares' and 'pools' sovereignty among its members (Wallace 1999). Such a structure could support effective policy-making in conflict-ridden regions such as the Balkans. EU member states delegated some sovereign prerogatives to European institutions, thus removing potentially problem-atic issues from local decision-making. By taking decisions in many areas on the basis of majority rule, the EU Council of Ministers allows for pol-icy-making even in the absence of a local agreement. The participation of Western Balkan states into the 'EU framework' (Hill 2001) was expected to add a new layer of governance potentially multiplying the possibility for win-win agreements between the parties.

Fostering Stability and Regional Cooperation. Through its influence in the region, the EU hoped to stimulate respect for existing interna-tional borders and regional cooperation, a task previously attempted by the United States. For the best part of the post-Dayton period, it was the United States that applied pressure on Serbia and Croatia to respect Bosnia-Herzegovina's political integrity and internationally recognized borders. When American attention moved to Afghanistan and Iraq and, more broadly, to waging the 'war on terror', the EU's soft power and political conditionality began replacing American influence in stabilizing the Balkans. For Serbia and Croatia, the preservation of the EU horizon was more important than the partition of Bosnia-Herzegovina between the two. Significantly, Croatia's nationalist-led government went to great lengths to reassure sceptical EU institutions that the country's reforms would proceed apace—in particular since it applied for EU membership in early 2003. Similarly, in early 2005 European conditionality paid off when the government in Belgrade surrendered several war-crime indictees to the International Criminal Tribunal for the Former Yugoslavia (ICTY) in The Hague, paving the way for the opening of SAA negotiations. The SAA was signed in April 2008, but the failure to arrest high-profile indicted war criminals, including Radovan Karadzić and Ratko Mladić, blocked the agreement's implementation. In May 2008 a pro-western government came to power in Belgrade and in July, on the eve of an EU foreign ministers' meeting in Brussels scheduled to discuss Serbia's bid to join the Union, Karadzic was arrested in Belgrade (Whitmore 2008).

Moreover, at the regional level the EU supported cross-border trade and cooperation. In early 2006 the EU proposed the creation of a regional free-trade agreement among the countries of the Western Balkans—including Bosnia-Herzegovina, Serbia, Montenegro, Croatia, Albania and FYROM. This proposal led to extending the Central European Free Trade Area (CEFTA) to the region, an extension nego-tiated under the auspices of the Stability Pact for Southeast Europe and aimed at favouring legitimate travel and economic development (McTaggart 2006b; see, more broadly, Dangerfield 2006). This agree-ment, which replaced the matrix of bilateral free trade agreements, aimed to achieve a free trade zone for all countries by the end of 2010. A large portion of CEFTA foreign trade was (and remains) with EU states.

CEFTA's impact in terms of economic growth was positive, although probably not too extensive.[5] Border checks remained necessary in order to implement rules of origin—with the related long lines at the border and costs to trade. In addition, political tensions impacted negatively on intra-CEFTA trade. The 2008 independence of Kosovo compli-cated CEFTA's operation, since neither Serbia nor Bosnia-Herzegovina recognized this new state and, as a result, boycotted Kosovo's prod-ucts. In response, Kosovo retaliated by imposing its own blockade on imports from Serbia and decided to boycott CEFTA Secretariat meetings (A'Mula 2009). This escalation even led to clashes at border posts in July 2011, and highlighted how political difficulties remained the key prob-lem in the region, hindering progress in the economic sphere as well.

In addition to fostering cross-border trade, European funds also required aspiring EU members to devise multi-year develop-ment plans to address collaboratively trans-border issues, such as the fight against organized crime, illegal trade and human trafficking.

Despite the fact that local illegal transnational networks in the mid-2000s remained more effective and better organized than the EU's own transnationalism (Kostovicova and Bojičić-Dželilović 2008), the EU's efficiency in this area gradually improved. In the long-term, the Balkans' inclusion into European institutions is expected to improve the effectiveness of the fight against organized crime and illegal migration, since the region will be part of the EU's law enforcement space (Pond 2006: 253).

Softening Nationalist Identities. Ultimately, European integration provides the opportunity to transform conflictual identities (Diez et al. 2008). Inclusion into European institutions could soften exclusive, nationalist identities by adding a new layer of identification. For example, a citizen of Sarajevo could possess simultaneously a Serb, Bosnian and European identity (and citizenship)—a situation of multiple layers common to most individuals living in European capitals (see, in general, Brewer 2001). Not only do such multiple identities lead to greater acceptance of diversity (Diez 2002), but also they can sustain a pragmatic attitude in addressing group differences.

Perhaps more importantly, integration into European institutions could provide an avenue for increasing contacts among the countries in the region, and contribute to de-politicize potentially explosive border issues. Indeed, despite the signing of the DPA, borders have remained contested. Since 2006, Serb nationalists in Bosnia-Herzegovina have flirted with the possibility of calling a referendum on independence that would detach their semi-autonomous republic from Bosnian common institutions and trigger a likely military reaction from Bosniaks (Belloni 2008: 162). Kosovo's independence became a *fait-accompli* in 2008, but this new state was initially recognized by only a minority of states in international society while Serb areas remained de facto autonomous within the newly constituted independent state. In FYROM, the inclusion of Albanians in the political system following the 2001 Ohrid Agreement contributed considerably to a decrease in ethnic tensions, but occasional outbreaks of localized violence signalled the presence of a persisting malaise. For all of these states, it was believed that rapid integration into the EU would have undermined the nationalists' call to redraw the regional political map. The answer to the problem of borders was not to redraw them, but to make them increasingly irrelevant by recognizing allegiances to overlapping polities and thus de-politicize the significance of (hard) borders. By supporting functional rather than geographical exercises of authority, soft borders could encourage the multiplication and pluralization of allegiances historically linked to the Westphalian state and encourage regional and municipal cooperation across dividing lines (Mostov 2007).

5.5   EU MEMBER STATES AND THE ENLARGEMENT *PROBLEMATIQUE*

The EU trusted that its open-door policy would have provided the Balkans with a long-term and coherent perspective, favouring domestic ownership, supporting institutional development and even softening nationalist identities. However, no sooner was such a policy declared than it was undermined by competing interests. The Stability Pact was quite effective in directing resources to the Balkans, but less so in providing unity to the European effort. The Pact was launched in June 1999 at the time when Germany held the EU Presidency, and since then was dominated by German-speaking officials, many of whom had little experience in Balkan politics. Two structural problems further complicated the Pact's effectiveness. First, the initial exclusion of the rump-Yugoslavia (and later Serbia) due to President Milosevic's indictment for war crimes severely damaged the Pact's regional ambitions. Second, the focus of the Stability Pact on working with legitimate governments could only have a limited impact on domestic civil society.[6] Moreover, the Commission's launch of its own SAP was widely interpreted as openly antagonistic to the Stability Pact (Gallagher 2005: 168–170). Although the supposed antagonism between the two initiatives was sometimes exaggerated, it is undeniable that the proliferation of initiatives undermined the clarity and unity of EU policies (Friis and Murphy 2000: 777).

This clarity and unity were further challenged by the difficulties experienced by the EU in the attempt to reform itself by acquiring more effective institutions. The spring 2005 rejection of the proposed new EU Constitutional Treaty by French and Dutch voters poured cold water on the aspirations of would-be members. Although the question of further enlargement was not a key factor in determining these votes,[7] for many commentators and policy-makers the rejection of the Treaty signified also the rejection of enlargement, complicating the prospect of the Western Balkans' accession to the EU. In the absence of constitutional reform, further enlargement could dangerously strain the existing modus operandi. The Western Balkans comprised seven countries (including newly independent Kosovo) which, added to the 27 states which were members of the Union in the late 2000s (until 2013 when Croatia joined the EU as the 28th member), could potentially paralyze future EU decision-making.

Because unanimity is required for EU membership to be granted, each existing member state has a veto power on accession. For this reason, when in 2005 the French government amended its country's constitution to require ratification by popular referendum of all future EU enlargements, aspiring new EU members immediately recognized the consequences of this decision. Although Western Balkan states were the immediate casualties of French reluctance to accept new members into the EU, French opinion was shaped more by the membership aspiration of Turkey (a big, poor and predominantly Muslim state) than by any other issue. In May 2008 France altered again its constitution by retaining the referendum clause only for countries whose population is greater than 5% of the total EU population—thus effectively singling out Turkey, while signalling a new political openness towards the Balkans. However, the June 2008 Irish dismissal of the Lisbon Treaty, which replaced the defunct proposed constitution, further sidelined the enlargement agenda.

Several EU member states, led by France, joined EU officials in opposing further enlargement in the absence of a new treaty. José Manuel Barroso, then President of the European Commission, suggested that, in order to ensure the Union's functionality with an even bigger number of members, institutional reform should have preceded any future enlargement. In a context of increasing doubts about the benefits of admitting new states into the EU, several high-profile EU politicians proposed alternatives to EU membership. In 2006, well before the outbreak of the Euro crisis, German chancellor Angela Merkel went on record as the first EU leader to publicly suggest a privileged partnership for the Western Balkan states (Krasniqi and Beunderman 2006). Although the proposal was not followed by concrete indications of what it entailed, it revealed the level of disillusionment with the prospect of further enlargement. At roughly the same time, French President Nicholas Sarkozy advanced the idea of 'strategic partnership' between the EU and aspiring member states. These proposals were meant primarily to keep Turkey at arms-length from the EU, but their entry into the public debate did not reassure Western Balkan states about the EU commitment to enlargement. According to a Gallup poll, by the late

2000s Western Balkans citizens were disillusioned about the prospect of joining the EU. Only a minority of respondents in all countries believed that their state could become a full EU member in the following few years, and few had confidence in the usefulness of accession into the EU (Gallup Balkan Monitor 2009).

French pressure ultimately led the EU to adopt a tougher stance on future enlargement. The EU wearily confirmed its readiness to accept new states, but specified that future admissions would be granted on a country-by-country basis and not in groups. The fulfilment of specific criteria for admission would be monitored more closely, and the EU would be less accommodating towards potential members (Phinnemore 2006). At the EU-Balkan meeting in Salzburg in March 2006, EU foreign ministers confirmed their more stringent approach. They watered down previous commitments with reference to the EU's 'absorption capacity' and to an 'internal European debate' on the future of enlargement as potential barriers to accession (EU/WB 2006). European Commission President Barroso acknowledged the growing 'enlargement fatigue' by announcing that the accession of Romania and Bulgaria (which joined on 1 January 2007) was the last enlargement—at least in the absence of an institutional reform capable of streamlining the decision-making process of a much larger EU (McTaggart 2006a). The 2006 enlargement strategy paper released by the European Commission advised against further enlargement (EU 2006), while the same document the following year demanded full attention be paid to the 'EU's integration capacity'.

In practice, both new and aspiring candidates were put on hold and the prospect of admission into the EU club became very distant. The long-term time frame complicated the short-term local endorsement of reforms, since local leaders needed to deliver tangible results to their constituencies in order to push through sometimes painful restructurings. Crucially, because the EU's 'absorption capacity' could not be influenced by aspiring EU member states, meeting EU criteria was not enough for accession, and the goal of EU membership thus turned into a moving target. As a result, local politicians became increasingly tempted to renege on previous commitments and delay further reform.

The direct link between the EU's accession prospects and domestic reform was perhaps most visible in Bosnia-Herzegovina. The day after the French referendum on the EU constitution, the RS Parliament rejected once again a policy reform package demanded by European institutions. By late 2007 Bosnia-Herzegovina was the only country in the region without a prospect of membership. Only after the EU decided to initiate a SAA did Bosnian authorities accept the reform package proposed by Brussels. In sum, the credibility of EU condition-ality necessitated an active presence and careful distribution of rewards (Schimmelfennig 2008). As the experience with the admission process of CEE states into the EU confirms, the introduction of 'intermediary rewards', such as substantial economic aid, greater access to EU markets, and visa-free travel was important to strengthen the push for reforms and the viability of pro-EU parties (Vachudova 2005).

5.6   CONCLUSIONS

Academic literature of the 1990s frequently described the European view of the Balkans as based on Orientalist ideas, part of a dichotomy between the rational and enlightened West and the feminine, emotional and irra-tional Orient (Bakić-Hayden and Hayden 1992; Todorova 1997). While this description captured a lasting attitude with deep historical roots, with the adoption of the EU's open-door policy in the early 2000s the Balkans turned into a transitional concept, something not yet Europe, or not quite European, but on its way to European integration. In advanc-ing an integration prospect, in effect the EU replaced space with time, suggesting that the region could move from a Balkan past to a European future (Jeffrey 2008). The Balkans was still perceived as politically, eco-nomically and socially backward, but they had the potential of entering the European mainstream, defined by progress, stability and prosperity.

To turn this vision into reality, the EU (then European Community) had to reform itself. When the wars of Yugoslav dissolution began in the early 1990s, Europe was politically, diplomatically and militarily unpre-pared to confront the worst crisis on European territory since World War II. Since then, the EU has developed and deployed an impressive range of different tools aimed at moving the region politically and economi-cally towards the European mainstream, teleologically understood to be the only and inevitable end-point of the region's multiple transitions. As a result, the Balkans changed the EU, in particular by accelerating the development of the CSDP, at least as much as the EU has contributed to changing the Balkans.

Since the mid-1990s an increasing number of political, economic, mil-itary and development programmes have been deployed to increase the

links between Europe and its south-eastern neighbours. This process culminated in the early 2000s with the affirmation of an open-door policy vis-
à-vis the Balkans, which quickly turned the EU into the most important
peacebuilding actor in the region. The EU's new role was widely praised.
Several academics and policy-makers alike identified the Balkans' integration into Europe as the long-term answer to this region's recent instability
and conflict. The integration perspective provided the region with a stimulating vision that should have supported the adoption and implementation
of domestic reforms without the brazen imposition of policy frameworks.

As a whole, the process of European integration has proved useful to
guide international involvement in the region and has constituted a step
forward compared to previous international practice. However, the effort
to promote peace, democracy and stability through integration soon faced
considerable obstacles. Most notably, shortly after declaring its open-door
policy, the EU found itself internally torn by competing visions. The inca-
pacity of the EU to give itself a Constitutional Treaty testified to the differences among member states about the Union's future role. As the next
chapter will show, with the outbreak of the economic and financial crisis in
2007–2008, the Union further downgraded its enlargement agenda among
its foreign policy priorities. As a result, the Balkans remained in a limbo.

Notes

1. The 'dual key' was abandoned on 21 July 1995 at the London Conference,
   opening the way for more assertive (and ultimately successful) diplomacy
   (Burg and Shoup 1999: 344).
2. This is also true for NATO (2005).
3. All documents related to the Pact are available at www.stabilitypact.org.
   For an assessment of the Pact's political significance, see Cremona (2000).
4. Although the Stability Pact was criticised for its scarce attention to civil
   society, it did achieve its objective of fostering local ownership. In February
   2008 its competences and activities were transferred to the Regional
   Cooperation Council (RCC), a new institution under regional ownership.
5. Interview with Renzo Daviddi, Deputy Head of the EU Delegation to
   Bosnia-Herzegovina-Herzegovina, Sarajevo, July 2013.
6. Interview with Erhard Busek, Stability Pact's Coordinator, Cambridge,
   MA, October 2003.
7. In the Netherlands only 6% and in France only 3% of respondents
   stated opposition to future enlargement as the reason for voting 'no'
   (Eurobarometer 2005).

REFERENCES

A'Mula, S. (2009, May 27). *Kosovo boycott CEFTA meeting* (Resource document). https://balkaninsight.com/2009/05/27/kosovo-boycotts-cefta-meeting/. Accessed 2 April 2013.

Ashdown, P. (2004, May 12). From Dayton to Brussels. *Reporter.* http://www.ohr.int/ohr-dept/presso/pressa/default.asp?content_id=32492. Accessed 12 March 2012.

Ashdown, P. (2007). *Swords and ploughshares: Bringing peace to the 21st century.* London: Orion.

B92 News. (2007, December 23). *Bosnia-Herzegovina in 2007: Highs and lows* (Resource document). www.b92.net/eng/news. Accessed 12 March 2012.

Bakić-Hayden, M., & Hayden, R. M. (1992). Orientalist variations on the theme 'Balkans': Symbolic geography in recent Yugoslav cultural politics. *Slavic Review, 51*(1), 1–15.

Batt, J. (Ed.). (2004, October). *The Western Balkans: Moving on* (Chaillot Paper No. 70). Paris: Institute for Security Studies.

Bechev, D., & Andreev, S. (2005, February). *Top-down vs bottom-up aspects of the institution building strategies in the Western Balkans* (Occasional Paper No. 3/05). Oxford: St. Antony's College.

Belloni, R. (2008). *State building and international intervention in Bosnia-Herzegovina.* London and New York: Routledge.

Brewer, M. B. (2001). The many faces of social identity: Implications for political psychology. *Political Psychology, 22*(1), 115–125.

Burg, S. L., & Shoup, P. S. (1999). *The war in Bosnia-Herzegovina: Ethnic conflict and international intervention.* Arnmonk, NY: M. E. Sharpe.

Busek, E. (2004, March). *Five years of stability pact for Southeast Europe: Achievements and challenges ahead* (Discussion Paper 70). Centre for the Study of Global Governance, London School of Economics.

Caplan, R. (2005). *Europe and the recognition of new states in Yugoslavia.* Cambridge: Cambridge University Press.

Capussela, A. L. (2015). *State-building in Kosovo: Democracy, corruption and the EU in the Balkans.* London: I.B. Tauris.

CEPS (Centre for European Policy Studies). (2005, July). *The reluctant debutante: The European Union as promoter of democracy in its neighbourhood* (CEPS Working document 223). Brussels.

Chandler, D. (2006). From Dayton to Europe. In D. Chandler (Ed.), *Peace without politics? Ten years of international state-building in Bosnia-Herzegovina* (pp. 30–43). London and New York: Routledge.

Cooley, L. (2019). *The European Union's approach to conflict resolution: Transformation or regulation in the Western Balkans?* London and New York: Routledge.

Coppitiers, B., Emerson, M., Huysseune, M., Kovziridze, T., Noutcheva, G., Tocci, N., et al. (2004). *Europeanization and conflict resolution: Case studies from the European periphery.* Gent: Academia Press.

Council of the European Union. (2000, June 19–20). *Presidency conclusions.* Santa Maria de Feira European Council Meeting, Press Release Nr: 2000/1/00.

Council of the European Union. (2003, June 19–20). *Presidency conclusions.* Thessaloniki European Council Meeting, 11638/03.

Crawford, B. (1996). Explaining defection from international cooperation: Germany's unilateral recognition of Croatia. *World Politics, 48*(4), 482–521.

Cremona, M. (2000). Creating the new Europe: The stability pact for South-Eastern Europe in the context of EU-SEE relations. *Cambridge Yearbook of European Legal Studies, 2,* 463–506.

Dangerfield, M. (2006). Subregional integration and EU enlargement: Where next for CEFTA? *Journal of Common Market Studies, 44*(2), 305–324.

Diez, T. (2002). Why the EU can nonetheless be good for Cyprus. *Journal of Ethnopolitics and Minority Issues in Europe* (2) (Resource document). www.ecmi.de. Accessed 10 June 2009.

Diez, T. (2005). Constructing the self and changing others: Reconsidering 'normative power Europe.' *Millennium: Journal of International Studies, 33*(3), 613–636.

Diez, T., Albert, M., & Stetter, S. (2008). *The European Union and border conflicts: The power of integration and association.* Cambridge: Cambridge University Press.

Eurobarometer. (2005, June). *The European constitution: Post-referendum survey in the Netherlands* (No. 172).

European Commission. (1999, May 26). *Communication from the commission to the council and the European parliament of 26 May 1999 on the stabilisation and association process for countries of South-Eastern Europe.* COM (1999), 235 final, Brussels.

European Commission. (2001). *The stabilisation and association process and CARDS assistance 2000 to 2006.* European Commission paper for the second regional conference for South East Europe. http://www.seerecon.org/region/documents/ec/ec_sap_cards_2000-2006.pdf. Accessed 5 June 2009.

European Commission. (2006). *Western Balkans: Prospect of EU membership incites peace in the Western Balkans.* http://ec.europa.eu/world/peace/geographical_themes/west_balk/index_en.htm. Accessed 20 November 2006.

ESI (European Stability Initiative). (2005a, June). *Breaking out of the Balkan ghetto: Why IPA should be changed.* Berlin, Brussels, and Istanbul: ESI.

ESI. (2005b, December). *Moment of truth: FYROM, the EU budget and the destabilisation of the Balkans.* Berlin, Brussels, and Istanbul: ESI.

ESI. (2005c, February). *The Helsinki moment: European member-state building in the Balkans.* Berlin, Brussels, and Istanbul: ESI.

EU/WB (European Union/Western Balkans). (2006, March 11). *Joint press statement*. Salzburg.

EU/World Bank Joint Office for South East Europe. (2008). *How much money is being given?* (regularly updated, resource document). www.seerecon.org. Accessed 18 December 2018.

Friis, L., & Murphy, A. (2000). 'Turbo-charged negotiations:' The EU and the stability pact for south Eastern Europe. *Journal of European Public Policy, 7*(5), 767–786.

Gallagher, T. (2005). *The Balkans in the new millennium: In the shadow of war and peace*. London: Routledge.

Gallup Balkan Monitor. (2009). *Perceptions of the EU in the Western Balkans* (Resource document). www.balkan-monitor.eu. Accessed 2 April 2013.

Gordon, C. E. (2009). The stabilization and association process in the Western Balkans: An effective instrument of post-conflict management? *Ethnopolitics, 8*(3), 325–340.

Hill, C. (2001). The EU's capacity for conflict prevention. *European Foreign Affairs Review, 6*(3), 315–333.

ICB (International Commission on the Balkans). (2005). *The Balkans in Europe's future* (Resource document). www.balkan-commission.org. Accessed 5 June 2009.

Jarstad, A., & Sisk, T. D. (Eds.). (2008). *From war to democracy: Dilemmas of peacebuilding*. Cambridge: Cambridge University Press.

Jeffrey, A. (2008). Contesting Europe: The politics of European integration. *Environment and Planning D: Society and Space, 26*(3), 428–443.

Juncos, A. (2018). EU security sector reform in Bosnia and Herzegovina: Reform or resist? *Contemporary Security Policy, 39*(1), 95–118.

King, I., & Mason, W. (2006). *Peace at any price: How the world failed Kosovo*. Ithaca and London: Cornell University Press.

Knaus, G., & Cox, M. (2005). The Helsinki Moment in Southeast Europe. *Journal of Democracy, 16*(1), 39–53.

Kostovicova, D., & Bojičić-Dželilović, V. (2008). Europeanizing the Balkans: Rethinking the post-communist and post-conflict transition. In D. Kostovicova & V. Bojičić-Dželilović (Eds.), *Transnationalism in the Balkans* (pp. 7–25). London and New York: Routledge.

Krasniqi, E., & Beunderman, M. (2006, March 17). Merkel moots 'privileged partnership for Balkans'. *EU Observer* (Resource document). http://euobserver.com/enlargement/21163. Accessed 5 June 2009.

Latifi, V. (2007). Preventive engagement of the international community: The model case of FYROM? *Foreign Policy in Dialogue, 8*(2/3), 32–38.

Lehne, S. (2004, October). Has the 'hour of Europe' come at last? The EU's strategy for the Balkans. In J. Batt (Ed.), *The Western Balkans: Moving on* (Chaillot Paper No. 7, pp. 111–124). Paris: Institute for Security Studies.

Leroux-Martin, P. (2014). *Diplomatic counterinsurcency: Lessons from Bosnia and Herzegovina*. Cambridge: Cambridge University Press.

Manners, I. (2002). Normative power Europe: A contradictions in terms? *Journal of Common Market Studies, 40*(2), 235–258.

Manners, I. (2006). The European Union as a normative power: A response to Thomas Diez. *Millennium: Journal of International Studies, 35*(1), 167–180.

McTaggart, A. (2006a, October 5). *Crossfire over enlargement confuses Balkans*. Balkan Insight.

McTaggart, A. (2006b, October 26). *EU hails Balkan free trade deal as milestone*. Balkan Insight.

Mostov, J. (2007). Soft borders and transnational citizens. In S. Benhabib, I. Shapiro, & D. Petranović (Eds.), *Identities, affiliation, and allegiances* (pp. 138–158). Cambridge: Cambridge University Press.

Mulchinock, N. (2017). *NATO and the Western Balkans: From neutral spectator to proactive peacemaker*. Houndmills: Palgrave.

NATO (North Atlantic Treaty Organization). (2005, February). *Bringing peace and stability to the Balkans*. Brussels: Briefing.

Noutcheva, G. (2012). *European foreign policy and the challenges of Balkan accession: Conditionality, legitimacy and compliance*. London and New York: Routledge.

Petruseva, A. (2004, November 12). *Macedonians turn away from ethnic divisions*. Institute for War and Peace Reporting.

Phinnemore, D. (2006). Beyond 25—The changing face of EU enlargement: Commitment, conditionality and the constitutional treaty. *Journal of Southern Europe and the Balkans, 8*(1), 7–26.

Pond, E. (2006). *Endgame in the Balkans: Regime change, European style*. Washington, DC: Brookings Institution Press.

Rehn, O. (2005, January 4). Values define Europe, not borders. *Financial Times*.

Reljić, D. (2007). A long way towards EU accession? Membership perspectives and the stabilisation and association process for the Western Balkan countries. *Foreign Policy in Dialogue, 8*(2/3), 16–23.

Sampson, S. (2002, June). *Weak states, uncivil societies and thousands of NGOs: Western democracy exported as benevolent colonialism in the Balkans*. Lund, draft.

Schimmelfennig, F. (2008). EU political accession conditionality after the 2004 enlargement: Consistency and effectiveness. *Journal of European Public Policy, 15*(6), 918–937.

Schimmelfennig, F., & Sedelmeier, U. (Eds.). (2005). *The Europeanization of central and Eastern Europe*. Ithaca and London: Cornell University Press.

Sebastian Aparicio, S. (2014). *Post-war statebuilding and constitutional reform: Beyond Dayton in Bosnia-Herzegovina*. Houndmills: Palgrave.

Solana, X. (2003, December 12). *A secure Europe in a better world: European security strategy* (Resource document). http://ue.eu.int/uedocs/cmsUpload/78367.pdf. Accessed 10 November 2004.

Subotić, J. (2011). Europe is a state of mind: Identity and Europeanization in the Balkans. *International Studies Quarterly, 55*(2), 309–330.

Todorova, M. (1997). *Imagining the Balkans.* New York: Oxford University Press.

Vachudova, M. A. (2005). *Europe undivided: Democracy, leverage and integration after communism.* Oxford: Oxford University Press.

Van Meurs, W. P. (2003). The next Europe: South-Eastern Europe after Thessakoniki. *South East Europe Review, 6*(3), 9–16.

Wallace, W. (1999). The sharing of sovereignty: The European paradox. *Political Studies, 47*(4), 503–521.

Weaver, O. (1998). Insecurity, security and asecurity in the West European non-war community. In E. Adler & M. Barnett (Eds.), *Security communities* (pp. 69–118). Cambridge: Cambridge University Press.

Whitmore, B. (2008, 22 July). *Karadzic arrest in Serbia shows power of elections.* Radio Free Europe/Radio Liberty.

Wolff, S., & Peen Rodt, A. (2007, March). *The reactive conflict management of the EU in the Western Balkans.* Paper presented at the International Studies Annual Meeting, Chicago.

Woodward, S. L. (2017). *The ideology of failed states: Why intervention fails.* Cambridge: Cambridge University Press.

Yusufi, I. (2004). Europeanizing the Western Balkans through military and police missions: The cases of concordia and proxima in FYROM. *European Balkan Observer, 2*(1), 8–12.

Zielonka, J. (2006). *Europe as empire: The nature of the enlarged European Union.* Oxford: Oxford University Press.

CHAPTER 6

Western Balkans Transitions and the Role of the European Union

6.1 Introduction

As Chapter 5 argued, with its promise of eventual membership the EU aimed at sustaining a process of political, economic and social transformation without, however, the blatant top-down policy imposition which characterized the early peacebuilding years in both Bosnia-Herzegovina and Kosovo. This chapter discusses the main economic, security and political issues emerging in the region following the EU's new, ambitious role.

The Western Balkans made considerable progress since 2000, when the EU recognized that the future of this region as a whole resides in integration with European institutions. The death of Croatian President Franjo Tudjman in late 1999 and the fall from power of Slobodan Milosevic, President of the rump Yugoslavia, in late 2000, created favourable conditions for the development of democratic institutions and practices. As a result, the region experienced an unprecedented blossoming. Formally democratic institutions were established everywhere, and were generally recognized as legitimate by both citizens and by international organizations operating in the region. Despite the enormous economic, political and social setback caused by the wars of the 1990s, the overall level of recorded development reached more than acceptable levels. For example, the 2008 Human Development Index, which combined levels of per capita income, adult literacy and life expectancy into one indicator, found that all Western Balkan states were 'highly developed' (UNDP 2008).

© The Author(s) 2020
R. Belloni, *The Rise and Fall of Peacebuilding in the Balkans*, Rethinking Peace and Conflict Studies,
https://doi.org/10.1007/978-3-030-14424-1_6

Yet, despite the considerable progress, by the late 2000s the region still experienced significant difficulties. In the economic sphere, high levels of unemployment remained the key challenge for most states. Moreover, corruption became increasingly entrenched, while the outbreak of the global financial crisis in 2007–2008 impacted EU member states, with negative repercussions in the Balkans as well. In the security sphere, the situation of both hard security (involving military issues) and soft security (involving crime both inside and across national borders) greatly improved. Yet, organized crime maintained deep roots in the region as well as significant economic interests in western Europe. From a political perspective, the February 2008 independence of Kosovo was by and large the most significant event of the late 2000s, raising troubling and potentially destabilizing questions about who and under what conditions had a right to self-determination. The Serb Republic of Bosnia claimed such a right, to the dismay of international officials who feared the consequences a declaration of independence could bring about for the stability of the region.

The common thread linking economic, security and political issues was found in the important and increasing role played by the EU in attempting to ameliorate them. Since the early 2000s, the perspective of European integration sustained a process of reform in the region, but did not transform the underlying political dynamics (Cooley 2019). Above all, with the exception of Croatia which joined the Union on 1 July 2013, for the other states the European promise remained too distant and intangible. With the outbreak of the economic and financial crisis in Europe in 2007–2008, the EU's main concern became the management of the crisis, relegating enlargement to the bottom of its priorities, and thus severely demoralizing aspiring new members.

This chapter begins with a discussion of the main economic, security and political developments throughout the 2000s. Although the region achieved considerable progress in all areas, hard-to-resolve problems continued to hinder the peacebuilding transition. Then, it focuses on the EU's attempt to formulate a viable policy to address the remaining challenges. The contradictions and hesitations of the EU approach are identified and assessed. Finally, the chapter explains how by the end of the decade the enlargement prospect became increasingly intangible. Western Balkan states became stuck in a grey zone between integration into the EU and isolation. They lived in a condition of 'permanent transition' without any certainty about their political future.

6.2   The Economy: Growth with Unemployment and Corruption

Since 2000, the Western Balkans began experiencing good economic growth. Even though the imperfect and politicized nature of statistical production in 'fragile states' settings suggests caution in assessing economic progress (Rocha de Siqueira 2017), the overall trend has been positive. The general improvement of the political situation contributed to this development, which allowed liberal peacebuilders to claim a degree of legitimacy for their policies. In 2000 both Croatia and Serbia entered a phase of democratization; the Macedonian crisis in 2001, involving rising tensions between the Slavic majority and the Albanian minority, was addressed and resolved before it could spiral out of control; the independence of Montenegro in 2006 and that of Kosovo in 2008 provided an answer to self-determination claims and, in so doing, laid the foundation for better economic cooperation and development.

Often led by new political elites influenced by neo-liberal ideas, states emerging from the dissolution of Yugoslavia adopted their own privatization and market reform programmes in the late 1990s and early 2000s (Bartlett 2008). Since 2003 and until the end of the decade, the region as a whole experienced economic growth averaging between 4 and 6% per year (Gligorov 2008). In 2007 Bosnia-Herzegovina experienced the highest GDP growth in the region with 6% while Croatia, Serbia and FYROM had a 4%, with the remaining countries somewhere in between. In Kosovo, however, growth was significantly lower than the rest of the region. Accordingly, the distance between Kosovo and its neighbours widened (Capussela 2015: 40).

Not only did the Western Balkans benefit from the improvement in the political situation but also from greater trade opportunities. In 2000 the EU granted states in the region a preferential treatment involving zero tariffs for almost all exports. The Union established exceptional unlimited duty-free access to the EU market for nearly all products originating from Albania, Bosnia-Herzegovina, Croatia, FYROM, Montenegro, Serbia and Kosovo. Only wine, sugar and certain beef and fisheries products entered the EU under preferential tariff quotas, as negotiated under the Stabilization and Association Agreements (SAAs) with each individual state. Significantly quota restrictions did not impact exports from the Western Balkans: throughout the year 2000s quotas were not even reached most of the time, leaving room for future export increases. Moreover, as mentioned in Chapter 5, the region liberalized intra-regional trade through the Central European Free Trade Agreement (CEFTA), a multilateral free trade agreement signed in December 2006, and which came into effect the following year for Albania, Bosnia-Herzegovina, Croatia, Kosovo, FYROM, Moldova, Montenegro and Serbia.

By the late 2000s, the question of how to consolidate economic progress, improve local and cross-national stability, and further sustain EU integration remained central for both commentators and policy-makers. On the one hand, some commentators argued that the Western Balkans should have entered into a customs union with the EU, involving the adoption of the EU's common external tariff with third countries (Emerson 2008). This option presented two main advantages: it would have done away with the complicated rules of origin in place for Western Balkans goods and it would have prepared the region for the adoption of common external tariffs and administrative customs procedures. In this way, not only would trade have been favoured, but also foreign direct investment. However, the Commission reasoned that Western Balkan states could make good use of tariffs in the process of negotiation and implementation of their SAAs and in trading with third countries. On the other hand, a more limited proposal, espoused by the World Bank, aimed at strengthening regional economic integration by developing human capital and reducing telecommunication costs (Kathuria 2008). In light of the Commission's views, this second proposal carried the day. Only in 2017 did Johannes Hahn, the Commissioner for European Neighbourhood Policy and Enlargement Negotiations again raise the idea of a custom union and common market but, by early 2019, it remained unimplemented. On balance, throughout the year 2000s the macroeconomic situation in the Western Balkans improved considerably as a result of post-war recovery, overall political stability, and increased opportunities for trade and investment. The prospect for the region as a whole was reasonably bright: by the turn of the decade the Western Balkans seemed to be repeating the Central European development experience with a time lag of about 10 years (Cohen and Lampe 2011).

However, when compared to western Europe and more broadly to countries competing in the global economy, the Western Balkans remained a laggard. Even though economic growth rates in the 2000s were significant, they could hardly fill the gap with the rest of Europe. By 2008 it was projected that the region still needed over 50 years to reach the economic levels of western Europe (UNODC 2008: 104). Moreover, national economies remained uncompetitive internationally. In 2010 Albania was ranked at 108 out of 134 in the global competitiveness ranking of the World Economic Forum, Bosnia-Herzegovina at 107, Croatia at 61, Montenegro at 65, Serbia at 85, and FYROM at 89 (Kosovo was not yet included).

This troubling data reflected the continuing influence of severe economic constraints. Western Balkan countries maintained substantial trade deficits in their balance of payments as a result of a large influx of goods from abroad and the difficulty of competing internationally. The elimination of tariffs on goods imported from the EU to the Western Balkan states opened the doors to a flood of imports. All states experienced large deficits in the balance of trade in goods and services, reflecting their low levels of competitiveness and the shortcomings of the neo-liberal transition process after two decades of implementation (Bartlett 2015). Because of extensive corruption and time-consuming bureaucratic obstacles, foreign direct investment was low, particularly in Bosnia-Herzegovina, FYROM and Serbia. Especially worrisome was the high level of unemployment. Economic growth produced little corresponding growth in employment, leading to 'jobless growth' (Bartlett 2008: Chapter 7). Unemployment in 2007 ranged from 9% in Croatia, to 15% in Albania, 20% in Serbia, 25% in Montenegro, 30% in Bosnia-Herzegovina, 35% in FYROM and 45% in Kosovo. Although Croatia fared better than the other Western Balkan states, its unemployment rate was still high compared to most of the EU countries.

Above all, the case of the Western Balkans confirms that 'growth-oriented' policies are not enough to address the socioeconomic and social stratifications underlying conflict. Neo-liberal economic policies were generally not developmental and pro-poor, and did not address entrenched high structural unemployment. The economic growth that took place during the 2000s was driven largely by inflows of external capital that fuelled a consumer boom, rather than investment in assets and infrastructure (Bartlett 2015: 223).

These policies did little to ameliorate poverty levels. Kosovo had the unenviable record of being the poorest country in Europe. According to the World Bank's 2008 Kosovo Poverty Assessment Report, about 45% of the population had consumption levels below the poverty line (set at 45 Euros per person per month). About 14% of the population was considered to be extremely poor, having difficulty meeting their basic nutritional needs. The average salary was just 200 Euros per month. In all Western Balkan states, the informal economy played a fundamental role in sustaining individuals and families. In Bosnia-Herzegovina, for example, it was estimated that the informal sector was over 50% of the total economy. Despite its positive role in supporting the livelihood of individuals with no other economic opportunities, the informal economy deprived the state of considerable resources due to missed taxation.

In addition to informal economic activities, which were not necessarily criminal, there existed widespread corruption and illegal economic practices. Transparency International's Corruption Perceptions Index regularly identified Bosnia-Herzegovina as the most corrupt country in the Western Balkans and more broadly in Europe. A survey focusing on *actual* experiences of corruption affecting the daily lives of ordinary people documented how a remarkable eight out of ten Bosnian citizens interacted with corruption in the course of the year (UNODC 2011). As argued in Chapter 3, in most cases corruption was instrumental to political stability. Although no international official would have openly admitted it, there existed a tacit understanding that office holders would have exploited economic opportunities to the fullest. Despite protests to the contrary, peacebuilding officials often turned a blind eye to these practices on the grounds that their first priority was the maintenance of political and economic stability, at the cost of tolerating the misuse of international aid and the exploitation of the process of economic privatization for personal advantage. Milorad Dodik, elected in 1998 and again in 2006 as RS Prime Minister, exemplified this symbiosis between domestic and international actors. Dodik was a darling of international donors, making his government a large recipient of international funds. Because Dodik appeared to be a 'moderate' politician, at least compared to the political alternatives available in the RS, the international community did not make much of a fuss when embezzlement scandals tainted his government. In the Bosniak-Croat Federation, Prime Minister Haris Silajdžić, Dodik's mirror image, also managed to deflect criticism for surrounding himself with cronies with less than pristine credentials.

The fight against corruption rose to the top of the list of EU priorities in October 2008, when the issue became a key benchmark in the visa liberalization process (discussed below).[1] Under international pressure Bosnian authorities adopted a legal framework modelled on the best practices of western democracies, including several strategic documents and new legislation such as the 2009–2014 Anti-Corruption Strategy and

Action Plan and the Law on Conflict of Interest. In 2010 the Council of Ministers decided on the establishment of an Agency for Corruption Prevention and the Coordination of the Fight against Corruption. Both the 2009–2014 Strategy and the Anti-Corruption Agency were part of Bosnia-Herzegovina's obligations under the roadmap for EU visa liberalization. While the adoption of these and similar initiatives occurred without major snags, implementation was inconsistent and ineffective.[2] Poor implementation and lack of enforcement reflected not so much capacity problems as limited political will to address the situation (Transparency International 2013: 35, 40). The executive increasingly introduced changes to dilute anti-corruption laws, roll back transparency requirements and undermine different checks and balances (Perry 2015: 22).

In general, public procurement is where the greatest corruption took place.[3] The Law on Public Procurement adopted in 2014 introduced a series of new provisions which, however, were largely cosmetic (Voloder 2015). A number of civil society actors, including Transparency International, the NGO Tender, the RS Employers Association, and ACCOUNT (discussed in Chapter 4), submitted a draft proposal with the amendments to the Law which were not adopted (Perry 2015: 97). As a result, public tenders/procurement continued to be a lucrative activity prone to abuse (Perry 2015: 60). For civil society watchdog organizations it was actually complicated to document irregularities, since frequently tenders were negotiated in advanced behind closed doors.[4]

Corruption problems persisted when the world economic crisis broke out in 2008, contributing to the worsening of the economic situation in the region (Matutinović 2009). The crisis of the Eurozone revealed that the economic growth of the 2000s was built on thin foundations (Bartlett and Prica 2013). In February 2008 local stock markets melted. In the following few months, the indices lost between 60 and 76% of their value. The export industry, which was highly dependent on western European markets, also suffered a setback as a result of declining demand (Marusić 2009). The impact of the crisis was most acute in increased job losses and soaring rates of unemployment especially among young people, further complicating a chronically difficult social situation and casting a dark shadow on the future (Barlett and Uvalić 2013).

The region experienced a double-dip recession with the initial recession in 2008–2009 followed by another recession in 2012 with devastating social effects, in particular in terms of growing poverty, unemployment and income inequality (Sotiropoulos 2014). Economic downturns have been severest in Slovenia and Croatia, both negatively impacted by their close ties to the eurozone. Only Kosovo did not suffer directly from the crisis, since it was effectively isolated from the global economy, it received modest direct investment and was not exposed to international capital markets (Pula 2014). As argued in the next chapter, the most far-reaching consequence of the global economic crisis lay in the region's prospects for EU integration: since western European citizens feared for their jobs, identity and security, they increasingly opposed further enlargement. The worry that the Western Balkans' accession to the EU would favour a new influx of economic migrants from the region contributed to pour cold water on the accession aspirations of candidate states.

6.3   Security: Stabilization and Crime

Since the beginning of the process of Yugoslav dissolution in the early 1990s, security has constituted the main problem both for the Western Balkans and Europe as a whole. All European security organizations, including NATO, the EU and the Organization for Security and Cooperation in Europe (OSCE) dedicated much energy and attention to hard security issues, in particular to the task of improving cooperation between former warring parties. The most important initiatives were reactive, that is, they developed after major crises took place, and comprised of an increasingly regional approach (Delević 2007: 28). Following the hard-won peace in Bosnia-Herzegovina the EU developed a regional approach focused on the 'Dayton triangle' (after the 1995 DPA) and involving Sarajevo, Belgrade and Zagreb. Several articles in the DPA addressed issues of arms control and confidence-building, both within Bosnia-Herzegovina and regionally, and provided an opportunity for peacebuilding actors to deploy a large contingent of military and police forces and to adopt a wide range of security measures (Belloni 2008: 20–23). By the early 2000s, following the 1999 NATO war over Kosovo and the 2001 Albanian uprising in FYROM, a second group of states was included in the list of security priorities. The presence of a sizable Albanian minority in FYROM and of an Albanian majority in Kosovo made it indispensable to approach regional stabilization by adding Albania, FYROM and Serbia to the Dayton Triangle (Delević 2007: 15).

Accordingly, the EU launched several initiatives to help stabilize the region. As discussed in Chapter 5, through the Stabilization and Association Process (SAP) the EU promised Western Balkan states that they were 'potential candidates' for membership. The SAP assumed that regional stabilization and EU integration could proceed hand in hand, with one reinforcing the other and vice versa. However, stabilization and integration reflected different logics and in practice they often worked at cross-purposes (Elbasani 2008). Stabilization appropriately included a regional dimension. Both hard and soft security issues had important cross-border dimensions, and the EU took a regional approach to address them. At the same time, the process of integration developed bilaterally between aspiring member states and EU institutions. In this process, some countries started from better initial conditions, or developed faster than others. Accordingly, stabilization and integration were, by definition, goals impossible to achieve simultaneously. Unsurprisingly Croatia, which in the second half of the 2000s became the most advanced state in the process of EU integration, resisted the regional approach at stabilization, preferring a fast track negotiation process where each country could be considered individually. Since the initial stages of its relationship with the EU, Croatia suggested that the 'regatta principle', requiring that each state should progress towards integration at its own pace, should have replaced the 'caravan principle', according to which countries should be admitted to the EU in bloc, forcing more advanced states to wait for laggards (Gogova and Radoslavova 2001).

The 'regatta principle' prevailed. During the 2000s, all Western Balkan states signed a SAA with the EU, but the accession process remained everywhere in some degree of difficulty. The Dutch government refused to ratify the agreement with Serbia until Ratko Mladić, a former Serbian General who led the war in Bosnia-Herzegovina, was arrested (which eventually occurred in May 2011).[5] Several EU member states did not recognize Kosovo as an independent state, thus preventing the EU from entering into legal obligations with this newly created state. Since its independence, FYROM had a dispute with its southern neighbour and EU member Greece over the name 'Macedonia', and Croatia a boundary dispute with Slovenia, an EU member since 2004. In both cases, Greece and Slovenia enjoyed a veto right over accession and, as a result, accession negotiations stalled for years.

In addition to hard security problems, the Western Balkans experienced soft security issues, involving the corrosive influence of organized crime groups. Organized crime structures developed considerably following the collapse of the communist regime and the outbreak of the wars of Yugoslav dissolution in the 1990s. Porous borders, weak rule of law and dire economic conditions all contributed to create suitable circumstances for the strengthening of well-organized gangs and mobs, often with strong political links. With the end of the wars criminal networks became further entrenched in economic and political life. Since the end of the 1990s and early 2000s, the Western Balkans as a whole became a hub for organized crime and a major source and transit for trafficking in human beings, drugs, and other illicit goods. As discussed in Chapter 3 with regard to Bosnia-Herzegovina and Kosovo, criminal networks took advantage of the opportunities available in the transition to market economies, such as the process of privatization, whereby state assets were sold at bargain prices to politically connected individuals. In addition, in those areas devastated by armed violence, the availability of considerable amounts of reconstruction aid provided an additional opportunity for enrichment.

The presence of organized crime structures, widespread corruption, porous borders and illegal immigration all contributed to prevent a timely liberalization of the EU visa regime. Paradoxically, Western Balkans citizens' freedom to travel was more restrictive during the 2000s than it was under the Yugoslav communist regime. Those individuals who wished to enter the Schengen area, which covered most of the EU, had to undergo a time-consuming and costly process to obtain a short-stay visa. This visa regime prevented people-to-people contacts between the EU and the Western Balkans (Lobjakas 2009). In addition, not only did it create widespread resentment but also it was politically counter-productive. Given the EU's open-door policy towards the region, it was plainly incongruous to prevent citizens from the Western Balkans to see first-hand what Europe and the EU were made of.

The EU stated two main reasons for preserving a strict visa regime: fears of opening the door to organized crime and illegal work migration into the EU. Both reasons, however, were unconvincing. Despite its reputation for crime and lawlessness, the region slowly 'normalized' during the 2000s. A 2008 United Nations report concluded that the Western Balkans did not suffer from high rates of any kind of conventional crime, either murder or rape, assault, robbery, theft and the like, but rather was one of the safer areas of the world, and certainly safer than western Europe (UNODC 2008). The smuggling of humans, weapons and drugs through the region was also on the decline. In addition, not only fears of opening the door to organized crime through a visa-free regime were overstated, but so were concerns about illegal work migration, given the relatively small number of people living in the region (about 20 million).

Although the situation improved considerably, criminal groups continued to have a strong influence on both politics and the economy. Part of the reason why their influence lessened but was not eradicated lay in the state of local police forces. Some members of the paramilitary units that terrorized the civilian population during the wars of the 1990s became members of the state security forces. In Serbia, paramilitaries and crime syndicates went as far as assassinating the Prime Minister Zoran Đinđić in March 2003. Among those convicted for the assassination was Milorad Ulemek, better known as 'Legija' (the Legionnaire) because of his time past in the French Foreign Legion. Legiija was not only a former paramilitary fighter, but most importantly the head of the elite Special Operations Unit of the Ministry of the Interior as well as of the 'Zemun Clan', the best known organized crime group in Serbia. In Bosnia-Herzegovina, the police in both entities was described as 'heavily involved in organized crime'. The police in the RS was also filled with individuals suspected of war crimes (ICG 2007: 14).

Unsurprisingly, Security Sector Reform became a key demand of both the EU and NATO to grant accession to aspiring new member states (Bieber 2011b). The presence of democratic governance of the defence and security sector became an important criterion in the process of membership into NATO and especially the EU (Hänggi and Tanner 2005). The two organizations developed a division of labour whereby the EU focused on internal issues, such as border security and policing, while NATO concentrated on defence affairs, the restructuring and downsizing of the defence forces, and the strengthening of democratic control of the military. Given their complementary roles in promoting security and stabilization, the two organizations developed a framework for cooperation under the so-called Berlin-plus formula, whereby the United States allowed EU members to act with NATO assets without US participation (Mulchinock 2017: 171). As of the EU in particular, the promotion of security sector governance was advanced through a variety of different programmes, each reflecting different policy discourses: security policy, development cooperation and democracy promotion. Still missing was a coherent strategy on security sector governance within the broader EU external relations framework (Hänggi and Tanner 2005: 41).

General improvements in the security situation convinced the EU to ease its admission rules. Visa Facilitation Agreements entered into force for Bosnia-Herzegovina, FYROM, Montenegro and Serbia in January 2008 but for the first couple of years the situation on the ground did not change significantly (ESI 2008: 6). The most important aspect of these agreements involved the repatriation of those individuals from the Western Balkans who, escaping war in their homelands, were temporarily admitted to western Europe. Because Serbia received the most repatriated individuals, this country's re-admission policy was particularly noteworthy. Serbia signed re-admission agreements with 17 EU member states, as well as with the EU itself. Most of those repatriated (or 're-admitted') were Serbs of Roma origin with no cultural, social or economic links with Serbia itself. The re-admission agreements did not stipulate the condition for the humane reception of the returnees nor did they provide for the state's responsibility for the re-integration of the returnees. As a result, once back to Serbia these individuals received little or no assistance, were often discriminated against, and in all cases unemployed. Despite its apparent flaws, repatriation agreements reflected the EU's interests which included the protection of the EU's territorial space from unwanted outsiders, such as migrants and drug traffickers (Hills 2004). To put it bluntly, the EU policy constituted an attempt to replace poor migrants, often escaping dangerous conditions and/or abject poverty, with middle class tourists travelling to western Europe for shopping and sightseeing.

6.4   Political and Legal Issues: Still Backward Looking

From a political point of view, throughout the 2000s the region was still affected by unfinished business from the wars of Yugoslav dissolution. In December 2004 the Prosecutor of the ICTY in The Hague signed the final indictments (for a total of 161) and aimed to complete trials as soon as possible. The Tribunal begun phasing out its activities and handing them over gradually to local tribunals in the post-Yugoslav states but two issues hampered this process. First, in the absence of enforcement powers of its own, the ICTY had to engage in prolonged political struggles and negotiations to convince targeted states to fulfil their legal obligations (the most important of which entailed the handover of indicted war criminals). A clear domestic constituency in support of tribunal prosecutions in post-Yugoslav states was often missing, and thus even sympathetic politicians assessed carefully the repercussions of their decisions, in particular the possibility that cooperation with the ICTY could cost them domestic support. For this reason, even with the end of authoritarian government in both Serbia and Croatia, cooperation with the ICTY could never be taken for granted, despite international actors' insistence that cooperation with the Hague Tribunal would be a precondition for advancing EU integration (Peskin 2008).

Croatian and Serbian cooperation greatly improved over the years with the arrest and handover of many indicted war criminals, but not all problems were solved. Most notably, Serbia's signature of a SAA with the EU remained on hold until Ratko Mladić was arrested in 2011. Second, the existing legal framework did not allow for the prosecution of indicted war criminals locally. In particular, since victims, perpetrators and witnesses were found in different countries, regional cooperation was indispensable but inadequate (Delević 2007: 74–75; Husejnović and Ahmetasević 2006).

Perhaps most importantly from a peacebuilding perspective, the reconciliatory effects of the ICTY have been limited (Fischer and Petrović-Ziemer 2013). The limits with the ICTY's work stimulated civil society's search for restorative forms of justice and truth-finding (Yakinthou 2018). The campaign for a Regional Commission for Truth-seeking and Truth-telling about War Crimes in the Former Yugoslavia (REKOM) aimed at establishing a set of undeniable facts about war events, as well as giving a voice to the victims. In addition, it attempted to avoid the simplistic ethnic narratives dominant in every country of 'us' victim and 'them' aggressor. Especially worthy of note was the Women's Court for the Former Yugoslavia, a bottom-up, truth-telling initiative organized by a coalition of civil society activists and women's organizations to achieve justice for women affected by armed conflict (O'Reilly 2016). The Court aimed at making violence committed against women visible, understanding the social, economic, cultural, political and family context where violence takes place, giving women the opportunity to voice their grievances, including them in the public memory and supporting the creation of civil society networks of international solidarity (Duhacek 2015).

Furthermore, in addition to the problems raised by transitional justice, another important problem caused by the wars of the 1990s was not yet solved by the early 2000s, with about one million refugees and displaced persons still in the region. With the January 2005 'Sarajevo Declaration' Bosnia-Herzegovina, Croatia, Serbia and Montenegro agreed to resolve the issue by the end of 2007, but this deadline was not met.

In the late 2000s war crimes prosecution and refugee return consti-tuted difficult political problems not amenable to easy and fast solutions. While important, these problems were overshadowed by Kosovo's dec-laration of independence in February 2008 (Ker-Lindsay 2009). From a doctrinal point of view, Kosovo's independence embodied a complex process of evolution of the doctrine of self-determination, a process which can only be summarily mentioned here. With the establishment of the modern state system in the seventeenth century, and more recently with the principles enshrined in the UN Charter, the doctrine of self-determination was skewed in favour of the maintenance of terri-torial integrity. According to the UN Charter, 'peoples' do have a right to self-determination, but only as independence from colonial control, from military occupation, and from regimes that practise apartheid (such as Rhodesia and South Africa during the Cold War). In all other cases, national governments may grant various degrees of autonomy to eth-nic groups concentrated in parts of the state territory, but they have no international legal obligation to do so.

For a variety of complex reasons, since the end of the Cold War the self-determination principle began to change. The practice of 'interim settlements' (Weller 2009: 269, 276) contributed considerably to this change. Such settlements typically involved a period of self-governance within established political boundaries. At the same time, these set-tlements included the possibility that a referendum on independence was carried out. The examples of Bougainville, Southern Sudan and Northern Ireland all testified to the growing influence of this trend. As of the former Yugoslav states, the case of Serbia and Montenegro was most relevant. These two states subscribed to an interim settlement in 2002 through the creation of a Federation. In 2006 Montenegro voted on a referendum and reached independence from Serbia, which in turn acknowledged and recognized the newly created state. The practice of interim settlements undermined the presupposition that a change in boundaries was objectionable, and made the independence of Kosovo more acceptable internationally.

By mid-2009 Kosovo was recognized by some 60 countries and was able to join the IMF and the World Bank. Serbia, together with its ally Russia, denounced Kosovo's independence as an unlawful act but inter-national legal doctrine seemed to be moving in a new direction. In October 2008 the UN General Assembly, prompted by a request from Serbia, voted to ask the International Court of Justice an opinion on the legality of Kosovo's independence. In its advisory opinion delivered on 22 July 2010, the Court declared that 'the adoption of the declaration of independence of the 17 February 2008 did not violate general international law'. Thus, the Court affirmed a right to independence and prompted a debate on whether or not the case of Kosovo set a precedent that could apply to other separatist regions as well. In an apparent contradiction, while Serbia refused to recognize the independence of Kosovo, it also operated to favour the de facto partition of the north of Kosovo, an area with a Serb majority and bordering Serbia itself (Capussela 2015: 68–74, 80–82).

After the Declaration of Independence international supervision continued but the peacebuilding presence was split into two different missions, the European Union Rule of Law Mission in Kosovo (EULEX) and the International Civilian Office (ICO), led by the International Civilian Representative (ICR). EULEX was tasked with monitoring, mentoring and advising Kosovo's rule-of-law authorities and to exercise certain judicial and police powers. In practice, EULEX exercised unprecedented executive functions, including enforcing the law on Kosovo's citizens (Capussela 2015: 107).

Despite these powers, EULEX has been mostly unwilling to confront corrupt members of the Kosovo Albanian political elite for fear of triggering violent protests (Visoka 2017: 52). Distrusted by the population, EULEX was politically vulnerable and in need of a degree of political support by Kosovo's authorities (Radin 2014). Accordingly, it preferred to remain focused on the less controversial task of advising the police or the customs service, leaving serious crime, including corruption, 'virtually untouched' (Capussela 2015: 143).

Unsurprisingly, the EU Commission stressed that corruption remained prevalent in many areas in Kosovo, thereby continuing to be 'a very serious concern' (European Commission 2009). Accordingly, tackling corruption and organized crime was considered as an indispensable step in order to improve the rule of law. Following heavy international pressure Kosovo police and prosecution were reorganized through the establishment of a new anti-corruption task force (which included EULEX officials), and a new Directorate against Economic Crime and Corruption. In 2012 Kosovo's President set up a National Anti-Corruption Council, which aimed at policy coordination. Most importantly, Kosovo adopted a package of laws (on declaration of assets, conflicts of interest, whistle-blowers, public procurement and the financing of political parties) that the EU considered strong enough to bring tangible results. However, similar to the Bosnian case, Brussels noted limits in implementation, due essentially to lack of inter-institutional cooperation and of commitment by senior leadership in public institutions (European Commission 2012).

Despite Kosovo's persisting governance problems, its independence triggered debates about the right to self-determination, in particular whether or not the Serb RS could also claim a right to self-determination, secede from Bosnia-Herzegovina and establish a new state (Bieber 2011b). Since Montenegro's declaration of independence in 2006, and even more forcefully since the Kosovo declaration of independence in 2008, the RS leadership had been calling for a referendum to determine its own independence (Toal 2013). Serbs engaged in what Philippe Leroux-Martin (2014: 146–147) described as a 'non-violent insurgency', that is, 'non-violent actions that seek, in violation of a peace process, to undermine or overthrow the existence of authorities that are essential for preventing a slide back into a state of generalized violence'.

Although the referendum was not held, it appeared that the Serb entity had been positioning itself to secede from Bosnia-Herzegovina if the opportunity arose. By contrast, the Bosniak leadership favoured the strengthening of the central institutions in Sarajevo and provocatively called for the abolition of the Serb entity. In judging between these competing claims, some international analysts and diplomats supported the creation of more new states, and thus they implicitly sided with the RS. William Montgomery, former US ambassador to Bulgaria, Croatia and Serbia/Montenegro advocated what he considered an 'achievable policy', that is, the partitioning of Bosnia-Herzegovina and Kosovo along ethnic lines. The international community should have recognized that multi-ethnic coexistence was wishful thinking, granted independence combined with pledges for full rights for the remaining minorities, and been ready to use military force to prevent violence during the process of dissolution (Montgomery 2009). Indeed, in the case of further border changes the resumption of armed violence would have been very likely, since the Bosniak leadership vehemently opposed this solution (Chivvis 2010: 98).

As the Pandora's box of border (re)arrangement seemed to open again by the end of the decade, both Bosniak and Serb politicians accused each other of re-arming, while denying their side was doing so. Foreign intelligence personnel in Sarajevo warned that hunting clubs, veterans' organizations and private security companies appeared to be arming with machine guns, automatic weapons and grenade launchers (Latal 2009). If armed conflict flared up again, the international capacity to stop it would have been insufficient, given the military presence in the country. The European Force (EUFOR), a weak EU-led mission that replaced the NATO-led Stabilization Force, maintained fewer than 2000 soldiers. Accordingly, the EU and NATO devised preliminary plans to deal with any possible outbreak of hostilities (Mulchinock 2017: 172).

Not only militarily, but also politically the international community was unable to respond effectively to this deteriorating situation. The OHR lost much of its power to impose a solution on the parties when they failed to reach one on their own. For much of the post-Dayton period, the OHR enjoyed the so-called Bonn Powers whereby the High Representative could impose legislation on the Bosnian Parliament and even sack local officials when he deemed it necessary to keep the peace process on track. However, starting from mid/late 2008, these powers became increasingly unusable. The High Representative attempted to impose a series of solutions, particularly a much-contested police reform, but was not effectively supported by top western countries (Leroux-Martin 2014). As a result, the High Representative had to retreat from his requests, effectively recognizing that his powers had been eroded to the point that their use became a political gamble. As the High Representative stated in 2009, the international presence in Bosnia-Herzegovina was a 'dead horse'.

In retrospect, although it is undeniable that Bosnia-Herzegovina was dangerously weak and that a clear international policy was much needed, the warnings about the possibility of a new outbreak of violence as a result of the RS moves towards independence were overstated. The RS is made up by two non-contiguous territories divided by the town of Brčko. In March 2009 the RS Parliament recognized Brčko as an independent district not under Serb control, thus implicitly renouncing to a sovereign claim over the town. The western part of the RS does not even border with Serbia proper, complicating any prospects of reunification with the 'homeland'. Serbia itself showed little appetite for changes to the territorial status quo, particularly since its bid to join the EU gained grounds internationally (that is, after the arrest of indicted war criminal Karadzić in 2008 and of Mladić in 2011).

Furthermore, from a normative point of view a few important issues militated against the possibility of independence for the RS. First, while

Kosovo had a long historical existence, which was also acknowledged by the Yugoslav constitution, the RS came into existence only in the 1990s as a result of ethnic cleansing. Thus, its claim to independence was tainted by this factor. The other critical difference between Kosovo and the RS was that the former could be considered as a legitimate case of 'remedial self-determination' (Weller 2009: 239, 272), while the latter could not. In the Kosovo case Serbia's claims over the province were undermined by its mistreatment and repression of the Albanian population. It was precisely this mistreatment and repression that, according to many analysts, gave rise to a right of secession. In the case of the RS it would have been difficult to put forward a similar argument. Rather than being subjected to repression, the RS itself mistreated the non-Serb population that lived on its territory before the war. Furthermore, not only were RS authorities implicated in the wartime policy of ethnic cleansing, but also they did not fulfil their obligations to create the conditions for the return of refugees and displaced persons after the end of the Bosnian war.

To counter the secession threat, peacebuilders engaged in a 'diplomatic counterinsurgency', that is, they waged a non-violent operation against Dodik by approving an investigation by senior US prosecutor at the State Court Corruption Chamber against Dodik and his party/business network (Kostic 2017: 127). Only after Dodik committed to a 'Structured Dialogue' on Bosnia-Herzegovina's justice sector, and agreed not to call a referendum in RS, international peacebuilders agreed to remove all international judges and prosecutors from the State Court by the end of 2012, and the EU Police Mission in the country apparently stopped building its corruption case.[6] With the Structured Dialogue the EU engaged in a water down process, and effectively backed down from its own conditions. Ultimately, the EU's softer stance did not stop the RS challenge to the Bosnian state. Indeed, in November 2015 the Constitutional Court abolished celebrating the date of RS's foundation, January 9, as the annual Republic Day holiday because this date discriminates against non-Serb citizens. In response, in complete disregard to the state's highest court, the RS held a referendum in September 2016 asking voters if they wanted to preserve the state holiday. This move has been widely interpreted as a step towards future referenda which may include questions of secession (Rose 2016).

6.5   The European Union in Search of a Policy

Since the EU promised states in the Western Balkans a prospect of membership, it put forward an impressive array of initiatives to steer Western Balkan states towards reform in the economic, security and political sphere. However, the Union has not always been able to exert a positive influence on those problems and issues, discussed above, which affected the area throughout the 2000s and beyond. Although the EU's support contributed to stabilize the situation, and to meet some of the challenges and promises discussed in Chapter 5, it also showed room for greater clarity of purpose.

In the economic sphere generous European aid, as well as free access to the EU market, sustained the restructuring of the economy and the rebuilding of the infrastructure. EU policy, however, discriminated between new EU members and non-members, and even between EU candidate states and aspiring candidate ones. To begin with, European structural funds were allocated more generously to recent UE members, such as Bulgaria and Romania, rather than aspiring new ones. During the 2007–2013 period Bulgaria and Romania received per capita roughly three times what they received in their last pre-accession period (that is, before 1 January 2007), while the Western Balkans obtained only a modest increase. The proportion of per capita aid per annum between Romania and Bulgaria and the Western Balkans was over 4:1 (Emerson 2008: 6). As a result, the gap between new member states and the Western Balkans widened.

In addition, the funding criteria increased the economic and social gap between early candidates for EU admission (such as Croatia and FYROM) and underdeveloped regions (such as Bosnia-Herzegovina and Kosovo). The Instrument of Pre-Accession (IPA)—the European funding mechanism for the region which came into effect on 1 January 2007—was open to all Western Balkan countries, but differentiated between candidate countries (Croatia and FYROM) and potential candidate countries (Albania, Bosnia-Herzegovina, Kosovo, Montenegro and Serbia) until they were upgraded to candidate status (European Commission, no date). This variation reflected a different scope in assistance, since candidates had the most demanding task of adopting and implementing the *acquis communautaire* while potential candidates should have only reached an 'alignment' with the *acquis*.

In practice, the former benefited from much more substantial assistance than the latter. For example, for the 2006–2009 period Croatia was granted €575.7 million and Bosnia-Herzegovina €277 million (EU/World Bank Joint Office for South East Europe, 2007). More generally, for the period 2007–2010 candidate states received more than 3 billion Euros, while potential candidate states received 1.7 billion Euros (DG Enlargement, no date). This allocation diminished the EU's political influence over potential candidate states, and left them with fewer resources to face the economic downturn resulting from the outbreak of the global economic and financial crisis in 2007–2008. The paradox of the EU assistance programme was that the most advanced countries got the lion's share of EU assistance, leaving laggards like Bosnia-Herzegovina further behind. Lines of division between 'candidates' and 'potential candidates' were thus reinforced.

As for security issues, coordination between the EU and NATO improved dramatically throughout the 2000s (Simón 2013). Security in Bosnia-Herzegovina was guaranteed by a declining number of EU peacekeepers, reduced in September 2012 to 900 soldiers from 19 nations—too small of a number to contain hostilities if they had broken out. The EU remained militarily dependant on NATO, which, in turn, relied heavily on American assets. Following the events of 11 September 2001, these assets were used primarily in the 'war on terror'. While the EU frequently showed lack of purpose and limited ability to act decisively and cohesively, the United States took the lead in searching for a durable solution to difficult political/security problems, and thus, similarly to the 1990s period, the United States continued to be the most consequential security actor in the region. In the absence of a coherent European policy, American leadership remained indispensable. Most notably, Albanian authorities in Kosovo relied on American, not European, support in order to push for a solution to the question of the final status of this former Serbian province (Ker-Lindsay 2009).

Above all, despite its promise to aspiring new EU member states that the doors to the European club were open, the EU struggled to project a clear vision of the process that should accompany the Western Balkans towards membership. As discussed in Chapter 5, one of the key promises of the European integration process lied in its potential for minimizing differences likely to be exploited by domestic actors. However, despite the considerable progress achieved by the CFSP, EU member states struggled to maintain a semblance of unity. One key issue involved the question of further enlargement and the doubts this matter raised about the EU's so-called absorption capacity, which was defined in the Copenhagen criteria as the 'Union's capacity to absorb new members, while maintaining the momentum of European integration' (European Council 1993: 14).

Beyond this broad strategic problem, EU member states were divided on specific policy issues. The conundrum of Kosovo's final status mercilessly displayed European divisions. The EU supported Kosovo's independence but a number of EU members led by Greece and Cyprus—in addition to Russia—objected to this solution. As a result of these divisions, the debate among the EU's member states about the opportunity of recognizing or not the independence of Kosovo was limited to a dull and lengthy paperwork over whether to 'acknowledge' Kosovo's will to independence or just 'take note' of it. Five EU members did not recognize the birth of the new state, and thus the EU was left unable to formulate a coherent position.[7] A position of 'status neutrality' agnostic about whether Kosovo should be regarded as an independent state, a province of Serbia or a UN protectorate, emerged as the only position that could allow Kosovo to cooperate with international organizations after the declaration of independence (Capussela 2015: 67).

Likewise, in Bosnia-Herzegovina the EU did not provide adequate leadership, hiding behind the mantra of 'domestic ownership' of the much-needed process of constitutional reform (Belloni 2008: 160–172; Sebastian Aparicio 2014). An alternative approach would have clearly laid down the boundaries of such a reform (such as acknowledging that the existence of the RS was not subject to discussion), while leaving to the Bosnian authorities the responsibility of working out the details of a new constitutional charter. This indecisive style reflected one of the many instances when the EU proved unable to project a credible image, reinforcing the feeling among international observers, citizens and leaders in the region that the EU lacked a real strategy to address the region's problems.

The issue of conditionality, the most powerful tool available to the EU to demand the implementation of reform policies, further highlighted the difficulty in devising a shared approach. Conflict between EU member states over accession have weakened the EU's leverage and reduced the credibility of conditionality (Bieber 2011a). Conformity and compliance have been frequently 'faked', with actors succeeding in enjoying the benefits of apparent compliance but still managing to produce superficial obedience while circumventing power structures (Noutcheva 2012: Chapter 6). Local elites' compliance game has been facilitated by the difficulties in setting and maintaining clear conditions. For example, part of the EU's conditionality towards the region involved the requirement of 'full cooperation' with the ICTY. In practice, this request meant that the Tribunal and its chief prosecutor Carla Del Ponte became the main gatekeepers in the process of European integration. In particular, in her assessment of the degree of cooperation of Croatia and Serbia with European demands, Del Ponte frequently oscillated between intransigent and more flexible positions. Del Ponte's wavering and the blurring between legal and political roles raised many eyebrows among the members of the EU General Affairs and External Relations Council, led to the embarrassment of political institutions, and occasionally stirred acrimonious debate among EU member states.[8] In particular, with regard to Serbia, Austria, Slovenia and Italy supported Belgrade's quick upgrade to candidate status (which was granted only in 2012) as an 'indirect' reward for the loss of Kosovo, while the United Kingdom and the Netherlands advocated stronger terms of conditionality. The lack of clarity about the respective responsibilities of the EU and of the Tribunal in ascertaining compliance created an impression of indecisiveness. The problem with diverging assessments of compliance between the Tribunal and EU member states was mooted by events when the final fugitive was arrested on July 20, 2011 but the impression of hesitation remained among all domestic actors in the region. More generally, EU foreign policy institutions, the ICTY, the Stability Pact and the SAP were all criticized for focusing obsessively on the political leadership, and for contributing to a polarization between an Europeanized elite and non-Europeanized and alienated citizens (Grabbe 2006).

Not only did international/EU institutions fail to provide a semblance of unity, but also they did not reverse the top-down style which characterized the previous international approach, and which was explicitly rejected by European officials when the EU declared its own open-door policy. Despite the EU's emphasis on partnership, the process of European integration showed some of the limits of earlier approaches. Because the integration process was structured around the idea of the increasing involvement of the EU in the Balkans with the intent of including this region into European institutions and socializing it by means of European norms, it reflected the same approach to regional development grounded on external initiative that characterized international intervention since the beginning of the peacebuilding transition from the mid-1990s onwards. This approach made Bosnia-Herzegovina, FYROM, Kosovo and the other countries of the Western Balkans the objects of international attention, that is, the recipients of strategies developed elsewhere with little or no domestic input.

Overall, by the turn of the decade all Western Balkan states had developed various links with the EU, progressed in their contractual relation with it—above all by signing SAAs—and, in the process, settled some of their outstanding disputes. The 2009 border demarcation agreement between FYROM and Kosovo and, above all, the 2013 Serbia-Kosovo agreement which granted extensive local autonomy to Serbian municipalities in Northern Kosovo while formally integrating these municipalities into the Kosovar state, would have been impossible without a significant EU involvement (Visoka 2017: Chapter 6; Capussela 2015: 74–78).[9] EU officials defined the 'historic agreement of Serbia and Kosovo' as 'proof of the transformative power of the European Union perspective' (Füle 2013).

This agreement was reached after the EU's use of strong leverage on both sides. The EU engaged in heavy-duty mediation which included the setting of the agenda and the elaboration of solutions, while relying on carrots and sticks. The EU's particular mediation style combined technical and political negotiations aimed at deconstructing political questions into manageable piecemeal agreements which could pave the way for a wider solution (Visoka and Doyle 2016). The agreement, entitled 'First Agreement of Principles Governing the Normalization of Relations' is a 15-point document that, among other issues, recognizes the inclusion of Northern Kosovo within Pristina's legal framework while increasing the autonomy of the four Serb-dominated municipalities in the north; it foresees the dismemberment of the Serbian security structures and their absorption into Kosovo's equivalent structures and the creation of the Association/Community of Serb majority municipalities with governing authorities in economic development, health, education, urban and rural planning; and it commits both Kosovo and Serbia not to block each other on their EU integration path. As a result of the agreement, Kosovo is allowed to participate in various regional organizations and meetings provided that the word 'Kosovo' is accompanied by an asterisk and the footnote: 'This designation is without prejudice to status, and is in line with UNSC 1244 Resolution and the ICJ Opinion on the

Kosovo Declaration of Independence'. This formulation testified to the EU approach to the Kosovo problem which has been underpinned by constructive ambiguity or, in the words of Krasniqi and Musaj (2015: 152), by 'creative obscurity'.

The ambiguity of the agreement reflects a common element of liberal peacebuilding which enables the continuation of transitional processes even in cases of apparently irreconcilable interests and views (Pospisil 2019). This ambiguity allowed both sides to interpret it in utterly different ways. While Belgrade understood the agreement as a means to continue its control within Kosovo, Pristina interpreted it as Serbia's de facto acceptance of Kosovo's sovereignty. These different understandings allowed all parties, including the EU as the mediator, to declare it as a 'historic success' (Subotić 2017: 179). Even though implementation of the agreement has proved challenging (Beha 2015), both Serbia and Kosovo were rewarded with an advancement in their EU integration process: Serbia was at last declared an official EU candidate state, and Kosovo received a positive assessment for the start of formal talks on a SAA. In the process, Serbia apparently changed its political focus from the non-recognition of the new Kosovo state to solidifying its control of the Serbian population in Kosovo's northern provinces.

6.6   Turning Enlargement into a Mirage?

Although still able to remain an important actor as in Kosovo, the EU since the outbreak of the global financial and economic crisis in 2007–2008 has progressively downgraded enlargement among the list of its foreign policy priorities and thus weakened its leverage and local appeal. As Dimitar Bechev (2012: 1) argued, the Euro crisis did not kill the EU enlargement policy, but it relegated the Western Balkans to 'the outermost circle in a multi-speed Europe—the periphery of the periphery'[10]—while strengthening a 'wait-and-see' attitude towards the region (Grabbe et al. 2010). While Germany remained a staunch supporter of EU enlargement, conditional upon the fulfilment by aspiring EU members of strict criteria, many EU member states believed that they should have focused their energies on sorting out their own internal economic and financial mess before seriously considering how (and whether) to proceed with accepting new members. This diffuse indifference combined with European citizens' scepticism in turning enlargement into anything but a priority (Balfour and Stratulat 2015). Since 2007, when the economic and financial crisis broke out, support for EU enlargement quickly decreased: in Cyprus, the Czech Republic, Italy, Spain, Slovakia and Slovenia, opposition to enlargement increased by more than 20% in 5 years. Overall, in 2011 popular opposition to enlargement was 49% throughout the 28 EU member states. Some differences existed with regard to this hostility vis-à-vis new aspiring members, with most opposition being expressed towards Albania and Kosovo (Eurobarometer 2011).

Not only did EU member states and their citizens show limited enthusiasm about accepting new member states from the Western Balkans, but also the European Commission lowered its level of activism in favour of and commitment to enlargement—at least compared to the important, supportive and instrumental role it previously played in the process of accession of CEE states. The EU commitment to the region has been more ambiguous than it is often asserted in academic analysis, eschewing both explicit indications of accession and even references to membership timetables. Indeed, as David Phinnemore (2013: 29) has argued, the European Council has promoted the region's 'European perspective', but has not spoken of 'either destiny or that the Western Balkan countries "shall" become members', raising questions about the idea of a supposed inevitability of accession to the Union or, as Phinnemore (2013: 34) put it, 'about when—indeed if—all the Western Balkan countries will actually achieve their goal of EU membership'.

This lack of a clear commitment reflected both member states' preferences and the need to strengthen EU structures after the Union quickly grew to 28 members (or 27 after the UK exit). As explained in Chapter 5, since 2006 the Commission has linked future EU expansion to no less than the comprehensive reform of the EU's institutions, policies and budget (European Commission 2006)—a view that did not change significantly among policy-makers in Brussels even after the coming into force of the Lisbon Treaty on 1 December 2009. Not only was the Union's integration capacity greatly tested by several rounds of enlargement, leading to a sort of 'Balkanisation of the EU' rather than a 'Europeanisation of the Balkans', but also difficulties experienced with some of the latest arrivals to the EU club—such as Bulgaria and Romania, who joined the Union in 2007—contributed to raising the bar for later candidates (O'Brennan 2014). As a result, while the EU made accession conditional on the fulfilment of criteria first outlined at the 1993 Copenhagen Council, it drew lessons from past enlargement mistakes and turned these criteria into an obstacle for aspiring new members, rather than a guide to carry out domestic reforms needed to obtain membership.

Since their initial formulation in 1993, the Copenhagen criteria expanded considerably. While becoming more detailed, they were paradoxically subjected to increasing differences in interpretation, thus failing to be a reliable tool by which to measure candidate countries' progress (Kochenov 2004). In addition, because of the disappointing situation of both Bulgaria and Romania—both plagued by serious governance problems—since the late 2000s the negotiation with candidate states started with the chapters on judiciary, justice and home affairs, which were generally the most difficult topics to address. Most importantly, besides the Copenhagen criteria member states within the European Council have put forward different conditions for each candidate country, inevitably raising questions about the fairness and credibility of the accession process and prompting aspiring new members to complain about double standards and moving targets being applied to them (ESI 2014: 5).

The difficulty to comply with European demands augmented on the ground, where European institutions were frequently unable to project a coherent vision and strategy. In Kosovo, for example, the intervention machinery was divided between the ICR, which was charged with supervising and supporting Kosovo's institutions while EU activities were scattered across six different institutions, with significant problems of coherence and coordination (Papadimitriou and Petrov 2013: 123). In Bosnia-Herzegovina, a turf war among EU member states (above all between Germany and the UK) weakened the effectiveness of European actors who, faced by domestic resistance to change, eventually refrained from applying conditionality and even abandoned or ignored previously stated reform priorities, criteria and conditions (Bassuener and Weber 2013). In Montenegro, local NGOs discredited EU staff by criticizing accession reports for being too soft with the Montenegro government. Likewise, in FYROM EU bureaucrats were reproached for ultimately focusing more on self-adulation with regard to their contribution to the development of a success story in the Western Balkans, rather than providing a genuine assessment of the situation in the country (ESI 2014: 15–17).[11]

In this context of uncertain and wavering commitment by both EU institutions and member states, compounded by significant implementation problems, '[t]he UK's departure from the EU may be the last nail in the coffin for accession' (Bieber 2016: 2). As a result of the so-called Brexit the EU's ability to exert a positive influence on the region has further decreased. First, the UK's departure from the EU means the loss of one of the few remaining advocates of enlargement. Second, the process of separation between the UK and the EU will absorb the political and bureaucratic energies of officials in Brussels for the foreseeable future. Third, the EU's existential crisis is likely to strengthen the perspectives of those in the Western Balkans who question the wisdom of implementing painful reforms in order to accede to an institution whose survival in the current form is increasingly called into question by its own current members (Bieber 2016; Ker-Lindsay 2017). In light of this situation, it is unsurprising that some leaders in the region have reacted to Brexit by challenging the EU's celebrated transformative power (Kostovicova 2016).

While the EU is torn by a profound crisis, the stubborn persistence of bilateral issues among states in the region contributes to complicate the integration process further. These disputes have deep roots, frequently predating even the break-up of Yugoslavia, and including a number of problematic issues such as border demarcation, property rights, the recognition of minority rights, the rights of refugees and displaced persons, and hard-to-reconcile interpretations of history (Fouéré 2014). Since FYROM declared independence in 1991, Greece has opposed the new state's name, claiming that it infers a claim on the eponymous Greek province and it monopolizes the Macedonian identity. In addition, the 'normalization' process between Serbia and Kosovo has contributed to improving or even resolving some outstanding issues affecting citizens' everyday lives across the border, such as property matters, freedom of movement, and cross-border trade and communication. However, many issues are not being implemented and, in the absence of a consensual peace settlement, continuing improvement cannot be taken for granted. In particular, '[t]here is no agreement on Kosovo's recognition, a genuine process of inter-societal reconciliation is constantly undermined by nationalist forces, and the shallow incentives for European integration and external geopolitical interferences could wash away the progress made so far' (Visoka 2017: 214).

In sum, the economic and financial crisis beginning in 2008 has severely weakened the EU enlargement enthusiasm. While it is undeniable that enlargement policy has not been discarded per se, it is also excessive to argue that, as a result of the geopolitical benefits enlargement brings to EU member states, 'the underlying dynamics of enlargement remain largely the same' (Vachudova 2014). Rather, with various degrees of regional stability in place, and with strategic attention focused on areas like the Middle East, North Africa, and those states lying between the EU and Russia, the geopolitical benefits of enlargement are both decreasing and changing. Rather than being primarily concerned with stability and democratic consolidation—issues that have driven Europe's approach to the region since the early 2000s—it is Russia's offensive in Ukraine in 2014 which has revived some European interest towards the Western Balkans (BiEPAG 2015), as further discussed in the next chapter. Serbia's increasingly strong political and economic ties with Russia, as well as with China (von Homeyer 2015), represent an alarm bell for European policy-makers about the dangers that a stalemate in the accession process might bring about.

6.7   Conclusions

From the early 2000s onwards, the EU pioneered a 'permanent transition strategy', which did not foresee a clear temporal end point in the process that should lead the Western Balkans to join the Union. Rather, politicians and citizens in the region were expected to believe in the truth of the EU promise, much the same way Catholics are expected to believe in the dogma of the Church, and regardless of the EU's actions. However, as with the more famous Leninist concept of 'permanent revolution', so 'permanent transition' presented considerable flaws.

To begin with, there was a temporal problem: politicians were expected to adopt politically risky reforms that were likely to undermine their domestic support, while the rewards of such reforms would be reaped at least several years on, if ever. This timetable was incompatible with domestic electoral deadlines. Unsurprisingly, the attitude of politicians in the Western Balkans has often been summed up by the sentence 'you pretend to be serious about integrating us in the EU and we pretend to reform'. In addition, the 'permanent transition' strategy was tainted by its lack of a clear offer of guidelines and incentives to local reformist forces. Since the EU enlargement process stalled as a result of the Union's enlargement fatigue, in particular with the outbreak of the economic and financial crisis in 2007–2008, this process could not be influenced by aspiring member states, regardless of their reformist efforts, but depended upon political developments within the EU itself. Third, although the EU attempted to reach and involve citizens, its enlargement process has been squarely focused on local elites, whose commitment to change could never be taken for granted. Overall, by the early 2010s peacebuilding progress in the Western Balkans stalled. Even international officials recognized that 'the enlargement strategy does not work, but the EU does not have alternative means to pressure domestic political leaders'.[12] This situation has been perfectly clear to the domestic political class in the region at least since the early 2010s, when the awareness of the structural problems involving the enlargement process became increasingly evident. The next chapter discusses the growing Euroscepticism within Western Balkan states which emerged as a result of the disappointment with the Union's approach towards the region.

NOTES

1. Interview with Chloé Berger, Head of Operation Section for Justice and Home Affairs and Public Administration Reform, Delegation of the European Union to Bosnia-Herzegovina and Herzegovina, Sarajevo, July, 2016.
2. Interview with Srdjan Blagovcanin, Executive Director of Transparency International Bosnia-Herzegovina Herzegovina, July 2015; see also Blagovcanin and Divjak (2015: 7–8).
3. As confirmed, for example, by Jasna Kilalić, USAID, Deputy Democracy Office Director, interview, July 2016.
4. Interview with Azhar Kalamujić, journalist, Center for Investigative Reporting, Sarajevo, July 2015.
5. On November 22, 2017, the ICTY found him guilty of genocide, war crimes and crimes against humanity and sent him to prison for life.
6. Confidential interview with an Italian police official, Sarajevo, June 2011.
7. For an up-to-date analysis of EU member states' position towards Kosovo, see Ker-Lindsay and Armakolas (2017).
8. For her part, Del Ponte often complained that western powers displayed 'grave systemic deficiencies' in their pursuit of war crimes indictees (Del Ponte 2009).
9. While the EU pushed hard for a solution along these lines, it was not the only one. Acting outside the EU foreign policy structures, important EU member states such as Germany played an important role (Hamilton 2014).
10. Along similar lines, Bartlett and Prica (2013) define the region as the 'European Super-periphery'.
11. The shortfalls of the Commission's reports have been discussed in 'Experts react: EU Enlargement and EU progress reports 2016'. LSEE European Politics and policy blog. http://bit.ly/2hyqb12.

12. Interview with Renzo Daviddi, Deputy Head of the EU Delegation to Bosnia-Herzegovina-Herzegovina, Sarajevo, July 2013.

References

Balfour, R., & Stratulat, C. (Eds.). (2015). *EU member states and enlargement towards the Balkans*. Brussels: European Policy Centre.

Bartlett, W. (2008). *Europe's troubled region*. Abingdon: Routledge.

Bartlett, W. (2015). The political economy of accession: Forming economically viable member states. In S. Keil & Z. Arkan (Eds.), *The EU and member state building: European foreign policy in the Western Balkans* (pp. 209–232). London and New York: Routledge.

Bartlett, W., & Prica, I. (2013). The deepening crisis in the European super-periphery. *Journal of Balkan and Near Eastern Studies, 15*(4), 367–382.

Barlett, W., & Uvalić, M. (Eds.). (2013). *Social consequences of the global economic crisis in South East Europe*. London: London School of Economics and Political Science.

Bassuener, K., & Weber, B. (2013). *House of cards: The EU's 'reinforced presence' in Bosnia and Herzegovina*. Sarajevo/Berlin: Democratization Policy Council.

Bechev, D. (2012). *The periphery of the periphery: The Western Balkans and the Euro crisis*. Bruxelles: European Council on Foreign Relations.

Beha, A. (2015). Disputes over the 15-point agreement on normalization of relations between Kosovo and Serbia. *Nationalities Papers, 43*(1), 102–121.

Belloni, R. (2008). *State building and international intervention in Bosnia-Herzegovina*. London and New York: Routledge.

Bieber, F. (2011a). The Western Balkans after the ICJ opinion. In J. Rupnik (Ed.), *The Western Balkans and the EU: 'The hour of Europe'*. Paris: Institute for Security Studies.

Bieber, F. (2011b). Building impossible states? State-building strategies and EU membership in the Western Balkans. *Europe-Asia Studies, 63*(10), 1783–1802.

Bieber, F. (2016, June). Ever farther union: Balkans and the Brexit (Resource document). *Nations in Transit Brief*. www.freedomhouse.org. Accessed 2 November 2016.

BiEPAG (Balkans in Europe Policy Advisory Group). (2015). *Western Balkans and the EU: Beyond the autopilot mode*. Graz.

Blagovcanin, S., & Divjak, B. (2015). *How Bosnia's political economy holds it back and what to do about it?* Washington: John Hopkins University-Center for Transatlantic Studies.

Capussela, A. L. (2015). *State-building in Kosovo: Democracy, corruption and the EU in the Balkans*. London and New York: I.B. Tauris.

Chivvis, C. S. (2010). The Dayton dilemma. *Survival, 52*(5), 47–74.

Cohen, L. J., & Lampe, J. R. (2011). *Embracing democracy in the Western Balkans: From post-conflict struggles to European integration.* Washington, DC: Woodrow Wilson Centre Press; Baltimore: The Johns Hopkins University Press.

Cooley, L. (2019). *The European Union's approach to conflict resolution: Transformation or regulation in the Western Balkans?* London and New York: Routledge.

Del Ponte, C. (2009). *La caccia. Io e i criminali di guerra.* Milano: Feltrinelli.

Delević, M. (2007, July). *Regional cooperation in the Western Balkans* (Chaillot Paper no. 104). Paris: Institute for Security Studies.

DG Enlargement. (no date). *The instrument for pre-accession assistance: An overview.* Brussels: Financial Instruments Directorate.

Duhacek, D. G. (2015). The women's court: A feminist approach to in/justice. *European Journal of Women's Studies, 22*(2), 159–176.

Elbasani, A. (2008). EU enlargement in the Western Balkans: Strategies of borrowing and inventing. *Journal of Southern Europe and the Balkans, 10*(3), 293–307.

Emerson, M. (2008, October). *Recalibrating EU policy towards the Western Balkans* (Policy Brief No. 175). Brussels: Center for European Policy Studies.

Erceg, T. (2008, July 8). *Less than a third of Croats favour EU.* Balkan Insight.

ESI (European Stability Initiative). (2008). *The white list project: EU policies on visa-free travel for the Western Balkans.* Berlin, Brussels, and Istanbul: ESI.

ESI (European Stability Initiative). (2014). *Vladimir and Estragon in Skopje.* Berlin, Istanbul, and Sarajevo: ESI.

Eurobarometer. (2011). *Public opinion in the European Union.* August, no. 75.

European Commission. (no date). *Instrument for pre-accession assistance (IPA).* https://ec.europa.eu/regional_policy/en/funding/ipa/. Accessed 9 June 2013.

European Commission. (2006, November 8). *Enlargement strategy and main challenges 2006–2007.* COM (2006) 649, Brussels.

European Commission. (2009, October 14). *Kosovo under UNSCR 1244/99 2009 progress report* (Commission staff working document). COM (2009) 533.

European Commission. (2012, October 10). *Commission communication on a feasibility study for a SAP between the EU and Kosovo* (Commission staff working document). COM (2012) 602.

European Council. (1993, June 21–22). *Presidency conclusions, Copenhagen.* http://ue.eu.int/ueDocs/cms_Data/docs/pressData/en/ec/72921.pdf. Accessed 5 June 2009.

Fischer, M., & Petrović-Ziemer, L. (Eds.). (2013). *Dealing with the past in the Western Balkans: Initiatives for peacebuilding and transitional justice in*

Bosnia-Herzegovina, Serbia and Croatia (Berghof Report 18). Berlin: Berghof Foundation.

Fouéré, E. (2014). *Bilateral disputes—A dark cloud over the Balkans*. Brussels: Centre for European Policy Studies.

Füle, S. (2013, October 16). *Enlargement package 2013*. Speech by EU commissioner Stefan Füle, European Parliament Committee on Foreign Affairs, SPEECH/13/816/. http://europa.eu/rapid/press-release_SPEECH-13-816_en.htm. Accessed 4 April 2015.

Gligorov, V. (2008, March 27). *Trade, investments and development in the Balkans*. Vienna: The Vienna Institute for International Economic Studies.

Gogova, I., & Radoslavova, B. (2001). Croatia on the road to EU membership. *Central Europe Review, 3*(14), 3–5.

Grabbe, H. (2006). *The EU's transformative power: Europeanization through conditionality in central and eastern Europe*. London: Macmillan.

Grabbe, H., Knaus, G., & Korski, D. (2010). *Beyond wait-and-see: The way forward for EU Balkan policy*. Bruxelles: European Council on Foreign Relations.

Hamilton, A. (2014). *Germany's foreign policy towards Kosovo. A policy perspective*. Pristina: Pristina Council on Foreign Relations.

Hänggi, H., & Tanner, F. (2005, July). *Promoting security sector governance in the EU's neighbourhood* (Chaillot Paper no. 80). Paris: EUISS.

Hills, A. (2004). *Border security in the Balkans: Europe's gatekeepers* (Adelphi Paper 371). Oxford and New York: Oxford University Press for International Institute for Strategic Studies.

Husejnović, M., & Ahmetasević, N. (2006, September 21). Regional justice: Bosnia-Herzegovina holds back from prosecution agreement. *BIRN*.

ICG (International Crisis Group). (2007, February 15). *Ensuring Bosnia-Herzegovina's future: A new international engagement strategy*. Sarajevo: ICG.

Kathuria, S. (2008). *Western Balkan integration and the EU: An agenda for trade and growth*. Washington, DC: The World Bank.

Ker-Lindsay, J. (2009). *Kosovo: The path to contested statehood in the Balkans*. London and New York: I.B. Tauris.

Ker-Lindsay, J. (2017). The United Kingdom and EU enlargement in the Western Balkans: From ardent champion of expansion to post-Brexit irrelevance. *Southeast European and Black Sea Studies, 17*(4), 555–569.

Ker-Lindsay, J., & Armakolas, I. (2017). *Lack of engagement? Surveying the spectrum of EU member state policies towards Kosovo*. Pristina: Kosovo Foundation for Open Society.

Kochenov, D. (2004). Behind the Copenhagen façade: The meaning and structure of the Copenhagen political criterion of democracy and the rule of law. *European Integration Online Papers, 8*(10), 1–24. http://www.eiop.or.at/eiop/pdf/2004-010.pdf.

Kostic, R. (2017). Shadow peacebuilders and Diplomatic counterinsurgencies: Informal networks, knowledge production and the art of policy-shaping. *Journal of Intervention and Statebuilding, 11*(1), 120–139.

Kostovicova, D. (2016). Reaction to Brexit around Europe: How the result affects the Balkans. *LSE Blogs.* www.blogs.lse.ac.uk. Accessed 15 December 2016.

Krasniqi, G., & Musaj, M. (2015). The EU's 'limited sovereignty-strong control' approach in the process of member state building in Kosovo. In S. Keil & Z. Arkan (Eds.), *The EU and member state building: European foreign policy in the Western Balkans* (pp. 140–162). London and New York: Routledge.

Latal, S. (2009, March 10). *Bosnians hope threat of new war will fade.* Balkan Insight.

Leroux-Martin, P. (2014). *Diplomatic counterinsugency: Lessons from Bosnia and Herzegovina.* Cambridge: Cambridge University Press.

Lobjakas, A. (2009, April 13). *The EU's invisible 'Schengen wall.'* Radio Free Europe/Radio Liberty.

Marusić, S. (2009, April 3). *FYROM trade in alarming fall.* Balkan Insight.

Matutinović, I. (2009, February 19). *Western Balkan transition countries faces their first recession.* Heinrich Böll Stiftung.

Montgomery, W. (2009, June 5). The Balkan mess redux. *The New York Times.*

Mulchinock, N. (2017). *NATO and the Western Balkans: From neutral spectator to proactive peacemaker.* Houndmills: Palgrave.

Noutcheva, G. (2012). *European foreign policy and the challenges of Balkan accession: Conditionality, legitimacy and compliance.* London and New York: Routledge.

O'Brennan, J. (2014). On the slow train to nowhere: The European Union, 'enlargement fatigue', and the Western Balkans. *European Foreign Affairs Review, 19*(2), 221–241.

O'Reilly, M. (2016). Peace and justice through a feminist lens: Gender justice and the women's court for the former Yugoslavia. *Journal of Intervention and Statebuilding, 10*(3), 419–445.

Papadimitriou, D., & Petrov, P. (2013). State-building without recognition: A critical perspective of the European Union's strategy in Kosovo (1999–2010). In A. Elbasani (Ed.), *European integration and transformation in the Western Balkans* (pp. 121–137). London: Routledge.

Perry, V. (2015). *A cross-cutting survey of corruption and anti-corruption issues in Bosnia and Herzegovina: Overview, challenges and recommendations.* Sarajevo: USAID.

Peskin, V. A. (2008). *International justice in Rwanda and the Balkans: Virtual trials and the struggle for state cooperation.* Cambridge: Cambridge University Press.

Phinnemore, D. (2013). The stabilization and association process: A framework for European Union enlargement? In A. Elbasani (Ed.), *European integration and transformation in the Western Balkans: Europeanization or business as usual?* (pp. 22–37). London: Routledge.

Pospisil, J. (2019). *Peace in political unsettlement: Beyond solving conflict.* Houndmills: Palgrave.

Pula, B. (2014). Effects of the European financial and economic crisis in Kosovo and the Balkans: Modes of integration and transmission belts of crisis in the 'super-periphery.' *East European Politics, 30*(4), 507–525.

Radin, A. (2014). Analysis of current events: 'Towards the rule of law in Kosovo: EULEX should go'. *Nationalities Papers, 42*(2), 181–194.

Rocha de Siqueira, I. (2017). Development by trial and error: The authority of good enough numbers. *International Political Sociology, 11*(2), 166–184.

Rose, E. (2016, September 25). Bosnian Serbs defy state with referendum landslide. *BIRN.*

Sebastian Aparicio, S. (2014). *Post-war statebuilding and constitutional reform: Beyond Dayton in Bosnia-Herzegovina.* Houndmills: Palgrave.

Simón, L. (2013). *Geopolitical change, grand strategy and European security: The EU-NATO conundrum in perspective.* Basingstoke: Palgrave.

Sotiropoulos, D. A. (2014). The social effects of the economic crisis in the Western Balkans: A case study of unreconstructed welfare regimes. *Southeastern Europe, 38*(2–3), 250–266.

Subotić, J. (2017). Building democracy in Serbia: One step forward, three steps back. In S. P. Ramet, C. M. Hassenstab, & O. Listhaug (Eds.), *Building democracy in Yugoslav successor states: Accomplishments, setbacks, and challenges since 1990* (pp. 165–191). Cambridge: Cambridge University Press.

Toal, G. (2013). 'Republika Srpska will have a referendum': The rhetorical politics of Milorad Dodik. *Nationalities Papers, 41*(1), 166–204.

Transparency International. (2013). *National integrity system assessment: Bosnia and Herzegovina 2013.* Banja Luka and Sarajevo: Transparency International.

UNDP (United Nations Development Programme). (2008). *Human development report 2007/08.* New York: UNDP.

UNODC (United Nations Office on Drugs and Crime). (2008). *Crime and its impact on the Balkans and affected countries.* Vienna: UNODC.

UNODC (United Nations Office on Drugs and Crime). (2011). *Corruption in Bosnia and Herzegovina: Bribery as experienced by the population.* Vienna: UNODC.

Vachudova, M. A. (2014). EU leverage and national interests in the Balkans. *Journal of Common Market Studies, 52*(1), 122–138.

Visoka, G. (2017). *Shaping peace in Kosovo: The politics of peacebuilding and statehood.* Houndmills: Palgrave.

Visoka, G., & Doyle, J. (2016). Neo-functional peace: The European Union way of resolving conflicts. *Journal of Common Market Studies, 54*(4), 862–877.

Voloder, N. (2015). *Transparent public procurement in Bosnia-Herzegovina: New solutions for an old problem.* Sarajevo: Analitika Center for Social Research.

von Homeyer, H. (2015, March 27). Don't leave Serbia to Russia and China. *EuObserver.* https://euobserver.com/opinion/128157.

Weller, M. (2009). *Contested statehood: Kosovo's struggle for independence.* Oxford: Oxford University Press.

Yakinthou, C. (2018). Fighting windmills, ignoring dragons: International assistance to civil society in post-conflict Bosnia-Herzegovina. In C. Yakinthou & P. Arthur (Eds.), *Transitional justice, international assistance, and civil society: Missed connections* (pp. 52–85). Cambridge: Cambridge University Press.

PART III

Tuzla, or the Local Turn

CHAPTER 7

Local Views: Scepticism Towards Europe and Its Consequences

7.1 Introduction

Since 2003, when the EU formally declared that the future of the region is in the EU, most citizens in the Western Balkans believed that increasing integration into the Union would bring considerable benefits. As the previous two chapters have shown, this belief contributed to sustaining difficult post-socialist and, even, post-war transitions. In many cases, the 'European perspective' gave meaning, sense and direction to both political elites and ordinary citizens in their attempt to take control of and shape the new and challenging post-Cold War environment. Since the early 2000s, when the EU espoused an open-door policy towards the region, all states have developed various links with institutions in Brussels, and moved forward in the process of European integration. Croatia was the last state, after Slovenia, Bulgaria and Romania, to formally join the Union, doing so on 1 July 2013.

Despite this dynamic, the enlargement process was not always straightforward for aspiring new members. In the mid-2000s the debate on enlargement became entangled with the acrimonious dispute over the proposed new EU Constitution. The admission to the EU of both Bulgaria and Romania in 2007 was almost immediately criticized by several European capitals for being premature. After they joined the Union, Bulgaria and Romania failed to fulfil their remaining reform pledges, thus reinforcing the views of those critics who would have preferred the

© The Author(s) 2020
R. Belloni, *The Rise and Fall of Peacebuilding in the Balkans*, Rethinking Peace and Conflict Studies,
https://doi.org/10.1007/978-3-030-14424-1_7

postponement of these two states' membership. The outbreak of the economic and financial crisis in Europe in 2007–2008 further relegated enlargement to the bottom of EU priorities. As a result, by the turn of the decade the enlargement process was under severe strain. The pro-enlargement European Commission progressively lost control over the process to the member states, most of whom remained officially in favour of extending EU membership to Western Balkan states, but endorsed the stricter application of conditions (Balfour and Stratulat 2015). EU member states became more assertive in directing the process, thus leading to a 'creeping nationalization' of enlargement policy (Hillion 2010). At a time of profound economic and financial crisis, EU member states believed that they should have focused their energies on solving their own internal problems before considering how (and whether) to move ahead with further enlargement. Accordingly, enlargement was not even given a ministerial portfolio in the European Commission which took office in late 2014.

While this limited enthusiasm about accepting new member states has been manifest at least since the mid-2000s, the growth of euro-sceptical attitudes within the Western Balkan region itself has been less noticed and discussed. It has been simply taken for granted that Western Balkan states have no choice other than to accept that integration into Euro-Atlantic institutions is the 'only game in town'. Accordingly, European institutions have displayed a 'certain arrogance' (Subotić 2011) by simply assuming that any state, given the choice, will strive to become an EU member in order to enjoy the benefits that participation in the European club entails. In typical paternalist fashion, resistance to what European bureaucrats consider to be the best policies for Western Balkan states is puzzling to outside actors.

This mutual suspicion between external and internal actors has affected domestic views about Europe. Since the late 2000s the positive perception of the EU has gradually began to change, leading to increasing Euroscepticism. There were deep-rooted negative perceptions of Europe (and 'the West' more generally) in the Western Balkans before the outbreak of the 2007–2008 economic and financial crisis. But the crisis severely undermined the main supposed advantages of EU integration—economic development and prosperity—and thus intertwined with and reinforced lingering negative attitudes towards Europe. The difficulty in providing a solution to the problem of refugees stuck in the region throughout 2015 had a negative effect on the Balkan peoples' perception of the EU (Cocco 2017).

This chapter examines the causes and consequences of this rise of negative views about the EU. While the previous two chapters discussed the reasons for the enlargement fatigue within European institutions and member states, this chapter considers Western Balkan citizens, whose views are frequently neglected or marginalized in the analysis of EU enlargement processes. This shift of focus constitutes one way to operationalize the 'local turn' in peacebuilding research, and in particular its attempt to problematize the agency, expectations, needs and practices of domestic actors (Mac Ginty 2012; Mac Ginty and Richmond 2013). As Chapter 5 argued, the EU's involvement in the Western Balkans has been frequently assessed with reference to its 'transformative' (Grabbe 2014) or 'normative power' (Whitman 2011), with abundant allusions to their positive impact on the ground. When local views are considered, they are generally treated as 'domestic constraints' deriving either from the presence of authoritarian political structures or the opportunity costs of adopting reforms requested by Europe. Critics of the EU's peacebuilding and member state-building approach have highlighted the limits of this interpretation, arguing that external involvement has at best contributed to building the procedural elements of democracy and, at worst, has legitimized weak and unresponsive institutions failing to meet citizens' needs (Chandler 2010). However, while drawing attention to the limits of intervention, even critics have emphasized European agency while giving scant consideration to domestic expectations, views, and attempts to (re)appropriate internationally sponsored norms and institutions (Sabaratnam 2014). Accordingly, this chapter reverses this analytical perspective, which has been focused on the EU's actions and strategies, and investigates how external involvement is experienced and interpreted locally.

After a brief discussion of what is meant by Euroscepticism, the chapter provides some evidence of its growth in the region. Second, it offers an account of the main reasons for this trend—reasons which include not only socio-economic factors but also symbolic and identity issues. Finally, the chapter examines the consequences of the rise of Euroscepticism. While there are no short-term, realistic alternatives to further integration into the EU, other options—most importantly developing closer ties with Russia—are increasingly debated locally. Overall, growing levels of Euroscepticism reflect frustration with the EU's real and perceived failures to meet citizens' expectations, rather than a radical rejection of the institutions and principles underpinning liberal peacebuilding and the process of European integration.

7.2   Euroscepticism and European Integration

The term 'Euroscepticism' is imprecise and value-laden. In a seminal work on political parties, Taggart and Szczerbiak distinguished between a 'soft' and a 'hard' variant of the phenomenon. 'Hard' Euroscepticism involves outright rejection of the European integration process, including the existence of the EU, as well as the concepts underpinning the European project. The June 2016 UK vote in favour of leaving the EU well reflects this type of attitude. 'Soft' Euroscepticism denotes not a principled opposition to European integration or EU membership, but a position where 'concerns on one (or a number of) policy areas lead to the expression of qualified opposition to the EU, or where there is a sense that "national interest" is currently at odds with the EU trajectory' (Taggart and Szczerbiak 2002: 7). This distinction has generated lively scholarly debate. Above all, 'hard' and 'soft' variants of Euroscepticism have been criticized for being too vague. 'Soft' Euroscepticism is a broad category encompassing a wide range of actors, worldviews, attitudes and policies, and is thus conceptually and empirically problematic. Perhaps unsurprisingly given this lack of clarity, a number of neologisms—including 'euro-apathy', 'euro-cynicism', 'euro-realism', and the like—are often employed in studies of the phenomenon.

Besides being conceptually broad, the notion of Euroscepticism is also value-laden. Academic approaches to European integration have frequently adopted, at least implicitly, a functionalist and linear perspective, which has relegated critical and/or sceptical views to the margins of the debate (Gilbert 2008). Such approaches frequently interpret the evolution of European integration from the standpoint of institutions and think-tanks in Brussels; and, with regard to new or aspiring new member states, they brim with civilizing ideas on improvement of the human condition and the transfer of values and institutions (Klinke 2015). Neo-colonial overtones are apparent in the use of notions of 'Europeanization', 'modernization' and 'liberalization' in regard to actors involved in the enlargement process. In this discourse dominated by an underlying idea of progress, opposition in any form, including mild versions of Euroscepticism, is easily seen as bordering on irrationality. This attitude reflects a 'paternalist Eurocentrism' (Hobson 2012: 285–310), which gives Europe the progressive task of delivering rational institutions to states characterized by conditional or defective sovereignty.

While institutions and think-tanks in Brussels show forms of Eurocentrism, the literature on Europeanization and European integration has been more nuanced but similarly EU centred. A main concern of this literature has been the identification of the conditions favouring the transfer of EU rules to aspiring new EU members. In a widely cited work Schimmelfennig and Sedelmeier (2005) have argued that the EU impact on potential member states is greatest whenever it puts forward clear demands and applies credible conditionality (see Chapter 2). Through a strategy of 'reinforcement by reward' the EU provides external incentives for a target government to comply with its conditions. In this framework, limited compliance has nothing to do with the existence of legitimate views and interests in contrast with EU demands, but is explained through reference to authoritarianism and/or domestic adoption costs. Authoritarian governments may find the costs of complying with EU conditionality too high, and thus they turn into the main obstacles to their country's EU accession.

With its focus on political leaders and governmental actors, this rationalist-bargaining model provides important insights on the Europeanization process, its impact and the conditions for its success. For examples, the April 2013 agreement between Belgrade and Pristina (discussed in Chapter 6), through which Serbia implicitly recognized the existence of an autonomous Kosovo in return for the start of EU accession negotiations, can be explained by the cost-benefit calculations of all actors involved (Economides and Ker-Lindsay 2015). However, at the same time this model presents at least three major limits. First, it tends to overemphasize success stories by assuming that appropriate rewards and/or pressures on political leaders will change domestic politics. Little conceptual space is left for forms of Euroscepticism and/or identity politics (Subotić 2011). Second, this model focuses on the EU's superior bargaining power, and its capacity to monitor the target state and to sanction it in case of non-compliance, with modest consideration for internal developments in the 'target state' (Keil 2013). Finally, popular attitudes are either neglected or paid lip service to. Rationalist approaches fail to account for the possibility of an identity mismatch between the EU and aspiring new members and the possibility that this mismatch could undermine the effectiveness of conditionality (Stahl 2011).

In sum, Euroscepticism is a rather vague, value-laden, and conceptually marginal concept in the literature on Europeanization and European integration. In this chapter, Euroscepticism is understood as a broad polymorphous stance expressing popular opposition to the modes of European integration and its impact on aspiring new EU members, and involving latent or manifest behaviour ranging from apathy and detachment regarding the integration process to active contestation. In principle, citizens' attitudes to the broader European integration project may be distinguished from attitudes to the actual functioning of the EU, although in practice the two are closely linked. While Euroscepticism is hardly discernible from EU-scepticism, frequently it is the latter that comes to the surface in citizens' assessments. Citizens do not simply contest either the European project or the existence of the EU 'as it is'; rather, they assess evolving representations in a context—such as the one dominated by a severe economic crisis—where doubts about the impact of European policies have been growing both within and outside the Old Continent. In the Western Balkans this assessment has become increasingly critical.

7.3   EUROSCEPTICISM IN THE WESTERN BALKANS

The EU is less attractive today than it was in 2003 when it promised an open-door policy for the Western Balkan states. According to Tanja A. Börzel, 'whether the "golden carrot" [of EU accession] is big enough to draw the Western Balkans closer to Europe is still an open question' (Börzel 2013: 175). The attitude prevailing in the region is a mix of resigned and fatalistic Euro-realism and growing Euroscepticism. Most citizens still see further integration into the EU as inevitable, although support for the process has declined everywhere, in some places considerably (Belloni 2014).

The level of Euroscepticism is commonly measured through popular attitudes towards membership of the EU. The problem with this indicator is that citizens generally have modest knowledge about Europe, and thus they rely on shortcuts or heuristics—and project their views of the national government onto the EU (Anderson 1998). Moreover, citizens' attitudes frequently follow the ups and downs of the integration process. A decline in support for European integration may reflect delays in the accession process or the EU's apparently obstinate requests—in particular for the arrest of war criminals. With these caveats in mind, a longitudinal analysis of public attitudes demonstrates that the EU's popularity in the Western Balkans has been progressively declining, shifting from Euro-enthusiasm to various levels of Euroscepticism (Table 7.1).

Table 7.1 Positive answers to the question: 'do your think that (OUR COUNTRY)'s membership of the EU would be a good thing?'

	2006*	2010*	2015**	2018**
Albania	84	81	84	83
Bosnia-Herzegovina	70	75	30	45
Croatia	35	25	32	N/A
Kosovo	87	87	89	84
FYROM	76	60	41	59
Montenegro	64	73	35	53
Serbia	61	44	24	29

*Gallup Balkan Monitor (2010)
**Regional Cooperation Council (2015, 2018)
Note The results from the two polls are comparable considering that the sampling strategies have a similar level of reliability (in 2018 Croatia was not polled). It should be noted that Eurobarometer surveys show generally greater support for EU integration than surveys cited in Table 7.1. However, Eurobarometer surveys have not consistently polled all countries of the region overtime, and thus are of limited use to assess support for the EU diachronically. Above all, Eurobarometer surveys are carried out in member and candidate states. Accordingly, they have not yet polled citizens in Bosnia-Herzegovina and Kosovo on their views about EU membership

In Serbia, support for integration has reached a record low. For the first time since the democratic changes in 2000, parliamentary elections held in March 2014 produced a National Assembly composed of political parties all in favour of EU membership. At the same time, however, the percentage of citizens in favour of joining the EU dropped from 61% in 2006 to 29% in 2018. Opinion poll data from the Serbian government's Office for EU integration generally shows greater levels of support, but also discloses that the vast majority of Serbian citizens would not be in favour of joining the EU if recognizing the independence of Kosovo were a condition. Even states with a strong pro-European tradition like FYROM and Montenegro have registered significant changes. Both in FYROM, which became an official EU candidate in 2005, and in Montenegro, which began accession talks in 2012, support for EU membership declined considerably since 2006. Macedonians are frustrated and disappointed by the repeated postponement of accession talks due to a dispute with Greece over the country's name. The name dispute may upset the delicate balance between ethnic Macedonians and the Albanian community, which believes that the country's chances of joining the EU are being undermined by the Macedonian majority (Milevska 2013). After a sharp decline in 2015, support for EU membership rose again as a result of the Prespa Agreement, signed on 17 June 2018. The withdrawal of the Greek veto resulted in the EU approval of the start of the accession talks with FYROM under the condition that the country's constitutional name is changed to Republic of North Macedonia (Kitsantonis 2018).

As for Montenegro, this country was the first one to experience the Commission's new approach to negotiations requiring an early focus on the most difficult areas of reform and the application of strict conditionality. Perhaps unsurprisingly, these areas have proved rather problematic. The EU's criticisms of the Montenegrin government in relation to the fight against organized crime and corruption have irked the local politico-economic elites—whose interests would be threatened by genuine progress in the fight against criminality—but did not lead to any meaningful progress in improving the rule of law (Petrushinin 2016). By 2018, only 1 in 2 citizens thinks that membership of the EU is a 'good thing.'

In general, the states most advanced in the EU integration process—Serbia, FYROM and Montenegro—experience the highest levels of Euroscepticism. In a progression already observed with regard to EU accession by CEE states, as citizens learn more about the social and sovereignty-related costs of accession, they begin to wonder whether these costs outweigh the benefits, and frequently change their views. To counter this trend, governments have developed communication strategies aimed at 'better informing, educating and communicating with citizens in order to enable wider public support about EU integration process (*sic*)' (Center for Democracy and Human Rights 2014: 14). By contrast, support is highest where the prospect of accession is more distant: that is, where citizens are for the most part uninformed about the terms and procedures of accession (Belloni 2014). In such cases, aspiring new EU members are ready and willing to adopt exogenous models in a manner that has been efficaciously described as 'self-colonizing' (Kiossev 1999).

Croatia's trajectory from Euro-enthusiasm to widespread Euroscepticism exemplifies the process of disillusionment taking place in the course of the integration process. Croatia had been nurturing its European roots and traditions since the beginning of the process of dissolution of the Yugoslav Federation in the early 1990s (Ashbrook 2010). The invocation of Europe by Croatian politicians served both to mobilize popular support and to marginalize the few critics of the integration process, who were stigmatized as 'closed, xenophobic, anti-democratic, and provincial' (Šoštarić 2011). During the process of European accession, however, Croatia lost much of its Europeanist zeal, thus confirming that the EU is most attractive when it is distant. When Croatia applied for EU membership in 2003, support for Euro-integration was about 85%. Ten years later, whereas the political elite believed that accession would expand its economic opportunities and thus remained strongly pro-Europe, the majority of Croatian citizens remained rather aloof, if not sceptical or critical.

Two communication strategies in 2001 and 2006 attempted to inform citizens on the progress towards integration and to improve the quality of the discussion about the pros and cons of accession, but they garnered little interest. The conditions for EU membership—including facing the past, dealing with war crimes, and removing immunity for high profile politicians—were often perceived as insulting to Croatian national identity and pride, while requests of economic liberalization and privatization were seen by some as socially unacceptable. In March 2011 large 'facebook protests' for the first time in any post-Yugoslav country condemned neo-liberal restructuring and rampant corruption, while campaigning for a 'no' vote at the upcoming 2012 referendum on EU's accession (Stubbs 2012). Despite popular protest, in 2012, 66.1% of citizens voted in favour of accession, but only 43.5% of those entitled to vote actually cast their ballot (Maldini and Pauković 2015). This turnout was the lowest ever recorded in a referendum on EU membership. Overall, since the early 2000s Croatians' attitudes evolved from enthusiasm to 'EU indifferentism' (Jović 2018).

While Serbia, FYROM, Montenegro and Croatia have recorded relatively low and declining levels of Euro-enthusiasm, support for EU integration remains significant in the other Western Balkan states. In Albania, which was recognized as an official candidate in June 2014, citizens' support for European integration remains stable at over 80%. Similarly, in Kosovo, where the process of developing closer ties with the EU is in its initial stages, support for Europe is almost unanimous. The Kosovar (Albanian) population has some reasons for resentment towards Europe—above all the lack of a common European position in relation to the recognition of Kosovo after the 2008 declaration of independence. However, 89% of the population agree with Kosovo entering the EU. In Bosnia-Herzegovina, which applied for membership in February 2016, surveys indicate that pro-European sentiments have been consistently high for most of the post-war period, although respondents from the Croat-Bosniak Federation are significantly more supportive of EU accession than those from the RS (IRI 2017). In general, Bosnian citizens consider EU institutions positively when compared to the corruption and inefficiency of their own national-level institutions and support EU accession hoping to circumvent dysfunctional domestic political structures (Cohen and Lampe 2011: 288). However, as discussed in the next chapter, support for EU accession dropped dramatically since 2010 as a result of a deepening economic, political and social crisis (Belloni et al. 2016).[1]

For Albania and Kosovo, and for Bosnia-Herzegovina for most of its post-war period, the presence of various degrees of Euro-enthusiasm has not in practice translated into concrete reforms aimed at moving closer to Europe. Rather, the broad consensus on the goal of integration has removed the need for debate on the pros and cons of the process. It has thus sidelined the integration issue on the list of policy priorities. Given that all actors in society endorse the European integration project, electoral campaigns are rarely focused on Europe, and electoral results do not depend on taking a particular stance on the EU. Overall, while Euroscepticism tends to increase the closer a state approaches the EU, the reasons for this trend are complex, and they differ for each state. However, some generalizations are possible, and they are discussed in the next section.

7.4   Why Euroscepticism?

Studies on Euroscepticism in western Europe have attempted to identify the reasons for popular discontent towards the EU. These studies have demonstrated that Euroscepticism is generated by three main factors—all of which play a role in the Western Balkans. First, the utilitarian calculation of economic costs and benefits shapes attitudes towards Europe (Gabel 1998). Second, attitudes towards the EU are closely linked to the degree of attachment to national/ethnic identities and fear of being culturally under threat. The stronger the feelings of national identity, the more citizens consider the European integration process to be a threat to their community (Hooge and Marks 2004). Third, Euroscepticism can be a function of citizens' dissatisfaction with their own national-level institutions. Disappointment and frustration with how domestic institutions work negatively impact on perceptions of European-level institutions (Anderson 1998). The case of Croatia briefly outlined above shows that in practice these issues are intertwined and that attitudes towards Europe may change significantly along the way in the course of the dynamic process of European integration.

These factors all play a role in the Western Balkan context, but with some ambiguities. For example, dissatisfaction with national institutions does not necessarily translate into discontent towards Europe. In the case of Bosnia-Herzegovina, citizens' dissatisfaction with domestic institutions has triggered a 'mechanism of substitution' (Sánchez-Cuenca 2000) whereby the EU and its reforming efforts are supported as substitute for ineffective domestic institutions. In addition, Euroscepticism is further motivated by some conditions characterizing in particular the current accession experience of states from the region. To begin with, as frequently discussed in the literature (i.e., Grabbe 2014), the use of a strict conditionality has contributed significantly to increase scepticism and diffidence locally, in particular among political elites who are asked to implement painful and unpopular reforms. Above all, from a popular perspective Euroscepticism is fuelled primarily by economic and identity issues, by concerns related to the difficult situation of former 'Balkan' but current EU member states, as well as by resentment at the top-down, paternalistic character of the integration process.

Economic Troubles. Various forms of economic integration between the EU and the Western Balkans already exist (Bartlett and Prica 2012), making the lure of full membership less attractive. As explained in Chapter 5, trade liberalisation between the EU and the region has been achieved and has effectively eliminated all restrictions on the entry of Western Balkan products into the EU. Almost two-thirds of all commercial exchange takes place between the region and the Union. Both Montenegro and Kosovo have unilaterally adopted the euro as their currency, while Bosnia-Herzegovina's currency, the convertible mark, is pegged to the euro. A 2006 Treaty has created an internal market in electricity and natural gas between EU member states and seven states from the region. In addition, since December 2009 citizens of FYROM, Montenegro and Serbia enjoy visa-free access to the Schengen area—a privilege granted in late 2010 to both Albanians and Bosnians as well. In the area of research cooperation Western Balkan states (plus Turkey, minus Kosovo) have obtained a status of associated countries within the Framework Programme Seven, whereby they become eligible for funding on the same basis as legal entities from EU member states.

Thus, the Western Balkans are already largely integrated into Europe. The problem is not so much (or merely) a lack of progress in the integration process, but that in good times Europe exports prosperity to the region but in times of crisis it exports instability (Bechev 2012: 1). The economic and financial crisis which broke out in 2007–2008 has severely damaged the economic situation of Western Balkan states, which are closely integrated into the EU and thus heavily dependent on external developments. While this economic integration has favoured growth and development since the late 1990s, at the same time it has increased the region's vulnerability to external shocks, principally the repercussions of the euro's weakness and instability. The impact of the crisis has been significantly felt everywhere, but especially in those countries which have advanced most in the EU integration process (Bartlett and Prica 2012). The main effect has been the growth of unemployment. After a sharp rise in the jobless rate in 2009–2010, the situation has been improving, but very slowly. In late 2018 unemployment in Albania was at 12.9%, in Kosovo at 29.4%, in Bosnia-Herzegovina at 35.3%, in FYROM at 20.8%, in Montenegro at 18%, and in Serbia at 11.3%.[2] This difficult situation has undermined support for the reformist policies required by the EU integration process. As next chapter will discuss, a wave of protests throughout the region since 2011 testifies to the growing social discontent among the population, and expresses a far-reaching critique towards the economic and political systems nurtured by two decades of international peacebuilding.

Problematic Neighbours. The difficult situations of neighbouring EU member states ring loud alarm bells for aspiring new members (see, for ex., Center for Democracy and Human Rights 2014: 16). Above all, the devastating effects of the economic and financial crisis on Greece have exacerbated scepticism towards the Union. Until recently, Greece was cited as a model to imitate because of its apparently irreversible achievements in moving from relative backwardness and underdevelopment to the stability and prosperity that followed the country's entry into the EU. However, since 2009, when the Greek government first admitted the existence of an unsustainably high budget deficit and public debt, and began deep structural reforms and drastic deficit reduction policies, the presumed advantages and benefits yielded by integration into European institutions have been called into question. Citizens from the

Western Balkans acknowledge the responsibilities of the Greek economic and political leadership for the 'Greek tragedy', but at the same time they believe that the EU's austerity policies have played a fundamental role in the worsening of the crisis.

This assessment does not signal the affirmation of 'hard' Eurosceptic views. Even in Greece, the decline in EU support has been accompanied by increased support for the euro, suggesting that Greek citizens recognize that being in the EU is the only realistic alternative despite the pain of austerity measures (Clements et al. 2014). Yet, at the same time, both Greek and Western Balkan citizens have grown increasingly disenchanted and discontented with the way in which European institutions handle economic and social issues, and in particular with the fact that austerity measures ultimately have their most painful effects on vulnerable population groups such as the elderly and the young unemployed. While the situation in Greece is certainly the most glaring demonstration of the EU's inability to guarantee stability and growth, Croatia's economic performance as the newest EU member state is also a troubling reminder that membership cannot assure prosperity (Ilić and Radosavljević 2014).

Moreover, not only does joining Europe not guarantee economic development, but also it does not necessarily improve the quality of democratic governance (Zielonka 2007). The cases of Hungary and Poland, which joined the Union in 2004, testify to the fact that democratic transformation is hollow. In both countries the support to EU accession and democratization appeared to be deeply rooted, yet both countries have been experiencing a frontal assault on liberal democracy. The democratic performance in some former 'Balkan' states which have recently entered the EU has also deteriorated considerably. In Slovenia, the first former Yugoslav state to enter the EU in 2004, the uncritical Eurocentric meta-discourse that served to support the country's transition towards Europe (Velikonja 2005) has eroded considerably. The much-admired social and economic model based on gradual reforms, tripartite bargaining and modest privatizations (Crowley and Stanojević 2011) gradually unravelled, paving the way for the explosion of a number of economic, social, and political grievances. Mass demonstrations began in the winter of 2012 to protest against economic and social policies perceived as 'imposed' by European institutions with the goal of salvaging the banks while leaving ordinary citizens to fend for themselves (Kirn 2019). The former prime minister was forced to resign and was sentenced to two years in jail for corruption (Krašovec and Ramet 2017). Overall, the difficult situation in neighbouring EU member states is observed and assessed with growing levels of preoccupation by aspiring new members in the Western Balkans (Horvat and Štiks 2015).

Europe's Paternalism. The EU has taken upon itself the objective of promoting the development of its neighbours who until the early 1990s belonged to the socialist camp. Its civilizing mission recalls the colonial time 'white man's burden' involving a 'moral duty' to modernize and improve those societies lagging behind as a result of decades of totalitarian rule. As Hobson (2012: 315) explains, '[p]aternalist Eurocentrism for the most part entails a highly optimistic, and frequently triumphalist, "progressive" politics.' However, from the viewpoint of the 'beneficiaries' of European zeal, paternalism is a sin: 'it is disrespectful, infantilizing, violates someone's autonomy and dignity' (Barnett 2016: 24; see also Buden 2015).

Paternalist pressure on aspiring new EU member states reinforces a public sense of being subjected to a kind of 'democratic totalitarianism' (Volčič 2005: 164). In theory, the integration process should involve two sets of actors—EU officials and democratically elected representatives of aspiring new members—with formally equal status. In practice, the crucial decisions on where, how, and above all when enlargement will occur are taken by Brussels. The heavy emphasis on technocracy, standardization, and assessment according to pre-established criteria crowds out domestic perspectives and expectations (Mac Ginty 2018). The very length of the process contributes to intensifying public frustration, and to raising suspicions about Brussels' ultimate intentions. For instance, in Serbia 'a large share of the public... believes that the country will never be accepted to join in the Union, even if it fulfils all technical criteria' (Bandović and Vujačić 2014: 63).

The criteria adopted to assess the reform process in the areas of political stability, democratic governance, market economy, and rule of law are vague and subjected to multiple and perhaps arbitrary interpretations. Since mid-2000s onwards, not only is 'strict conditionality' (Council of the European Union 2006: point 7) the principle on which negotiation on membership is pursued, but also the number of conditions to be met has increased, the thresholds for compliance have been raised, and demands have been made at more points in the accession process. For example, with regard to the Copenhagen criteria for a functioning market economy, 'a conveniently elastic measure of compliance… gives the impression of an assessment process that has a strong political element rather than being based on a fully transparent and objective measurement' (Bartlett 2015: 214). Similarly, the notion of 'good governance' is rather elastic, and the EU interprets it according to its changing geopolitical understanding of the enlargement process. Meanwhile, the principle of 'good neighbourly relations' has gained prominence over time, whereby any border disputes should be resolved in conformity to the principle of peaceful settlement and, if necessary, submitted to the International Court of Justice (Içener and Phinnemore 2015: 36–40). The EU's increasing requests intended to ensure compliance with principles and values (including normative standards such as gay rights) under severe strain even within EU member states are perceived as moralistic, inappropriate and untimely (see, for example, Kuhar 2011).

Particularly worrying from the point of view of citizens in the region is the EU's wavering with regard to its visa policy. The 2009–2010 visa liberalization, discussed in Chapter 6, was achieved after decades of isolation and years of requests by Western Balkan states. It was received locally with excitement and thrill. Since then, tens of thousands have taken advantage of visa liberalization in order to enter the Schengen area and many have applied for political asylum, in particular in Germany, Sweden and Belgium (where, however, only 3% of applicants were granted the status of refugee). In order to block this movement of people in mid-September 2013 the European Parliament adopted a 'protection clause,' which was later endorsed by the European Council, which allows both member states and the Commission to suspend the visa-free regime in case the number of arrivals is judged to be a 'threat to the public order or security' of any EU state, or of the EU as a whole (Council of the European Union 2013). The suspending mechanism entered in effect in early 2014, and has not yet been activated. The practical implications of this clause may be minimal, but not its symbolic consequences, as citizens from Western Balkan states may interpret it as a sign that European institutions are aloof or even hostile.

Despite growing diffidence towards Europe, local political elites are careful not to antagonize their interlocutors—who provide them with both legitimacy and economic aid. In some cases, however, they do not hesitate to claim that European institutions and officials are ultimately responsible even for the difficult economic situation and for the lack of future prospects. For example, when violent protests broke out in

Bosnia-Herzegovina in February 2014 (discussed in Chapter 8), Bosnian Serb leader Milorad Dodik blamed the 'international community', including the EU, for failed privatization and the poor state of the economy (Balkan Insight 2014). This positioning contest, whereby European policy-makers try to assert their expert authority over national elites while domestic actors attempt to shift the blame for stagnating economies, has significant consequences on citizens' perceptions of Europe as not only distant, technocratic and opaque but also expressing the idea that the region should be supervised and administered by the European centre.

Overall, Western Balkan societies are critical of a ready-made version of Europe which sees them as 'objects' of Europeanization and passive receivers of values and frameworks coming from the European centre. Rather than accepting Brussels' demands uncritically, Western Balkan societies want to re-appropriate, modify and reorganize the relationship between centre and periphery on the basis of the principle that they are 'equal but unique' (Petrović 2014). They may not be necessarily against European integration, but they question a kind of Europe understood as the extension of authority and norms to their countries, rather than as a project to construct a genuinely pan-European edifice. Thus, despite the expropriation of domestic agency in the region through forms of post-liberal governance (Chandler 2010), in point of fact the values and norms on which the EU puts much emphasis—including what it means to be 'European'—are subjected to negotiation and mutual accommodation.

Identity Fears. These reasons for scepticism towards the EU and its institutions—deriving from the repercussions of the post-2008 economic crisis, the difficulties of neighbouring EU member states, and the top-down and judgmental character of the EU integration process—are intertwined with a deep-rooted diffidence towards the 'West,' and in particular towards the Christian-Catholic world. Even Muslims in the Western Balkans, and above all in Bosnia-Herzegovina, who are frequently Europeanist (Bougarel 2005), are slowly changing their attitude. Bosniak elites have interiorised a strong sense of victimization as a result of the 1992–1995 war, and are increasingly identifying Europe and the West as entities who betrayed their cause.[3] Accordingly, they turn with mounting interest to Turkey as an example of successful modernization occurring outside of the EU framework (Rucker-Chang 2014). As of Christian-Orthodox citizens (Serbs, Macedonians, Montenegrins), they are traditionally extremely suspicious of and sometimes hostile to the 'West'. From the late Byzantine period onwards, the West, and later Europe, was seen as the source of existential threats to the Orthodox world, inducing many citizens to prefer Ottoman rule to subordination to Rome (Makrides 2009: 213). Ottoman rulers occupied the region but left Orthodoxy intact, and this was frequently interpreted locally as God's plan to save the Orthodox East from subjugation to Roman Catholicism. This anti-western attitude was illustrated powerfully in a characteristic saying of the fifteenth and sixteenth century: 'Better a Turkish turban then a Latin tiara' (Makrides 2014).

Needless to say, this rooted suspicion towards the 'West' does not necessarily support a Huntingtonesque view of clashing civilizations. The fact that the EU has four Eastern Orthodox states as members (Bulgaria, Cyprus, Greece and Romania) testifies to the conceptual weakness of those approaches grounded on the supposed incompatibility of cultures. Rather, the lingering persistence of conceptual dichotomies of East versus West intertwines with a negative image of Europe as promoter of values—such as human rights, pluralism and the separation between church and state—which are supposedly in contrast with Orthodox culture (Lis 2014). In particular, while Orthodox Churches officially support the existing or future EU membership of their countries, they are associated with the political camp of EU sceptics (Olteanu and de Nève 2014). In some cases, as in Serbia, the Church has both condoned routine violence against various minority groups and vociferously opposed any Serbian compromise on the status of Kosovo (Vukomanović 2008). Opinion polls suggest that Kosovo constitutes the red line in public perception of Serbia's relationship with the EU (Jović 2018).

Recent European policies have reinforced a deep sense of mistrust among Orthodox nationalists. European members of NATO participated in the 1999 bombing of Serbia in order to protect the Albanian population of Kosovo. NATO airstrikes contributed to deepen a widespread resentment towards western European states. The alliance during the 1990s between Serbia and Greece, a EU member state, testified to the solidarity within the Orthodox world necessary to confront the perceived western/European quest for domination (Michas 2002). After the war, the EU imposed a number of conditions on Serbia in order to accept the country as a potential EU candidate, including full collaboration with the ICTY—an institution that has tried and condemned several Serbs responsible for crimes committed during the wars in the 1990s.

In addition, the EU's position on the question of Kosovo independence (which is supported by 23 member states) contrasts with the 'firm emotional resistance' of Serbian citizens, many of whom do not want to accept the 'loss of Kosovo' (Obradović-Wochnik and Wochnik 2012: 1167). The April 2013 Agreement between Serbia and Kosovo, which implicitly acknowledges the autonomous existence of Kosovo, reflects the pragmatic, short-term cost-benefit calculation of the actors involved, rather than normative adaptation or identity formation (Economides and Ker-Lindsay 2015). As a result, for many Serbs the most severe threats to their identity continue to come from Europe, which is still considered to be the 'other'—or something that lies outside their own realm (Makrides 2009: 216). To the extent that Orthodox citizens approve of European integration, they do so because of a sense of resignation based on the lack of feasible alternatives, rather than because of convinced adherence to what the EU supposedly stands for.

In sum, Western Balkan societies experience various degrees of Euroscepticism. It is impossible to identify a single type of Euroscepticism among the different Balkan countries, nor even within each of them. Euroscepticism is both polysemic and constantly evolving. Street protests (discussed in the next chapter) have carried forward a radical critique of the results of post-socialist transitions and, in this context, of the role played by European actors in promoting painful reforms. A general apathy and detachment from Europe suggest the existence of a widespread sense of fatigue with Europe's requests and procedures. To these expressions of Euroscepticism one should add a frequent nostalgia for both Tito and Yugoslavia, which was a sort of 'mini-EU' supposedly functioning better than contemporary post-Yugoslav states (Palmberger 2008). Importantly, nostalgia does not express glorification of the past and a longing for a socialist world, but a rejection of the current political situation with its economic uncertainties and political arrogance (Velikonja 2008). Right wing extremists are also increasingly expressing their own anti-European views. Neo-Nazis and neo-fascists in Serbia are especially admired by their ideological sympathizers throughout Europe because of their supposed role in 'protecting Christian Europe against the Muslim threat', as well as their staunch opposition to Europeanization processes and liberal values—above all lesbian, gay, bisexual and transgender (LGBT) rights (Tomić 2013). What unites most of the diverse expressions of Euroscepticism is the perception of the gap between the European ideal and the actual performance of integration. Rarely does criticism of Brussels go as far as rejecting the European project altogether. Rather, Western Balkan citizens are critical of particular policies or initiatives; but, for the most part, they continue to accept the European perspective. Their attitude can perhaps be described as a type of 'EU-scepticism'—a critical Europeanism which questions the methods, timing and rhetoric of the integration process but does not reject the European ideal altogether.

7.5   Geopolitical Competition

Although the growth of Eurosceptic attitudes in the region rarely involves unqualified opposition to the process of European integration, it has nonetheless developed jointly with increasing consideration of the alternatives.[4] Some voices on the left have called for the revival of the century-old idea of the Balkan Federation, which may lack political weight, but it expresses the need for an alternative to the EU-inspired neo-liberal restructuring (Živković and Medenica 2013). Besides this option, other alternatives are given consideration. Nearly half of the Macedonian population believes that its political elite should seek a different basis for political development outside the EU. In particular, local media frequently depict Turkey as a symbol of success without EU integration (Petkovski 2014). In Kosovo pro-European attitudes compete with equally strong pro-American sentiments. US-dominated NATO is very popular among the Albanian population, who think of American troops as their saviours from Serb oppression. Significantly, many streets are named after American politicians and commanders.

While Turkey, the United States and to an extent even China, exert some degree of influence in the region, it is Russia who has now become Europe's biggest competitor (Bechev 2017; Galeotti 2018; Lasheras 2016). Russia has been playing an increasingly assertive role in the area since the outbreak of the world economic and financial crisis in 2007–2008. Because of both strategic and economic interests, Russia has turned the Western Balkans into an important foreign policy priority. According to Russia's 2013 Foreign Policy Concept, 'Russia aims to develop comprehensive pragmatic and equitable cooperation with Southeast European countries. The Balkan region is of strategic importance to Russia, including its role as a major transportation and infrastructure hub used for supplying gas and oil to European countries' (Russian Federation 2013: point 66). Putin's framing of the world as a 'clash of civilizations' pitting

Russia and its allies against a hostile West bearing threatening values plays out in the region (Shlapentokh 2013; Lasheras 2016: 9).

Russian growing influence conflicts with norms and standards underpinning both liberal peacebuilding and Euro-Atlantic integration (including transparency, rule of law, human rights, democratic accountability and free markets). The spread of Russian opaque political and business practices is supposedly leading to a 'creeping oligarchisation' of the region (Stacey and Oliver 2014). Local leaders in the Western Balkans skilfully play one side against the other in order to extract resources and concessions by Brussels, in particular a more relaxed attitude with regard to accession conditions. As aptly argued by Dimitar Bechev (2017: 249), the new competition between the West/EU and Russia is 'a rivalry between an opportunist which has a clear set of goals though lacks the means to achieve them, and a terminally disoriented West that possesses the power assets but is not of one mind about how to respond to the challenge.'

Bosnia-Herzegovina and Serbia have been primary concerns of Russian foreign policy since the 1990s. Bosnia-Herzegovina is perhaps the weakest and potentially most unstable state in the region. Russia has long been a supporter of the RS and its President Milorad Dodik, who has systematically opposed social, economic, political, and above all judicial reforms demanded by the EU in order to make progress towards accession. As discussed in the previous chapter, Dodik has also threatened to hold a referendum on independence that, if held, would likely put an end to any prospect of EU integration for the Serb entity. Russian officials came out publicly in favour of a referendum. In addition, both in 2014 and 2015 Russia abstained from a Security Council vote on the extension of the EU's military mission in Bosnia-Herzegovina (Lasheras 2016). Similarly, when in September 2016 the Steering Board of the Peace Implementation Council condemned the referendum just held in the RS on the Constitutional Court's ban of the Statehood Day holiday, Russia refrained from endorsing such a statement. Although these moves had no immediate practical consequences, they signalled Moscow's increasingly unilateral approach to the region, as well as its support for the Bosnian Serbs.

Even in Serbia, while the political class is committed to Euro-integration, some scholars and pundits have been debating the possibility of abandoning EU integration in favour of closer ties with the Russian Federation (Marić 2014). The new Serbian leadership, which came to power after the 2012 elections, has tried to minimize the discussion on alternatives to Europe by staking its political capital on a pragmatic attempt to solve economic and social problems. The 'politics of alternatives' (Radeljić 2014), however, remains a major concern for the Serbian political class, which is divided between its wish to join the EU as quickly as possible and its worry about spoiling relations with Russia, which is a major trading partner and controls strategic companies in Serbia, including 56.5% of the state-owned oil company *Naftna Industrija Srbije*. Tellingly, Serbia is the only state outside the post-soviet area which enjoys a free trade zone with Russia. Moscow tacitly encourages Belgrade's aspirations to join the EU since, if successful, Russia would benefit from a 'Trojan horse' inside the Union (Galeotti 2018: 10–11).

Geopolitical issues also contribute to fostering the development of closer links between the two countries. In contrast to the EU, Russia has always supported Serbia's position on Kosovo, both condemning NATO's bombing in 1999 and refusing to recognize the province's self-declared independence in 2008. In late 2013 Serbia and Russia went so far as to sign a military cooperation agreement. At an event held in October 2014 in Belgrade to mark 70 years since Soviet troops helped liberate the city from Nazi occupation, President Putin re-affirmed that Russia's stance over Kosovo is 'a position of principle that is not to be subjected to any adjustments' (Radio Free Europe 2014). Putin's stance was motivated, among other reasons, by an attempt to justify Russia's annexation of Crimea on the basis of historical and cultural grounds— the same grounds that supposedly assign sovereign rights to Serbia over Kosovo. Yet, while Putin's position may be self-serving, Serbs have nonetheless assessed it positively, and raised Russia to the rank of most popular foreign power (Bechev 2017). In this context dominated by the presence of economic and geopolitical interests on both sides, Serbia has refused to accept the European economic measures adopted against Russia as a result of its involvement in eastern Ukraine since early/mid 2014. Meanwhile, Russia voted down a UN Security Council resolution marking the twentieth anniversary of the Srebrenica massacre, calling it 'anti-Serb.'

Thus, as in many other past instances, a situation of political-military crisis and the presence of real or perceived threats has strengthened Orthodox (and Slavic) brotherhood vis-à-vis Europe and the West. Russian, Belarus and Serbian military units even organized a joint military exercise in September 2015 named 'Slavic brotherhood' on Russian territory (Galeotti 2018). Worryingly, strong military ties may lead Belgrade to believe that Moscow could support it in a future conflict. In an apparent show of support for Moscow, both Serbia and Bosnia-Herzegovina abstained on the UN General Assembly Resolution 68/262, entitled 'Territorial Integrity of Ukraine.' In FYROM, citizens are reported to be sympathetic to the Russian version of the situation in Ukraine because of their frustration in relation to the 'name issue' and the related freezing of the EU integration process (Vankovska 2014). Likewise, in Montenegro there is considerable popular opposition to the government's decision to join the EU in introducing sanctions against Russia (Tomović 2014).

The mid- and long-term consequences of Russia's new role in the region are hard to gauge. Russia's main strength lies in its ability to exploit the EU's weaknesses (Bechev 2017). The United Kingdom's vote in June 2016 in favour of leaving the EU (the so-called 'Brexit') may both further weaken enlargement prospects and increase Russian influence in the region (Lasheras 2016). If the enlargement prospects for the Western Balkans become increasingly remote, then Serbia and other states may turn gradually more to Russia, whose 'soft power' involves not only economic instruments but also a variety of other initiatives and tools designed to generate goodwill in the region, including energy, diplomatic, military, and cultural policies (Galeotti 2018). While American and European sanctions against Moscow over the Ukraine affair have contributed to throw Russian economy sharply into reverse, Russian investment and influence remain substantial (Serra 2015). Russian diplomatic advance in the region may challenge the teleological narrative of transition towards the EU, already severely tested by the growth of Euroscepticism.

7.6   Conclusions

For much of the past 20 years, support for the EU has provided sense and direction during a period of often traumatic political, economic and social change. Much academic work has endeavoured to explain the conditions under which the EU can fulfil its progressive task of delivering modern and efficient rules and institutions to aspiring new EU member states. While insightful, this work has given little or no attention to the rise of sceptical views towards the EU. Indeed, particularly since the outbreak of the global economic and financial crisis, and the lack of seemingly efficient responses to it, the EU's attractiveness has lost much of its traction. The continuing crisis in Greece, as well as the outbreak in the summer of 2015 of a humanitarian crisis over refugees trying to reach Northern Europe through the Western Balkans, have fuelled further critical attitudes towards the EU, especially among the young population who sees Brussels as too distant and technocratic to solve pressing economic and social issues. In an unpredictable twist, the traditional roles between the EU and the Balkans have been reversed. Throughout 2015 the EU has turned into an exporter of instability to the region, since refugees entered it from Greece—an EU member state—and remained stuck in the Western Balkans as other EU member states in the area blocked their travel towards Central and Northern Europe (Lasheras 2016).

Advocates of integration both inside and outside the EU view Euroscepticism with concern. If citizens become disillusioned with European integration, this may also negatively affect the hope of reforming their own malfunctioning domestic institutions under the pressure of external demands. Moreover, Russia's new foreign policy assertiveness is a further cause of concern for those policy-makers and analysts who believe that the region, now encircled by EU borders, cannot be left out in the cold. In particular, the crisis in Ukraine has stimulated EU members in the region, such as Bulgaria and Romania, to ask Brussels for an accelerated EU accession process for their neighbours (Assenova 2014).

Needless to say, EU member states do not consider further enlargement to be one of their priorities. Despite this lack of political will, or perhaps because of it, some scholars have underlined the instability of the current situation, the need to re-launch the integration perspective, and the urgency of revitalizing Europe's celebrated transformative power. The old key words of 'prosperity,' 'growth,' 'stability', and the like, are unlikely to inspire disillusioned citizens in the region. According to Konitzer (2014: 29), if the EU is to have a credible chance of exerting a positive influence, it must project a concrete, post-crisis vision of what the European project is about and of the real benefits—material, but also in terms of values, identity, and belonging—that membership in the Union may bring.

It is unclear whether such a strategy can produce positive results. Communication campaigns of both the EU and national institutions have long attempted to fill the gap between elites and the public but they have had little success. By privileging the EU's actorness, its objectives and expectations, these programmes risk reinforcing the perception of a paternalistic attitude towards the Western Balkans. The focus on the EU, its values, its ability to communicate, and its related transformative powers marginalize domestic perspectives. In addition, not only does such a focus preserve unequal power relations vis-à-vis the Western Balkan states, but it also prevents thorough consideration and debate on the growing discontent with the costs of the seemingly never-ending transition towards Europe.

Moreover, the current low salience of European issues in the domestic politics of Western Balkan states makes it unlikely that another information strategy will stimulate and support the profound reformist actions expected by Brussels. Indeed, for both Euro-enthusiast states and for sceptical ones, Europe ranks low on the list of the most pressing political priorities. For the former, Euro-enthusiasm does not translate into a set of credible reforms aimed at removing domestic obstacles to European integration. Albania, Bosnia-Herzegovina and Kosovo testify to the difficulty of transforming widespread sentiments in favour of Europe into a workable pro-European strategy. For the latter, popular scepticism and/ or passive acceptance of European-mandated rules contributes to the formation of an environment where citizens find themselves increasingly bound by EU norms and constraints, with little or no access to political representation to express their dissatisfaction.

Above all, and somewhat counter-intuitively, Euroscepticism does not necessarily imply a dismissal of Europe, erosion in the belief of democracy, or even disengagement from politics. For example, declining electoral participation does not reflect an apathetic attitude; rather, it expresses a critique of the internationally sponsored procedural aspects of the democratic process, a rejection of what is perceived as a corrupt political sphere, and a call for substantive political programmes and commitments (Greenberg 2014). Thus, Euroscepticism is hardly the pathology that some arguments adopting a normative understanding of the term imply, but an inherent feature of democratic development. In the Western Balkans, as elsewhere, dissatisfied citizens can be instrumental in the construction of a viable and legitimate domestic and supranational democratic order. In a context where the economic policies of states are decisively shaped by Europe's requests and conditions (Bieber and Ristić 2012), Eurosceptic views can perform a positive function. If EU policies are no longer taken at face value, then debates on the pros and cons of European integration, including the impact of European policies on issues of social cohesion and economic justice within society, can contribute to supporting a re-politicization of questions important for citizens of the Western Balkans and help manage the tension between national democracy and European demands. They may also contribute to answering the demands of economic and social inclusion increasingly being voiced in the region, and which are discussed in the next chapter.

Notes

1. However, respondents from the Croat-Bosniak Federation remain significantly more supportive of EU accession than those from the RS (IRI 2017).
2. For up to date unemployment rates see Trading Economics at: www.tradingeconomics.com.
3. Interview with Srdjan Blagovcanin, Transparency International, Sarajevo, July 2015.
4. Needless to say, a full analysis of alternatives would require in depth comparative research, which is beyond the scope of this chapter. This section simply aims to draw attention to and briefly evaluate Russia's attempt to use a growing disillusion with the EU to forge new alliances in the region.

References

Anderson, S. J. (1998). When in doubt, use proxies: Attitudes towards domestic politics and support for European integration. *Comparative Political Studies, 31*(5), 569–601.

Ashbrook, J. E. (2010). Croatia, euroskepticism, and the identity politics of EU enlargement. *Problems of Post-Communism, 57*(3), 23–39.

Assenova, M. (2014). Southeast Europe: Reactions to the crisis in Ukraine. *Eurasia Daily Monitor, 11*(49). http://www.jamestown.org/single/?tx_ttnews%5Btt_news%5D=42094&no_cache=1#.VNyPX_0Q4go. Accessed 5 December 2016.

Balfour, R., & Stratulat, C. (Eds.). (2015). *EU member states and enlargement towards the Balkans.* Brussels: European Policy Centre.

Balkan Insight. (2014, February 14). *Protests show Bosnia-Herzegovina needs to dissolve, Dodik says.* http://www.balkaninsight.com/en/article/dodik-blaims-international-community-for-Bosnia-Herzegovinan-protests.

Bandović, I., & Vujačić, M. (2014). The European question in Serbia's party politics. In C. Stratulat (Ed.), *European integration and party politics in the Balkans* (pp. 47–67). Brussels: European Policy Centre.

Barnett, M. (2016). Peacebuilding and paternalism. In T. Debiel, T. Held, & U. Schneckener (Eds.), *Peacebuilding in crisis: Rethinking paradigms and practices of transnational cooperation* (pp. 23–40). Abingdon and New York: Routledge.

Bartlett, W. (2015). The political economy of accession: Forming economically viable member states. In S. Keil & Z. Arkan (Eds.), *The EU and member state building: European foreign policy in the Western Balkans* (pp. 209–232). London and New York: Routledge.

Bartlett, W., & Prica, I. (2012). *The variable impact of the global economic crisis in south east Europe*. London: LSEE.

Bechev, D. (2012). *The periphery of the periphery: The Western Balkans and the EURO crisis*. Brussels: European Council on Foreign Relations.

Bechev, D. (2017). *Rival power: Russia in Southeast Europe*. New Haven and London: Yale University Press.

Belloni, R. (2014). L'euroscepticisme croissant des Balkans occidentaux. *La Revue Nouvelle, 6–7*, 18–23.

Belloni, R., Kappler, S., & Ramović, J. (2016). Bosnia-Herzegovina: Domestic agency and the inadequacy of the liberal peace. In O. P. Richmond & S. Pogodda (Eds.), *Post-liberal peace transitions: Between peace formation and state formation* (pp. 47–64). Edinburgh: Edinburgh University Press.

Bieber, F., & Ristić, I. (2012). Constrained democracy: The consolidation of democracy in Yugoslav successor states. *Southeastern Europe, 36*(3), 373–397.

Börzel, T. A. (2013). When Europeanization hits limited statehood: The Western Balkans as the test case for the transformative power of Europe. In A. Elbasani (Ed.), *European integration and transformation in the Western Balkans*. London: Routledge.

Bougarel, X. (2005). Islam balkanique et intégration européenne. In R. Leveau & K. Mohsen-Finan (Eds.), *Musulmans de France et d'Europe* (pp. 21–48). Paris: CNRS Éditions.

Buden, B. (2015). Children of post-communism. In S. Horvat & I. Štiks (Eds.), *Welcome to the desert of post-socialism: Radical politics after Yugoslavia* (pp. 123–139). London and New York: Verso.

Center for Democracy and Human Rights. (2014, December). *National study/Montenegro*. Podgorica.

Chandler, D. (2010). The EU and South-Eastern Europe: The rise of post-liberal governance. *Third World Quarterly, 31*(1), 69–85.

Clements, B., Nanou, K., & Verney, S. (2014). 'We no longer love you, but we don't want to leave you': The eurozone crisis and popular euroscepticism in Greece. *Journal of European Integration, 36*(3), 247–265.

Cocco, E. (2017). Where is the European frontier? The Balkan migration crisis and tis impact on relations between the EU and the Western Balkans. *European View, 16*(2), 293–302.

Cohen, L. J., & Lampe, J. R. (2011). *Embracing democracy in the Western Balkans*. Washington, DC: Woodrow Wilson Center Press.

Council of the European Union. (2006, June 15–16). *Presidency conclusions—Brussels European Council*. 16879/06.

Council of the European Union. (2013, December 5). *Council amends EU visa rules*. Brussels, 17328/13.

Crowley, S., & Stanojević, M. (2011). Varieties of capitalism, power resources, and historical legacies: Explaining the Slovenian exception. *Politics & Society, 39*(2), 268–295.

Economides, S., & Ker-Lindsay, J. (2015). Pre-accession Europeanization: The case of Serbia and Kosovo. *Journal of Common Market Studies, 53*(5), 1027–1044.

Gabel, M. J. (1998). Public support for European integration: An empirical test of five theories. *The Journal of Politics, 60*(2), 333–354.

Galeotti, M. (2018). *Do the Western Balkans face a coming Russian storm?* Brussels: European Council on Foreign Relations, ECFR/250.

Gallup Balkan Monitor. (2010). *Survey reports.* http://www.balkan-monitor.eu/index.php/reports.

Gilbert, M. (2008). Narrating the process: Questioning the progressive story of European integration. *Journal of Common Market Studies, 46*(3), 641–662.

Grabbe, H. (2014). Six lessons of enlargement ten years on: The EU's transformative power in retrospect and prospect. *Journal of Common Market Studies, 52*(Issue Supplement S1), 40–56.

Greenberg, J. (2014). *After the revolution: Youth, democracy, and the politics of disappointment in Serbia.* Stanford: Stanford University Press.

Hillion, C. (2010). *The creeping nationalisation of the EU enlargement policy* (SIEPS Report 6). Stockholm: Swedish Institute for European Policy Studies.

Hobson, J. M. (2012). *The Eurocentric conception of world politics: Western international theory, 1760–2010.* Cambridge: Cambridge University Press.

Hooge, L., & Marks, G. (2004). Does identity or economic rationality drive public opinion on European integration? *PS, 37*(3), 415–420.

Horvat, S., & Štiks, I. (Eds.). (2015). *Welcome to the desert of post-socialism: Radical politics after Yugoslavia.* London and New York: Verso.

Içener, E., & Phinnemore, D. (2015). Building on experience? EU enlargement and the Western Balkans. In S. Keil & Z. Arkan (Eds.), *The EU and member state building: European foreign policy in the Western Balkans* (pp. 32–54). London and New York: Routledge.

Ilić, I., & Radosavljević, Z. (2014, May 4). *Croatia's economy sends troubling message to neighbouring EU wannabes.* Reuters.

IRI (International Republican Institute). (2017). *Bosnia and Herzegovina: Attitudes on violent extremism and foreign influence.* Washington, DC: Center for Insights in Survey Research.

Jović, D. (2018). Accession to the European Union and perception of external actors in the Western Balkans. *Croatian International Relations Review, 24*(83), 6–32.

Keil, S. (Ed.). (2013). *State-building in the Western Balkans: European approaches to democratization.* London: Routledge.

Kiossev, A. (1999). Notes on self-colonising cultures. In B. Pejić & D. Elliot (Eds.), *After the wall: Art and culture in post-communist Europe* (pp. 114–117). Stockholm: Moderna Museet.

Kirn, G. (2019). Maribor's social uprising in the European crisis: From antipolitics of people to politicisation of periphery's surplus population. In F. Bieber & D. Trentin (Eds.), *Social movements in the Balkans: Rebellion and protest from Maribor to Taksim* (pp. 30–47). London and New York: Routledge.

Kitsantonis, N. (2018, June 17). FYROM and Greece sign historic deal on name change. *The New York Times*.

Klinke, I. (2015). European integration studies and the European Union's gaze. *Millennium: Journal of International Studies, 43*(2), 567–583.

Konitzer, A. (2014). Croatia's party system—From Tuđmanism to EU membership. In C. Stratulat (Ed.), *EU integration and party politics in the Balkans* (pp. 13–29). Brussels: European Policy Centre.

Krašovec, A., & Ramet, S. P. (2017). Liberal democracy in Slovenia: From seventh heaven to the lobby of hell in only two decades? In S. P. Ramet, C. M. Hassenstab, & O. Listhaug (Eds.), *Building democracy in the Yugoslav successor states: Accomplishments, setbacks, and challenges since 1990* (pp. 257–285). Cambridge: Cambridge University Press.

Kuhar, R. (2011). Resisting change: Same-sex partnership policy debates in Croatia and Slovenia. *Südosteuropa, 59*(1), 25–49.

Lasheras, F. (2016). *Return to instability: How migration and great power politics threaten the Western Balkans*. Brussels: European Council on Foreign Relations.

Lis, J. A. (2014). Anti-western theology in Greece and Serbia today. In A. Krawchuk & T. Bremer (Eds.), *Eastern orthodox encounters of identity and otherness* (pp. 159–168). New York: Palgrave.

Mac Ginty, R. (2012). Between resistance and compliance: Non-participation and the liberal peace. *Journal of International and Statebuilding, 6*(3), 167–187.

Mac Ginty, R. (2018). The limits of technocracy and local encounters: The European Union and peacebuilding. *Contemporary Security Policy, 39*(1), 166–179.

Mac Ginty, R., & Richmond, O. P. (2013). The local turn in peacebuilding: A critical agenda for peace. *Third World Quarterly, 34*(5), 763–783.

Makrides, V. N. (2009). Orthodox anti-westernism today: A hindrance to European integration. *International Journal for the Study of the Christian Church, 9*(3), 209–224.

Makrides, V. N. (2014). 'The barbarian West:' A form of orthodox Christian anti-western critique. In A. Krawchuk & T. Bremer (Eds.), *Eastern orthodox encounters of identity and otherness* (pp. 141–158). New York: Palgrave.

Maldini, P., & Pauković, D. (Eds.). (2015). *Croatia and the European Union: Changes and development*. Aldershot: Ashgate.

Marić, S. (2014). Serbia. In Institut für Europäische Politik (Ed.), *EU-28 Watch*, no. 10.

Michas, T. (2002). *Unholy alliance: Greece and Milosevic's Serbia*. College Station: Texas A&M University Press.

Milevska, T. (2013, December 19). FYROM's ethnic albanians lose patience over EU accession talks. *EurActiv*. http://www.euractiv.com/section/enlargement/news/FYROM-s-ethnic-albanians-lose-patience-over-eu-accession-talks/.

Obradović-Wochnik, J., & Wochnik, A. (2012). Europeanising the 'Kosovo question': Serbia's policies in the context of EU integration. *West European Politics, 35*(5), 1158–1181.

Olteanu, T., & de Nève, D. (2014). Eastern orthodoxy and the processes of European integration. In A. Krawchuk & T. Bremer (Eds.), *Eastern European encounters of identity and otherness* (pp. 179–206). New York: Palgrave.

Palmberger, M. (2008). Nostalgia matters: Nostalgia for Yugoslavia as potential vision for a better future. *Sociologija, 50*(4), 355–370.

Petkovski, L. (2014). FYROM. In Institut für Europäische Politik (Ed.), *EU-28 Watch*, no. 10.

Petrović, T. (Ed.). (2014). *Mirroring Europe: Ideas of Europe and Europeanization in Balkan societies*. Leiden: Brill.

Petrushinin, A. (2016, March 11). In Montenegro, the emperor has no clothes. *Financial Times*.

Radeljić, B. (2014). The politics of (no) alternatives in post-Milošević Serbia. *Journal of Balkan and Near Eastern Studies, 16*(2), 243–259.

Radio Free Europe. (2014, October 16). *Putin vows to support Serbia on Kosovo* (Resource document). https://www.rferl.org/a/russia-serbia-putin-us-criticism-belgrade/26640165.html. Accessed 14 March 2018.

Regional Cooperation Council. (2015). *Balkan barometer: Public opinion survey*. Sarajevo: Regional Cooperation Council Secretariat.

Regional Cooperation Council. (2018). *Balkan barometer: Public opinion survey*. Sarajevo: Regional Cooperation Council Secretariat.

Rucker-Chang, S. (2014). The Turkish connection: Neo-Ottoman influence in Post-Dayton Bosnia. *Journal of Muslim Minority Affairs, 34*(2), 152–164.

Russian Federation. (2013). *Concept of the foreign policy of the Russian Federation* (Resource document). http://www.mid.ru/brp_4.nsf/0/76389FEC168189ED44257B2E0039B16D. Accessed 5 December 2016.

Sabaratnam, M. (2014). Avatars of eurocentrism in the critique of the liberal peace. *Security Dialogue, 44*(3), 259–278.

Sánchez-Cuenca, I. (2000). The political basis of support for European institutions. *European Union Politics, 1*(2), 147–171.

Schimmelfennig, F., & Sedelmeier, U. (Eds.). (2005). *The Europeanization of central and Eastern Europe*. Ithaca: Cornell University Press.

Serra, M. (2015, January 27). Reshaping the Balkans: Soft power after 'rubble diplomacy' (Resource document). *Aspenia Online*. https://www.

aspeninstitute.it/aspenia-online/article/reshaping-balkans-soft-power-after-%E2%80%9Cruble-diplomacy%E2%80%9D. Accessed 5 December 2016.

Shlapentokh, D. (2013). The death of Byzantine empire and the construction of historical/political identities in late Putin Russia. *Journal of Balkan and Near Eastern Studies, 15*(1), 69–96.

Šoštarić, M. (2011, September 12). *From Zagreb with love: On the bounded rationality of euroscepticism and europhilia in Croatia.* Balkan Analysis.

Stacey, K., & Oliver, C. (2014, April 15). William Hague warns against 'creeping oligarchisation' of Balkans. *Financial Times.*

Stahl, B. (2011). Perverted conditionality: The stabilisation and association agreement between the European Union and Serbia. *European Foreign Affairs Review, 16*(4), 465–487.

Stubbs, P. (2012). Networks, organizations, movements: Narratives and shapes of three waves of activism in Croatia. *Polemos, 15*(2), 11–32.

Subotić, J. (2011). Europe is a state of mind: Identity and Europeanization in the Balkans. *International Studies Quarterly, 55*(2), 309–330.

Taggart, P., & Szczerbiak, A. (2002). The party politics of euroscepticism in EU member and candidate states. *Opposing Europe Research Network* (Working Paper No. 6). http://www.sussex.ac.uk/sei/research/europeanpartieselectionsreferendumsnetwork/epernworkingpapers. Accessed 5 December 2016.

Tomić, Đ. (2013). On the 'right' side? The radical right in the post-Yugoslav area and the Serbian case. *Fascism, 2*(1), 94–114.

Tomović, D. (2014, August 25). *Montenegro Serbs rally for Russians in Ukraine.* Balkan Insight.

Vankovska, B. (2014). The echo of the Ukrainian crisis in FYROM. *Sudosteuropa, 62*(2), 221–237.

Velikonja, M. (2005). *Eurosis: A critique of the new Eurocentrism.* Ljubljana: Peace Institute.

Velikonja, M. (2008). *Titostalgia: A nostalgia for Josip Broz.* Ljubljana: Peace Institute.

Volčič, Z. (2005). The notion of 'the West' in the Serbian national imaginary. *European Journal of Cultural Studies, 8*(2), 155–175.

Vukomanović, M. (2008). The Serbian orthodox church as a political actor in the aftermath of October 5, 2000. *Politics and Religion, 1*(2), 237–269.

Whitman, R. G. (2011). *Normative power Europe: Empirical and theoretical perspectives.* Houndmills: Palgrave.

Zielonka, J. (2007). The quality of democracy after joining the European Union. *East European Politics and Societies, 21*(1), 162–180.

Živković, A., & Medenica, M. (2013, May 31). Balkans for the peoples of the Balkans. *LeftEast.* http://www.criticatac.ro/lefteast/balkans-for-the-peoples-of-the-balkans/. Accessed 5 December 2016.

CHAPTER 8

Undoing International Peacebuilding from Below?

8.1 Introduction

Since the early 2010s, a wave of protests advancing social, economic and political demands has erupted throughout the region. In Slovenia, Croatia, FYROM and Bosnia-Herzegovina, protests have denounced the political system, political elites, corruption, mismanagement and deteriorating economic and social conditions. In two instances—Slovenia and FYROM—protesters managed to out corrupt, autocratic governments and favoured the largely peaceful handover of power. Similar cases of malcontent, but with a different intensity, emerged in Albania, Kosovo, Montenegro and Serbia. Everywhere corruption and mismanagement have been central in public criticism (Bieber and Brentin 2019; Milan 2018; Mujanović 2018). In some of these protests Europe has been the direct target of public scorn, and on a few occasions the EU flag has been burned. More commonly, protests have been directed against governmental levels, which are seen locally as implementing the EU's peacebuilding/state-building agenda. Protests have not been always non-violent, progressive or emancipatory. For example, in Kosovo a populist movement called Lëvuzja Vetëvendosje (Movement for Self-Determination) grounded its case for self-determination on mono-ethnic criteria and exclusionary practices and ultimately contributed to entrench identity politics (Visoka 2017: Chapter 4). For the most part, however,

© The Author(s) 2020
R. Belloni, *The Rise and Fall of Peacebuilding in the Balkans*, Rethinking Peace and Conflict Studies,
https://doi.org/10.1007/978-3-030-14424-1_8

protest movements did not endorse ethnic politics, but rather subscribed to ideas of emancipation as equality and liberation.

In one of the best-known analyses of these street protests, Horvat and Štiks argued that these apparently isolated instances of social discontent are characterized not simply by anti-government rhetoric but also by a radical critique of the political and economic system (Horvat and Štiks 2015). In some instances, protesters strove for radical change and attempted to develop individual and collective subjectivities antagonistic to established political and economic relations (Razsa 2015). But with the exception of the most radical, anarchist wing of the movement, the protesters have generally not attacked values cherished by the EU, such as democracy and economic modernization; rather, they have demanded that these values be implemented by taking citizens' needs into account. They have offered a 'counter-transition' (Riding 2018) to the endless peacebuilding process involving a ruinous interconnection of ethno-national politics and neoliberal restructuring. Protests, together with sit-ins, demonstrations, appeals, boycotts, de-legitimation campaigns and all other forms of contentious politics have developed hand in hand with forms of solidarity and cooperation. This new, bottom-up civil society attempted to introduce structural and class concerns as legitimate issues of political action (Moraca 2016).

Ideologically and generationally heterogeneous, protesters have nonetheless shared some characteristics. First, protesters have denounced as sell-outs the type of civil society organizations which have been the main target of internationally led peacebuilding intervention (see Chapter 4). Individuals involved in NGOs are considered, at best, as inadequate bureaucrats working on projects with limited impact or, at worst, opportunists complicit with the political and economic elite in perpetuating a condition of widespread injustice and suffering. From the point of view of the protesters, the artificially created civil society has resulted in the formation of an NGO elite—dubbed as 'NGOniks', 'NGO compradors', 'merchants of fog' and the like—detached from everyday reality as much as the international community and the local political elite (Puljek-Shank and Fritsch 2018). Internationally funded NGOs are seen as predominantly resigned to the status quo and to the (nationalist) stance that 'there is no alternative' to ethnic politics, nationalism, patronage and clientelism (Arsenijević 2014b: 48).

Second, while for the most part protests constituted a reaction to the worsening social and economic situation, they also allowed for the emergence of new ideas and initiatives offering a more progressive and emancipatory vision of society alternative to the kind of status quo sponsored by peacebuilding agencies. Third, protesters either did not address directly the EU—seen as too distant and aloof—or, when they did, they demanded a EU with different political and social policies. The organization of plenums (akin to town hall meetings or general assemblies) in Croatia and Bosnia-Herzegovina, where citizens could debate any issue of public relevance, has furnished a platform from which to voice such demands, which have been directed primarily at local institutions but have called Europe as well into question. In the Western Balkans, as in many other regions in the Global South targeted by international intervention, these forms of political awakening have contributed to unmask the failings of neoliberal and state-centric political restructuring and its limits in addressing citizens' needs (Mac Ginty and Richmond 2013).

In dissecting these dynamics, this chapter focuses on the case of Bosnia-Herzegovina, which is particularly significant both because Bosnians have long been identified as passive and apathetic and because this country experienced in 2014 the most important social upheaval in the region. The chapter begins with a brief assessment of both the reasons for citizens' dissatisfaction with the peace process and why until the late 2000s public protests have been uncommon. Second, it discusses the February 2014 revolts and their social and political meaning. Finally, the chapter examines the response of international peacebuilding actors who engaged in forms of experimental governance to placate the protests.

8.2   The Roots of Popular Discontent

Although citizens of Bosnia-Herzegovina yearn for 'normal lives' entailing a developmentalist state able to ensure stability and predictability in social protection, they face ambiguity and flexibility (Jansen 2015). Institutions are widely perceived as inefficient, unfair, and unpredictable. The perception of the performance of public institutions and services is below the regional average on all indicators, including transparency, treatment of citizens, time required for getting information and obtaining services, and price of public services (RCC 2016: 105–112). This perception reflects the outcome of the complex, neoliberal redefinition of social protection after the war, which has shifted responsibility for welfare from the state to local level actors, including fourteen Bosnian governments and a countless number of NGOs.

This shift contributed to a pervasive ambiguity with regard to the responsibilities for welfare and pushed citizens to rely increasingly on *štela* (Brković 2015), a culturally embedded practice of having strong relations in society used in many aspects of public life, and involving a broad spectrum of behaviours from small favours to more blatant forms of corruption. Despite the fact that one can use *štela* to acquire possessions he/she is not entitled to, Bosnian citizens have relied on these connections mainly to fill the void that was created by the failure of public institutions' transition to democracy, especially in terms of service provision and employment opportunities. According to a UNDP report, an astounding 95% of over 1600 respondents believe that *štela* is required to access healthcare, education, employment, and documents (UNDP 2009: 75).

Practicing *štela* constitutes the citizens' response to the new neoliberal demands placed on them as a result of state restructuring driven by peacebuilding objectives. *Štela* is almost universally practiced to find employment, if necessary even across ethnic and religious lines (Ramović 2017; RCC 2016: 65). Indeed, the most important factor shaping the likelihood of finding a job is personal connections, followed by political links and bribery (UNRCOiBH 2015: 17). While perceived as necessary from the point of view of Bosnian citizens, in fact this practice reinforces inequalities and limits the possibility of improving the delivery of public services and the efficiency of the job market.

As discussed in Chapter 2, employment in the civil service (administration, education, health) remains largely under the control of nationalist parties and is used as a source of patronage. People employed in the public sector represent 27% of the total number of employed persons in Bosnia-Herzegovina (Papić 2015: 167). Unsurprisingly, political and social actors who benefit the most from the system, including politicians, administrators and service providers, work to maintain the status quo based on personal relationships. At the same time, clients of political parties' patronage networks choose pragmatically to support those leaders who guarantee them access to state jobs and other perks, such as pensions. Patronage helps discipline dissent by making many Bosnians invested in the existing system and discouraging their participation into challenges to it (Murtagh 2016: 160).

In this context dominated by patronage, clientelism and the need for personal connections to access services, trust towards institutions is at a record low. According to the Global States of Mind, published by Gallup in 2014, Bosnian citizens have a very low confidence in their institutions. With 91%, Bosnia-Herzegovina ranks second in the world (in the category of 'partly free countries') in the perception of government corruption. The country's government is the least popular worldwide, with the lowest approval among the general population, with just 8% (Gallup 2014). In addition, almost 9 out of 10 citizens, with no significant variation between different ethnic groups, believe that political elites represent the major problem (UNRCOiBH 2015: 15). The realm of politics and politicians is commonly opposed to the realm of 'ordinary people'. Bosnians maintain a deep scepticism towards the political process, as revealed by the common catchphrase 'politics is a whore' (Helms 2013: Chapter 5). The realm of official politics is thought to involve morally corrupted subjects who abandon personal ethics either out of opportunism or nationalist conviction. As a result, Bosnia-Herzegovina experiences two types of social contract. The first one involves the political-economic elites, and aims at freezing the status quo in order to maintain control over each respective community, i.e. to preserve elites' power and (mis)manage economic resources to the advantage of a relatively small clique of people. A second social contract involves citizens trying to make sense of and manage a social and economic environment heavily disrupted by the war (Belloni and Ramović 2019).

Given the overall modest performance of domestic institutions, combined with the widespread perception of unfairness and inefficiency in the delivery of services, it is puzzling that Bosnian citizens have continued to choose at the polls the same ethno-national political parties which are responsible for the country's mismanagement and failures. As explained in Chapter 3, peacebuilding agencies often lamented how Bosnians have regularly missed the opportunity to choose change, preferring instead to vote for their respective nationalist parties responsible for economic mismanagement and poor governance. As a result, since the beginning of the peace process policy-makers have frequently argued that Bosnians are passive, apathetic, apolitical and not capable of or willing to bring about political, economic and social change (Hulsey 2010). Needless to say, this type of assessment relieved international peacebuilding actors from their own responsibilities and mistakes committed during the endless post-Dayton transition. Above all, this assessment does not take into account three important elements, discussed below: the recent political history of the country, the disempowering role of the international community, as well as the presence of significant agencies and activities concentrated outside of the public sphere.

To begin with, the first experience of mass-scale protests played an important role in depressing public political participation for years to come. A series of demonstrations for peace were held at the time when Yugoslavia started to disintegrate and gathered an unprecedented number of people. The protests culminated on 5 April 1992, when approximately 100,000 people assembled in Sarajevo in front of the Parliament demanding peace. Nationalist snipers fired at protesters from the top floor of the Holiday Inn Hotel, introducing the siege of the city and the tragedy which was to engulf the entire country for three and a half years. This traumatic experience remained in the collective memory as a reminder of the powerlessness of the public vis-à-vis the nationalist agenda of political elites (Spaskokska 2012: 58; see also Bilić 2012). Both the conflict which ensued and the post-conflict years dominated by nationalist politics have served to engrain a mark of deep frustration in the memory of all citizens, and to restrict them to a voting body prey to manipulation by political elites.

Second, strong peacebuilding interventionism focused on partnership with political elites and obstructed citizens' activism. Formal peace negotiations excluded civil society (Belloni 2008), and led to a peace settlement which locked in a structure amenable to the predominance of nationalist political parties. With the basic parameters of the settlement established, the peace process was heavily path dependent and proved difficult to adapt to bottom-up needs and expectations. The manner in which peacebuilding was pursued further contributed to marginalize grassroots' initiatives and inputs. International actors almost exclusively focused on issues relevant for themselves, such as economic and political liberalization, with local voices reduced to artificially created NGOs. Approaches that could lead to long-term solutions and attention for the everyday have been neglected by the international agenda (Richmond 2011: 76). This heavy-handed style achieved some short-term positive results and led key international actors to perceive Bosnia-Herzegovina as a successful case of intervention. However, the resulting reduced role of the international community after 2006 allowed the defects of peacebuilding to surface (Bennet 2016).

Third, the assessment of the Bosnian population as 'apathetic' is based on the assumption that political mobilization happens in public spheres. The social movement literature has been primarily focused on the clearly visible manifestations of grievances and associated protest movements (Della Porta and Diani 2006). The more disguised spheres of social mobilization occurring in contexts where open protest may seem inappropriate or even dangerous have not been adequately accounted for. The public sphere in Bosnia-Herzegovina, with a history of socialism and a risk of censorship, has not always been the primary field of resistance. Indeed, public activity carries risks when directed against structural or governmental power (Richmond 2016: 23). Accordingly, the vocalization of grievances on the part of the population has traditionally not focused on public protest, but has taken on a coded form in alternative circles. As James C. Scott (1990) has masterfully shown, this is not unique to Bosnia-Herzegovina. Even when subordinate groups experience forms of domination including no political and civil rights, they still can create and defend a social space in which offstage dissent to power relations is voiced.

Similarly, in Bosnia-Herzegovina a number of informal or alternative spaces and venues have been in existence for some time. In those arenas, political discourses countering the elites had emerged. These spaces have served as microcosms of protest, but have often been overlooked as bearers of relevant agency. Above all cultural spaces, such as theatres and art galleries, and youth centres are particularly noteworthy. Drawing in particular from Lefebvre's (1991) notion of space, Stefanie Kappler (2014) has documented how local agency has evolved (also) through a withdrawal from the public sphere to avoid state censorship and control. Kappler has shown how these 'spaces of agency' have involved different actors able to express their needs and interests in subtle and even coded manners.

Above all, cultural and youth centres have acted as microcosms of an almost pan-Yugoslav nostalgia (Kappler 2014). The centres have brought together and mobilized young people beyond the nationalist discourses to create the basic stepping stones for cooperation along common interests, whether they be debate, cinema, music, or other activities. This has happened less specifically through political action, but represented an attempt to restore the politically lost freedom through creative activities around the needs of the surrounding community. It is exactly this notion of free thinking and expression without restrictions which has been missing in the political sphere, which has been seen as constrained and lacking trust on the part of the population (Chandler 2006). It was only a matter of time before this kind of hidden political activity would erupt in the public sphere.

8.3   Public Agency and Political Protests

From the mid-2000s onwards *Dosta!* emerged as a citizen movement aimed at encouraging citizens to become involved in social and political life. This group, which drew inspiration from the Serbian student movement *Otpor* which greatly contributed to the fall of President Milosevic in 2000, subscribed to values of solidarity and social justice and aimed at re-politicizing the public sphere. *Dosta!* did not develop a fully fledged political programme but through creative and public actions it aimed at affirming pro-democracy values and mobilizing the public at large (Touquet and Vermeersch 2008).

The background work of cultural and youth centres, as well as of citizens initiatives such as *Dosta!* culminated in public manifestations of discontent with protests erupting in Sarajevo in early 2008. Before this date, a number of small-scale workers' protests were held, but only gradually workers' frustrations merged with the exasperation of the pensioners and the youth—most of whom never even had a chance to find work. These frustrations came to the fore at the beginning of 2008. In February, Sarajevo experienced a wave of juvenile crimes which climaxed in the murder of a 17-year-old boy. Several thousands of Sarajevans took to the streets and demanded the improvement of the security situation. The protestors' complaints quickly evolved to include the incompetence and unwillingness of ruling elites to address issues of importance for the majority of the population, above all the difficult socio-economic situation (Richmond 2011: 77). Although the protests were essentially non-violent, they occasionally escalated and led to the throwing of rocks towards the building of the Canton Sarajevo Government. Protesters demanded the resignation of the Prime minister of the Sarajevo Canton Government and of the Mayor of Sarajevo both of whom denied responsibility and tried to discredit the demonstrators by qualifying them as a 'mob'.

Although these protests achieved little short-term success in changing public policy, they contributed to a subtle shift in popular consciousness. Citizens rediscovered the agency at their disposal, that had previously been suffocated by a Byzantine political system and a sense of powerlessness. They also set a precedent which would be followed by citizens in other parts of the country, as following sections will show. Additionally, the non-ethnic cause behind these protests confirmed that many Bosnians share the same concerns, and that they identified predatory elites and the neoliberal policies of the international community as the main immediate causes of their misfortune, rather than people from a different ethnic group.

The non-ethnic nature of the citizens' movement is perhaps best reflected by the protests that took place in Banja Luka (RS) in 2012 for the preservation of the Picin Park. The defence of public and common goods such as parks (in addition to urban space, public utility infrastructure, and nature) testifies to the presence in the region of a widespread concern involving the commons. The park in Banja Luke was set to be destroyed because one local businessman and close friend to RS President Dodik planned to build a residential and business complex. An informal citizen group called *Park je naš* (The park is ours) organized dozens of protest walks and demonstrations. One of the protesters' routines was to shout *lopovi* (thieves) in front of buildings hosting entity and local level institutions. While the park was eventually destroyed and part of the new building constructed, in June 2014 the businessman who masterminded the construction project was sentenced to 3 years in prison for manipulating the prices of *Medicinska Elektronika* company shares on Banja Luka Stock Exchange (Dragojlović 2015).

Another important wave of protests took place in June 2013 motivated by the widely held frustrations over political deadlock and bureaucratic red tape and their impact on newborns (Mujkić 2015). It focused on personal identification numbers and became known as 'baby revolution' or 'baby-lution'. Newborns were required to have an identification number in order to obtain documents such as birth certificates, medical cards and passports. The Parliamentary Assembly failed to adopt provisions regulating this matter and thus brought issuance of ID numbers to a halt for a few months. Belmina Ibrišević was one of the children who needed a passport to travel outside of Bosnia-Herzegovina to get a medical treatment that her life depended on (Jukić 2013). Political parties saw the issue of identity numbers as a vital national interest which had to be defended by all means, and thus ignored calls to solve the problem. Meanwhile, Berina Hamidović became the first victim of the ID numbers row, dying just before turning three months for lack of appropriate medical care.

On 5 June 2013 around 3000 citizens, many of whom were mothers with their strollers and babies, formed a chain around the Parliament building with the intention of preventing parliamentarians from leaving it until the new law on ID numbers was adopted. This action brought immense public support for the protesters—demonstrating the presence in the country of a non-ethnic solidarity unseen at a similar scale after the conflict (Al Jazeera 2013). High Representative Valentin Inzko, who perceived the protests as a security problem rather than a democratic asset (Wimmen 2019: 22), pressured local politicians to reach a temporary compromise. Even though politicians again tried to defend their actions with reference to national/ethnic causes, they eventually adopted a new version of the Law which enabled the issuance of ID numbers.[1]

The protests which erupted in February 2014 constituted a break from earlier instances of discontent, since they involved an unprecedented number of citizens beyond the capital city, led to the use of violent methods, and articulated radical requests that challenged the core tenets of the status quo endorsed by international actors. When the protests broke out, socio-economic problems had reached worrying levels, with the Labour and Employment Agency of Bosnia-Herzegovina recording an official unemployment rate at 44.1% and the unemployment rate among young people at 62%—the second highest level of youth unemployment in the world.[2] Led by laid-off factory workers, the protests began in Tuzla, where class-based politics is deeply rooted and where multi-ethnicity during and after the war was defended and, to an extent, preserved (Armakolas 2011). Before the war, Tuzla benefited from a thriving industrial sector which, however, was undermined through dubious privatization deals. This resulted in heavy job losses and contributed to high unemployment rates which, together with poor working conditions, motivated the 2014 protests.

The demonstrations were met with a brutal response from the police, provoking public outcry (Busuladžić 2014). The protests did not target any particular political party or politician but expressed the deeper grievances and frustrations against the entire political class. They quickly spread to other major urban centres, including Sarajevo, Mostar, Bihać, Bugojno, Travnik and Goražde. Some governmental buildings were set on fire, including the building of the

Canton Sarajevo Government, but also buildings of canton governments in Zenica, Tuzla, and Mostar. NGOs were barred from meetings to organize the protests (Puljek-Shank and Verkoren 2016). Three days into the protests governments of Zenica-Doboj Canton, Tuzla Canton, and Sarajevo Canton resigned. They were followed by the resignation of the Una-Sana Canton Government a few days later. Overall, the protests signalled that citizens were breaking out of the vicious cycle imposed on them by a political system unresponsive to their demands, which they denounced as a criminal system, and demanded the implementation of a kind of peace in accordance with their needs. Although the RS remained largely protest-free, opinion polls conducted shortly after the first wave of violence indicated the presence of high levels of support in both entities (Kurtović and Hromadžić 2017: 270).

The protests quickly evolved into plenums (informal citizens' councils) established throughout the Federation of Bosnia-Herzegovina. Plenums were *Eulogy for the Mêlée* (Riding 2018), that is, small eulogies for a Bosnia-Herzegovina, or even Yugoslavia, before ethnic cleansing and the peacebuilding process delineated nationalist segregation. Protestors sidelined much of the established civil society sector, described in Chapter 3 as part of the 'first Bosnia', and rather included impoverished workers, pensioners, grassroots activists, artists, students, war veterans, football hooligans and the unemployed—in other words, the so-called 'second Bosnia.' There was no formal leadership, but the organization of plenum activities rested on people who simply showed the best organizing skills and who had ideas on how plenums should be shaped. Plenums, rather than violence, represented the real political innovation during the uprising. The plenums called on the entire population to send in their requests, or to bring them in person to one of the plenum sessions.

Fear constituted the main obstacle in the mobilization of citizens. Citizens feared they would lose their jobs if they became actively involved in activities against authorities. In a country with high unemployment levels and where 56% of those individuals having a job work as public employees, the threat of losing employment proved very effective.[3] Some protesters were exposed to considerable pressure from the authorities, either directly or indirectly through frequent in-depth inspections of their businesses and the related threat to issue financial penalties or even to close their operations.

Plenums' meetings were comprised of two parts. In the first part, every citizen had three minutes to voice his/her concerns and requests. In the second part, the most common requests were discussed, adopted, and sent to various levels and branches of government, demanding their immediate implementation. The most common demands involved corruption issues, welfare and healthcare, transparency, the abolition of salary privileges for public officials and the reversal of privatization (Jansen 2014). Issues related to the vexed question of constitutional reform were evaded in order to avoid opening the Pandora's box of ethno-nationalist claims and counter-claims. Rather, the often-repeated assertion 'we are hungry in three languages' aimed at undermining ethno-national divisions and the ethno-territorial logic of the peacebuilding process and, through the subversive use of ethno-national categories, aimed at ridiculing dominant political and social frames. The use of humour and mocking differentiated the protests from standard NGO practice in the Western Balkans. Eventually, requests of all plenums were merged and submitted to the Government of the Federation.[4]

Framed as a space of 'unbribable politics' (Arsenijević 2014a) plenum participants quite explicitly refused the type of clientelistic relationships that have characterized Bosnian society throughout the endless peace-building transition (Milan 2018: 835). At the same time, with their demands to the authorities the plenums reduced the horizontal politics which characterized the protests, and involved a diversity of voices, to a relatively small number of requests. In other words, as experiments with direct democracy proceeded apace, the movement no longer appeared as radically different from established political practices but, paradoxically, it emerged as almost an another political party, or layer of governance (Riding 2018).

Established NGOs failed to offer support to plenums or to even sympathize with their cause. Similarly the media, which after the war was heavily supported by the international community, played a negative role during protests and plenums. There were very few media outlets which provided accurate reports of the evolving situation. To make things even worse, much of the media served the political elites to spin the protests towards their agenda. RS media accused protestors of being 'politically motivated' and even published stories on the alleged, and unfounded, arming of demonstrators, with the aim of preparing an attack on the Serb controlled part of the country. In the Federation the media reported on members of the main ruling Bosniak party accusing demonstrators of being 'hooligans' bent on creating chaos. Social Democratic Party leader and Foreign Minister Zlatko Lagumdžija even described the protests as an 'attempted coup d'etat'. In a particularly hideous instance, the media related President Izetbegović's unverified claim that 12 kilograms of drugs were found during the protests, only to clarify later that the drugs were actually seized by the police in an unrelated operation.

Additionally, some political parties tried to hijack plenums and protests in order to present themselves as the new emerging subject which could replace the old, corrupt one. Members of political parties infiltrated plenums either to make sure that they could be seen as leaders of changes or to undermine them. The pressure from political parties was also manifested in the fact that some participants of plenums were coerced into abandoning them. The attempt to undermine plenums, along with the media tirade, showed how big the stakes were for political elites, and how much they felt threatened by citizens' actions.

Because of a combination of media and police pressure, the anti-government momentum was difficult to maintain. In addition, devastating floods in May 2014 prompted plenums' members to direct their energies towards organizing volunteer activities. As a result, after a few months protests began to fizzle out. In its relatively brief life span, the protest movement stimulated political imagination and participation, and alimented the possibility of a long-term shift in civic consciousness (Murtagh 2016). If the economy continues to stagnate and the resources at the disposal of the political leadership diminish, social peace through patronage may be increasingly difficult to secure, and violent protests could become a feature of Bosnian politics.

Overall, the February 2014 events demonstrated the growing re-politicization of the public sphere. Apart from the immediate results evident in governments' resignations, protests provided a clear warning for political elites. They showed that public opinion matters much more than it did before 2008, when protests in Bosnia-Herzegovina had (re) surfaced in the public realm. Plenums provided a venue for citizens to voice their concerns and a medium through which they could take their concerns to appropriate institutions. In addition plenums, which were met with approval throughout the country, affirmed the importance of non-ethnic concerns among the population. As a whole, the heterogeneous group of the protesters and their supporters demanded nothing less than a new way of doing politics based on a shared concern and responsibility for the 'commons' and attention to socio-economic problems (Arsenijević 2014b). In this sense, protests signalled the emergence of a new kind of 'prefigurative politics' attempting to delineate and actualize alternative forms of political practices and sociability (Kurtović and Hromadžić 2017). While it remains to be seen whether economic malaise will strengthen working-class solidarity or will be absorbed by ethno-national dynamics, the February 2014 protests alimented a newly found sense that 'change' might be difficult, painful, and slow to come, but is possible.

8.4   Experimentalist Governance at Work

Faced with an unprecedented challenge to the impact of their policies, international actors were unable to address the rising tide of malcontent. Because the EU selects partners on the basis of their ability to engage in policy dialogues and/or advocacy with local governments, it has always found it problematic to interact with alternative, less structured forms of engagement (Kappler 2014: 126). High Representative of the International Community Valentin Inzko expressed well the discomfort common among international officials about the violent February 2014 protests when he suggested that, should the situation escalate, it might be necessary to send EU-troops to pacify trouble areas (Radio Free Europe 2014). His initial reaction was soon qualified in favour of citizens' right to protest peacefully, but nonetheless the reference to armed intervention revealed a profound confusion about the nature of the protests and how to address citizens' demands. Furthermore, in commenting on the revolts Inzko added how 'Muslims' were primarily involved. By so doing, Inzko involuntarily validated Bosnian leaders' self-serving claim that the protests should have been understood as an ethnic problem caused by 'hooligans' on the orders of other ethnic groups, and not as a social and economic one motivated by corruption and misrule. Unsurprisingly, emboldened by the international response, Bosnian authorities spent 23 million KM (approximately 12 million Euro) on crowd control equipment (Mujanović 2018: 154–155).

Confronted with mounting criticism about his inability to interpret and act upon the situation, Inzko rectified his views claiming that 'protests are not about who is a Bosniak, Croat, a Serb or an Other... [they are] about jobs and a normal, dignified life for all' (Selimbegović 2014). While this correction belatedly stated the obvious, it did little to restore legitimacy for international officials, who are widely perceived as being either complicit with ethno-nationalists, or aloof and unable to address citizens' needs and demands.[5] This episode confirmed the international community's inability, which characterized international actors' approach since the early 1990s, to recognize and support non-nationalist views. In order to undermine the political-economic system based on networks of patronage, international intervention 'ought to aim at stimulating the political agency of citizens and favouring the coordination of their political action' (Capussela 2015: 30). By contrast, for more than two decades, international civil servants and diplomats have focused their analysis of and approach to intervention relying on ethnic and national categories (Campbell 1998), and thus depressed civic notions of identity and citizenship.

Inzko's views highlighted two long-lasting, and problematic, priorities among international officials in their dealings with Bosnia-Herzegovina. First, peacebuilders have placed ethnic security at the top of their post-Dayton priorities—thus marginalizing other concerns and values, including justice, economic and social rights and, above all, the promotion of non-nationalist politics. No doubt, this prioritization has been largely due to the horrors of the 1990s war, and the related concern to avoid a relapse into conflict. At the same time, however, western anxieties about violence reflect a deeply ingrained orientalist or, to cite Maria Todorova, balkanist orientation towards the region (Todorova 1997). This orientation plays into the hands of ethno-nationalist leaders who have been simultaneously working to preserve ethnic divisions while presenting themselves as the solution to the problems they contribute to create. In suggesting the possibility that the EU could intervene to re-establish order and security, Inzko inevitably sided with the supporters of the status quo, that is, the very same nationalist elites Bosnian citizens have been protesting against.

Second, and consequently, by accepting and accommodating distinct ethnic identities the international community has primarily focused on stability instead of change (Cooley 2019). Although international officials have frequently called upon Bosnian citizens to 'make change happen' by rejecting nationalist programmes and worldviews at the polls (and, by extension, in every political, economic and social sphere) they have nonetheless been the staunchest guarantors of the nationalist ethnic (dis)order that emerged at Dayton. Not only have they stood behind the unresponsive, fragmented, and ethnically based constitutional framework drafted by international lawyers but also, as argued in Chapter 3, they have contributed to the consolidation of nationalist power and to the entrenchment of corruption and patronage by turning a blind eye to the misuse of international aid and resources.

As a result of this simultaneous, paradoxical role of both critics of ethno-nationalism and supporters of those structures and practices feeding ethno-nationalist politics, international peacebuilders have failed to listen and relate to Bosnian citizens. They have blamed citizens for not abandoning their nationalist leaders altogether—thus not recognizing that support for ethno-nationalist parties has been a rational response to both a condition of fragmentation and fear and the presence of forms of patronage (Hulsey 2010). Perhaps most importantly, when Bosnians have expressed clear non-nationalist views and demands, as with the February 2014 protests and in a variety of other instances described above, they have either ignored those demands or interpreted them as a threat to stability, rather than an opportunity for progressive change.

More broadly, the February 2014 protests revealed the bankruptcy of the international peacebuilding strategy based on an economic and political liberalization formula. To begin with, neoliberal economic restructuring did not lead to clear improvements in living standards for ordinary people. As mentioned, the difficult socio-economic situation affects in particular the youth, which endures the highest rate of unemployment in Europe (62.7%). In addition, Bosnia-Herzegovina holds the second highest rate of overall unemployment on the continent; the lowest ranking among European countries on the World Bank's Ease of Doing Business Indicators, and one of the lowest rankings in the Corruption Perceptions Index (Delegation of the European Union to Bosnia and Herzegovina 2015a).

The neoliberal reformist zeal in the political-institutional arena was similarly disappointing. During the first intervention phase, described in earlier chapters as the 'rise of peacebuilding', international officials engaged in assertive intervention imposing legislation, removing obstructionist elected officials and building the state bureaucratic apparatus. While this bold, forceful style achieved undeniable short-term positive results, it had a limited effect on both underlying power structures and citizens' daily struggle to make ends meet. Bosnians seemed to have barely noticed international efforts. Significantly, the early 2014 protests and plenums did not even address any of their demands to international institutions. While the protesters' choice to focus their attention on local authorities undoubtedly reflects a negative assessment of the work of international organizations, it also confirmed an engrained attitude deriving from Bosnians' long coexistence with foreign rule. While formally ruled by others, Bosnians of all faiths have generally been self-governing in day-to-day affairs. According to historian Emily Greble, while not displaying particular forms of insolence or disrespect, 'Sarajevans' customary response to foreign rulers [was] ignoring them' (Greble 2011: 63). Given this type of response, it is unsurprising that the international imposition of a variety of measures left most citizens fairly indifferent. As Oliver Richmond (2016: 16) confirms, 'the subaltern is practiced in evading top-down power'.

The internationally perceived need to reach out to wider sectors of the population in order to favour domestic legitimacy of internationally sponsored institutions has led to a change of strategy. As elaborated in Chapter 5, since the early 2000s, when the EU emphatically promised that the future of the region, including that of Bosnia-Herzegovina, lies in its progressive integration into European institutions, international officials laboured to support domestic change without imposing it. Despite its persisting orientalist underpinnings reflected in the need of continuing external assistance and guidance embedded in the process (Petrović 2011), Europeanization was expected to lead to the (more or less) voluntary adoption of liberal-democratic reforms by local elites without blatant top-down impositions by international officials. The EU's accommodating stance resulted into a power-vacuum and rule-free environment that gave uncompromising Bosnian politicians leverage to pursue their status quo agenda, and at the same time laid bare the weaknesses of the peace process (Weber and Bassuener 2014).

From 2006 onwards peacebuilders repeatedly asserted their willingness to accept any political compromise domestic leaders could agree on, in particular with regard to the implementation of the 2009 European

Court of Human Rights' Sejdić-Finci ruling. With this decision, the Court had condemned Bosnia-Herzegovina for the discriminatory practice whereby citizens not declaring themselves as belonging to one of the three Constituent Peoples are prevented from running for the Presidency and/or the House of Peoples. Because the ruling addressed the fundamental power-sharing structure that allowed ethno-nationalist parties and their clique to maintain power, it found a hostile domestic reception (Perry 2015).

Against the EU's expectations, the lure of getting closer to Europe has not convinced Bosnian elites of the need to abandon the most debatable ethnic-guarantees, frequently turned into privileges for personal gain, and to reform their Byzantine, rights-violating constitution. In February 2014, as protests were breaking out, the EU Commissioner for Enlargement, Stefan Füle, held unproductive meetings with party leaders in Sarajevo, but ignored the citizen plenums, only to announce a few days later that negotiations to amend the constitution in line with the Sejdić-Finci ruling failed (Jukić 2014; Cooley 2019: 73). This fiasco was only the last one in a series of international attempts to achieve the modification of the Bosnian Constitution. As a whole, neoliberal institution building has not led to the creation of an accountable state responsive to citizens' needs, but has played into the hands of predatory Bosnian elites. As a participant in the 2014 protests put it, 'the so-called post-socialist transition to liberal democracy has been experienced as a never-ending story of looting' (Husarić 2014: 67) within which ordinary citizens are stuck between a traumatic violent past and a future which still has to start. It is hardly surprising that this state of affairs has provoked strong criticism towards international organizations and officials—in particular towards the EU. In addition to accusing domestic political elites of corruption and incompetence, protesters have also criticized the type of neoliberal reforms brought to Bosnia-Herzegovina via international tutelage. Protestors' complaints have expressed a frustration about the EU's inability to address a painful and rapidly growing set of socio-economic problems.

In response to the February 2014 uprising, and the criticism it provoked towards international officials, peacebuilders led by the EU tried again to put Bosnia-Herzegovina on a reform course, while attempting to reach out to the most marginalized segments of the population. In July 2014, the EU Special Representative and his international partners (such as the IMF) launched a socio-economic reform programme, the Compact for Growth and Jobs, which proposed a reform agenda aimed at spurring investment, accelerating job creation, encouraging the fight against corruption, and achieving greater levels of social protection (European Union 2014). In November, the German and British foreign ministers presented an initiative aimed at supporting the political process and revitalizing Bosnia-Herzegovina's European accession path. The German–British Initiative proposed the 're-sequencing' of EU conditionality by recommending to delay implementation of the Sejdić-Finci ruling, which was previously considered as a precondition for entry into force of the SAA signed in 2008 but kept on hold. In this way, the EU backtracked from its own conditions, abandoning the constitutional reform agenda in favour of apparently more realistic socio-economic reforms. This new approach resulted from the failures of the enlargement perspective and the subsequent dynamics of experimentalist governance which put priority on socio-economic reforms. In practice, the German-British initiative both muddied international failures and rewarded established political parties keen to claim progress towards EU accession (Puljek-Shank and Fritsch 2018: 15).

By subscribing to the 'Reform Agenda for Bosnia-Herzegovina 2015 – 2018' (Delegation of the European Union to Bosnia-Herzegovina and Herzegovina 2015b), in early 2015 the government in Sarajevo committed itself to undertake economic and social reforms, and adopted the so-called 'coordination mechanism' aimed at streamlining the country's complex governance structure and allowing it to 'speak with a single voice'. In June of the same year, the European Council adopted the Decision for the SAA to enter into force, opening the door for Bosnia-Herzegovina's EU membership application in February 2016, which was accepted in September of the same year (European Council 2016).

Overall, the peacebuilders' new approach remained surrounded by widespread scepticism.[6] Despite the apparent progress, doubts persisted about both the EU and domestic institutions' commitment and clarity of purpose. The steps that preceded Bosnia-Herzegovina's EU application were not encouraging. For example, the Council of Ministers adopted the 'coordination mechanism' during a ministerial session held in secrecy, and lacking any official record. Meanwhile, millions of dollars of international aid allocated for the reconstruction following the devastating floods in 2014 were unaccounted for. And, finally, the new Labour Law adopted by Bosnian authorities as part of the internationally sponsored reform agenda prompted a thousand workers to protest outside the Parliament building (Mujanović 2018). The fact that Bosnia-Herzegovina's economy is unable to provide jobs and remains export-oriented and anchored to the control of wages and the reduction of consumers' purchasing power remains a problem for citizens (Radovanović 2015). The Compact for Growth and Jobs, with its call for 'short-term sacrifices… in pursuit of medium-term growth and jobs' appears hollow to the many citizens who lost social security and safety net in the long post-war transition.

More generally, scepticism towards international initiatives is rooted in years of failed reform attempts. Peacebuilders have long claimed their resoluteness in advancing an economic agenda able to overcome obstacles to growth and employment, but to no avail. Just to mention the most well-known instances, in 2002 five international agencies (IMF, World Bank, USAID, EU, OHR) initiated the Bulldozer Process aimed at bulldozing barriers to growth in all sectors of the economy through concrete legislative changes. The Poverty Reduction Strategy Program, supported by the World Bank and IMF from 2004 to 2007, put forward several macroeconomic reforms in numerous sectors (health, agriculture, social protection and so on), which were agreed upon by local governments. However, the dire state of the Bosnian economy testifies to the limited impact of these and other comparable initiatives. Predictably, plenum members advised international actors to stop 'interfering' with Bosnian politics (Kurtović 2014).

Similarly, the EU has long attempted to use conditionality in order to push the domestic reform agenda. When conditions proved unattainable, the EU set aside conditions while paradoxically claiming a policy victory. Despite the EU officials' claim to the contrary, the re-sequencing of EU conditionality adopted in the aftermath of the February 2014 uprising continues with the previous policy of flexibility in the application of conditions. It confirmed the principle that policy making is supposed to be conducted together with local elites, and not against them.[7] Accordingly, those issues threatening to domestic leaders were further downgraded in the list of reform priorities.

8.5   Conclusions

In sum, the modest efficiency in the delivery of services and the dire state of the economy have contributed to the disillusionment among Bosnians in relation to the seemingly endless post-war transition, which is experienced as a 'desert' (Horvat and Štiks 2015), an 'empty' political space (Hromadžić 2015), or even a 'swamp' full of crocodiles where the threat of sinking is ever-present (Jansen et al. 2017). Unsurprisingly, opinion polls find that 50% of Bosnians would consider living and working abroad—the highest percentage in the region (RCC 2016: 116). Citizens are so hapless that they either rely on clientelistic relations or have given up on asking even basic services from their government. In one reading of the situation, the vertical social contract is described as 'non-existent' (Hemon 2014: 54). Bosnians are so disillusioned that the majority (57% of them—once again the highest percentage in the region) do not even discuss government decisions anymore (RCC 2016: 116). In addition, citizens include the international community, together with local authorities and politicians, as most accountable for this state of affairs (UNRCOiBH 2015: 20). Increasingly, pro-democracy movements in Bosnia-Herzegovina as in the rest of the region see the EU as an impediment to democratization.

Faced with continuing socio-economic crisis and an unresponsive political system, citizens' re-politicization initially developed out of public view and, in Bosnia-Herzegovina as in the rest of the region, it attempted to reclaim the commons, including the parks, the museums, and above all the factories, which the post-war transition has alienated from them. The February 2014 protests and the related establishment of plenums across the country testified to the presence of growing socio-economic grievances in the country, as well as the desire to articulate and implement political forms of engagement alternative to the Dayton peacebuilding framework. In addition, they expressed the condemnation of the internationally led (neo)liberal focus on building democratic institutions and supporting a democratization and liberalization process which has not led to the creation of a responsive and accountable state. Indeed, liberal peacebuilding has neither made institutions responsive to citizens' needs, nor has it restrained Bosnian elites from their clientelistic, predatory, and ultimately self-serving approach at state-building. The 2015 Compact for Growth testifies to the fact that the EU does not have a grand strategy of intervention, but it adapts to changing circumstances. Not only reform attempts have hit the wall of domestic elites' resistance, but also they have remained framed within a problem-solving framework which does not challenge the structural limitations of governance. Despite its reformist ethos, liberal peacebuilding has remained focused on 'stability', as discussed in the next, concluding chapter.

NOTES

1. Unfortunately, it was too late for Belmina Ibrišević, who died in October, 2013 in a hospital in Germany.
2. In 2018 Bosnia-Herzegovina actually reached the first position. See World Bank/ILO compiled data 'Unemployment, Youth Total', available at: https://data.worldbank.org/indicator/SL.UEM.1524.ZS.
3. Interview with Renzo Daviddi, Deputy Head of the EU Delegation to Bosnia-Herzegovina, Sarajevo, July 2015.
4. The blog 'Bosnia-Herzegovina-Herzegovina Protest Files' (https://bhprotestfiles.wordpress.com) collected and translated into English the documents produced by the plenums between February–May 2014; https://www.transparency.org/news/feature/corruption_perceptions_index_2017.
5. A member of the Sarajevo Plenum asserted that the EU is guilty of 'not allowing Bosnia-Herzegovina to collapse on itself.' For him, expressing a sense of frustration shared by many plenums' members, 'reform is impossible'. Confidential interview, Sarajevo, July 2015.
6. For example, Srdjan Blagovcanin, Director of the BiH Transparency International described the German-British Initiative as 'good only for an op-ed on the local newspaper'. Interview, Sarajevo, July 2015. See also, IFIMES (2015).
7. Interview with Kurt Bassuener, Democratization Policy Council, Sarajevo, July 2015.

REFERENCES

Al Jazeera. (2013, June 11). *Thousands protest over Bosnia-Herzegovina baby ID row.*

Armakolas, I. (2011). The 'Paradox' of Tuzla city: Explaining non-nationalist local politics during the Bosniaan War. *Europe-Asia Studies, 63*(2), 229–261.

Arsenijević, D. (Ed.). (2014a). *Unbribable Bosnia and Herzegovina: The fight for the commons.* Baden-Baden: Nomos.

Arsenijević, D. (2014b). Protests and plenums: The Struggle for the commons. In D. Arsenijević (Ed.), *Unbribable Bosnia and Herzegovina: The fight for the commons* (pp. 45–50). Nomos: Baden-Baden.

Belloni, R. (2008). Civil society in war-to-democracy transitions. In A. K. Jarstad & T. D. Sisk (Eds.), *From war to democracy: Dilemmas of peacebuilding* (pp. 182–210). Cambridge: Cambridge University Press.

Belloni, R., & Ramović, J. (2019, forthcoming). Elites and everyday social contracts in Bosnia and Herzegovina: Pathways to forging a national social contract? *Journal of Intervention and Statebuilding.*

Bennet, C. (2016). *Bosnia's paralysed peace*. London: Hurst & CO.

Bieber, F., & Brentin, D. (Eds.). (2019). *Social movements in the Balkans: Rebellion and protest from Maribor to Taksim*. London and New York: Routledge.

Bilić, B. (2012). *We were gasping for air*. Baden-Baden: Nomos.

Brković, Č. (2015). Management of ambiguity: Favours and flexiblity in Bosnia and Herzegovina. *Social Anthropology, 23*(3), 268–282.

Busuladžić, E. (2014). Why? In D. Arsenijević (Ed.), *Unbribable Bosnia and Herzegovina: The fight for the commons* (pp. 11–26). Baden-Baden: Nomos.

Campbell, D. (1998). *National deconstruction: Violence, identity and justice in Bosnia-Herzegovina*. Minneapolis: University of Minnesota Press.

Capussela, A. L. (2015). *State-building in Kosovo: Democracy, corruption and the EU in the Balkans*. London and New York: I. B. Tauris.

Chandler, D. (2006). From Dayton to Europe. In D. Chandler (Ed.), *Peace without politics? Ten years of international state-building in Bosnia-Herzegovina* (pp. 30–43). London and New York: Routledge.

Cooley, L. (2019). *The European Union's approach to conflict resolution: Transformation or regulation in the Western Balkans?* London and New York: Routledge.

Delegation of the European Union to Bosnia and Herzegovina. (2015a). *Compact for growth and jobs—Youth unemployment and perspectives in Bosnia-Herzegovina*. Sarajevo.

Delegation of the European Union to Bosnia-Herzegovina and Herzegovina. (2015b). *Reform agenda for Bosnia and Herzegovina 2015–2018*. Sarajevo.

Della Porta, D., & Diani, M. (2006). *Social movements: An introduction*. Oxford: Blackwell.

Dragojlović, M. (2015, November 18). Mile Radisić willingly surrendered himself to serve his sentence. *Independent Balkan News Agency*.

European Council. (2016). *Council conclusions on the application of Bosnia and Herzegovina for membership of the EU*. Press Release, 525/16, 20/09/2016.

European Union. (2014). *Compact for growth and jobs: Brochure*. Sarajevo: European Union.

Gallup. (2014, October). *Global states of mind* (Resource document). www.gallup.com. Accessed 5 December 2016.

Greble, E. (2011). *Sarajevo, 1941–1945: Muslims, Christians and Jews in Hitler's Europe*. Ithaca and New York: Cornell University Press.

Helms, E. (2013). *Innocence and victimhood: Gender, nation and women's activism in post-war Bosnia and Herzegovina*. Madison: The University of Wisconsin Press.

Hemon, A. (2014). Beyond the hopelessness of survival. In D. Arsenijević (Ed.), *Unbribable Bosnia-Herzegovina* (pp. 59–64). Baden-Baden: Nomos.

Horvat, S., & Štiks, I. (Eds.). (2015). *Welcome to the desert of post-socialism: Radical politics after Yugoslavia*. London: Verso.

Hromadžić, A. (2015). *Citizens of an empty nation: Youth and statemaking in post-war Bosnia-Herzegovina*. Philadelphia: University of Pennsylvania Press.

Hulsey, J. W. (2010). 'Why did they vote for those guys again?' Challenges and contradictions in the promotion of political moderation in post-war Bosnia and Herzegovina. *Democratization, 17*(6), 1132–1152.

Husarić, H. (2014). February awakening: Breaking with the political legacy of the last 20 Years. In D. Arsenijević (Ed.), *Unbribable Bosnia and Herzegovina: The fight for the commons* (pp. 65–70). Baden-Baden: Nomos.

Jansen, S. (2014, February 13). *Can the revolt in Bosnia and Herzegovina send a message to the wider world?* Balkan Insight.

Jansen, S. (2015). *Yearnings in the meantime: 'Normal lives' and the state in a Sarajevo apartment complex.* New York: Berghahn Books.

Jansen, S., Brković, Č., & Čelebičić, V. (Eds.). (2017). *Negotiating social relations in Bosnia and Herzegovina: Semiperipheral entanglements.* Abingdon: Routledge.

Jukić, E. M. (2013, June 5). *Bosnia-Herzegovina's feuding leaders give ground on ID row.* Balkan Insight.

Jukić, E. M. (2014, February 18). *Füle Blames Bosnian leaders for rights logjam.* Balkan Insight. http://www.balkaninsight.com/en/article/no-results-in-rights-ruling-meeting-in-sarajevo.

Kappler, S. (2014). *Local agency and peacebuilding: EU and international engagement in Bosnia-Herzegovina, Cyprus and South Africa.* Houndmills: Palgrave.

Kurtović, L. (2014). The strange life and death of democracy promotion in Bosnia and Herzegovina. In D. Arsenijević (Ed.), *Unbribable Bosnia and Herzegovina: The fight for the commons* (pp. 97–102). Baden-Baden: Nomos.

Kurtović, L., & Hromadžić, A. (2017). Cannibal states, empty bellies: Protests, history and political imagination in post-Dayton Bosnia-Herzegovina. *Critique of Anthropology, 37*(3), 262–296.

Lefebvre, H. (1991). *The production of space.* Oxford: Blackwell.

Mac Ginty, R., & Richmond, O. P. (2013). The local turn in peacebuilding: A critical agenda for peace. *Third World Quarterly, 34*(5), 763–783.

Milan, C. (2018). Rising against the thieves: Anti-corruption campaigns in South-Eastern Europe. *Partecipazione e Conflitto, 10*(3), 826–849.

Moraca, T. (2016, August). *Between defiance and compliance: A new civil society in the post-Yugoslav space?* (Occasional Paper). Rovereto: Osservatorio Balcani e Caucaso.

Mujanović, J. (2018). *Hunger and fury: The crisis of democracy in the Balkans.* London: Hurst & Co.

Mujkić, A. (2015). In search of a democratic counter-power in Bosnia-Herzegovina. *Southeast European and Black Sea Studies, 15*(4), 623–638.

Murtagh, C. (2016). Civic mobilization in divided societies and the perils of political engagement. *Nationalism and Ethnic Politics, 22*(2), 149–171.

Papić, Ž. (2015). Consensus on the common good. In A. Kapetanović & J. Illerhues (Eds.), *The legacy of peace: Bosnia and Herzegovina 20 years after the Dayton peace accords* (pp. 161–180). Sarajevo: Friedrich Ebert-Stiftung.

Perry, V. (2015). Constitutional reform in Bosnia and Herzegovina: Does the road to confederation go through the EU? *International Peacekeeping, 22*(5), 490–510.

Petrović, T. (2011, September). Thinking Europe without thinking: Neocolonial discourse on and in the Western Balkans (Resource document). *Eurozine*. http://www.eurozine.com/articles/2011-09-22-petrovic-en.html. Accessed 5 December 2016.

Puljek-Shank, R., & Fritsch, F. (2018). Activism in Bosnia-Herzegovina: Struggles against dual hegemony and the emergence of 'local first'. *East European Politics and Societies, 20*(10), 1–22.

Puljek-Shank, R., & Verkoren, W. (2016). Civil society in a divided society: Linking legitimacy and ethnicness of civil society organizations in Bosnia-Herzegovina. *Cooperation and Conflict, 52*(2), 184–202.

Radio Free Europe. (2014, October 16). *Putin vows to support Serbia on Kosovo.*

Radovanović, M. (2015). Bosnia and Herzegovina's quantitative easing. In A. Kapetanović & J. Illerhues (Eds.), *The legacy of peace: Bosnia and Herzegovina 20 years after the Dayton peace accords* (pp. 143–160). Sarajevo: Friedrich Ebert Stiftung.

Ramović, J. (2017, April). *Maximum profit, minimal peace: Insights into the peacebuilding potential of peace.* Unpublished Ph.D. Thesis, University of Manchester.

Razsa, M. (2015). *Bastards of utopia: Living radical politics after socialism.* Bloomington and Indianapolis: Indiana University Press.

RCC (Regional Cooperation Council). (2016). *Balkan barometer 2016.* Sarajevo: RCC Secretariat.

Richmond, O. P. (2011). *A post-liberal peace.* New York: Routledge.

Richmond, O. P. (2016). *Peace formation and political order in conflict affected societies.* Oxford: Oxford University Press.

Riding, J. (2018). A new regional geography of a revolution: Bosnia-Herzegovina's plenum movement. *Territory, Politics, Governance, 6*(1), 16–41.

Scott, J. C. (1990). *Domination and the arts of resistance: Hidden transcripts.* New Haven and London: Yale University Press.

Selimbegović, V. (2014, February 16). Interview with HR Valentin Inzko. *Oslobođenje.* http://www.ohr.int/ohr-dept/presso/pressi/default.asp?content_id=48419.

Spaskokska, L. (2012). Landscapes of resistance, hope, and loss: Yugoslav supra-nationalism and anti-nationalism. In B. Bilić & V. Jankovic (Eds.), *Resisting the evil: (Post-)Yugoslav anti-war contention* (pp. 37–61). Baden-Baden: Nomos.

Todorova, M. (1997). *Imagining the Balkans.* Oxford: Oxford University Press.

Touquet, H., & Vermeersch, P. (2008). Bosnia and Herzegovina: Thinking beyond institution building. *Nationalism & Ethnic Politics, 14*(2), 266–288.

UNDP (United Nations Development Programme). (2009). *The ties that bind: Social capital in Bosnia-Herzegovina*. Sarajevo: UNDP.

UNRCOiBH (United Nations Resident Coordinator's Office in Bosnia-Herzegovina and Herzegovina). (2015). *Public opinion poll results*. Sarajevo.

Visoka, G. (2017). *Shaping peace in Kosovo: The politics of peacebuilding and statehood*. Houndmills: Palgrave.

Weber, B., & Bassuener, K. (2014). *EU policies boomerang: Bosnia and Herzegovina's social unrest*. Sarajevo and Berlin: Democratization Policy Council, Policy Brief.

Wimmen, H. (2019). Divided they stand: Peace building, state reconstruction and informal political movements in Bosnia-Herzegovina, 2005–2013. In F. Bieber & D. Brentin (Eds.), *Social movements in the Balkans: Rebellion and protest from Maribor and Taksim* (pp. 9–29). London and New York: Routledge.

CHAPTER 9

Conclusions

9.1　Peacebuilding and Its Discontents

More than two decades of post-war international intervention in the
Balkans revealed the difficulties with the implementation of the main
objectives of the liberal peacebuilding agenda, which included the development of legitimate domestic institutions, the support to civic coexistence, and the creation of a market economy. International actors' social
engineering-type understanding of domestic processes collided with
empirical realities such as the influence of hard-nosed domestic leaders,
inefficient bureaucracies, and difficult socio-economic conditions. This
domestic context has frequently led commentators to argue that peacebuilders' efforts to support the conditions for self-sustaining peace are
undercut by the nonliberal agents and conditions that generate and
sustain state weakness in the region, and more generally outside of the
western liberal core (e.g. Paris 2004, 2010). Accordingly, the crisis of the
liberal peace has been widely understood as nonliberal and illiberal resistance to the imposed emergence of liberal order and rule.

However, this crisis cannot be simply located in post-conflict spaces.
Peacebuilding intervention in the Western Balkans demonstrated how
the liberal/illiberal divide, discussed in Chapter 1, is rather simplistic,
for at least two reasons. First, the international cannot be associated with
liberalism and the local with traditionalism and conservative values. Not
only do both international and local actors alike include a wide range

© The Author(s) 2020
R. Belloni, *The Rise and Fall of Peacebuilding
in the Balkans*, Rethinking Peace and Conflict Studies,
https://doi.org/10.1007/978-3-030-14424-1_9

of agents with often conflicting interests, values, and priorities, but also none of these actors can be considered as a beacon of liberal aspirations. Second, peacebuilding develops in a context where power and authority are not exercised exclusively, or even predominantly, within formal democratic institutions. Thus, the formal authority spheres are not the only loci, and sometimes not even the most important ones, where political and social processes develop.

Because of widespread disappointment with the outcome of intervention, both the means and the ends of the peacebuilding framework have been increasingly called into question. With regard to the means, the experience in the region has highlighted the persistence of a long-standing dilemma in liberal theory and practice between restraint and imposition. As Sørensen (2011: 58) has noted, 'on the one hand, a strict Liberalism of Restraint may help very little in promoting western freedom because it respects the principles of sovereignty and non-intervention in nonliberal states. A vigorous Liberalism of Imposition, on the other hand, risks undermining what it seeks to achieve, because it invokes a liberal imperialism that removes the local responsibility that is the very condition of freedom'.

The choice between imposition and restraint ultimately involves different conceptions of how peace can be best consolidated. Supporters of a Liberalism of Imposition adopt a linear understanding of political, economic, and social processes based on the idea that war affected states can be transformed through well-sequenced policies (i.e. Paris 2004). In the Western Balkans this understanding led to a rather simplistic notion of how imported institutions, norms, and policies impact domestic realities. It translated into an initially assertive imposition of exogenous policies which led to some progress in (re)creating the conditions for peaceful coexistence but, as even backers of liberal peacebuilding would concede, with considerable costs. Not only did such an approach allow for the irresponsibility of domestic elites who could free ride on international initiatives, as noted by Sørensen above, but it also violated liberal norms involving autonomy and self-determination.

Faced with scathing criticism for the use of supposedly unsustainable illiberal methods, the international community declared the conclusion of the rising phase of peacebuilding, to be replaced with a novel approach focused on the importance of domestic ownership as a tool to create legitimate and accountable institutions. In this new phase, the EU became the most important peacebuilding actor in the region, where it deployed both its celebrated 'power of attraction' and the conditionalities related to the accession process, without blatantly imposing reform packages and policies on recalcitrant domestic officials. However, the EU's dismissal of colonial-style prerogatives in the name of a Liberalism of Restraint revealed the persistent influence of uncompromising local actors. Peacebuilding became increasingly highjacked by local gate-keepers bent on continuing the exploitation of economic and political opportunities afforded to them by permissive neo-liberal economic policies. Even though several of the reforms required to join the EU were adopted, they achieved mostly superficial changes that did not impact either the deeper societal structures or the domestic elites' power base.

As a result, increasingly since the early 2010s, citizens in the region have contested what they see as a political-economic system dominated by patronage, lack of transparency and inefficiency. Corruption became a sort of catch-all target of public disdain used to condemn the broader shortcomings of liberal peacebuilding. While corrupt practices have been widely known since the beginning of the peacebuilding process, and officially censured, they have proved resilient to judicial prosecution and governance reforms. The resulting citizen cynicism has not prevented the emergence of social movements demanding greater opportunities for political participation and attention to socio-economic issues. In particular, citizens have contested what they perceive to be unrepresentative leaders bent on plundering state assets and exploiting the commons, and put forward demands which testified to the desire to establish forms of social democracy. Their grievances called into question not only corrupt domestic leaders, but also international peacebuilding agencies, seen as distant and aloof, and ultimately responsible for setting the parameters of public policy.

Few of these citizen requests regarding the implementation of the liberal peacebuilding agenda have been adequately addressed. As explained in Chapter 1, the liberal peacebuilding framework functions according to an experimentalist logic that typically allows for only marginal operational changes. Sabel and Zeitlin have described experimentalist governance as a 'recursive process of provisional goal-setting and revision based on learning from the comparison of alternative approaches to advancing them in different contexts' (Sabel and Zeitlin 2012: 1). This process involves the setting of broad frameworks and joint efforts at different territorial levels (supranational, national and subnational), with local levels maintaining discretion in terms of implementation. The regular reporting by states on both process and results should encourage the development of diagnostic monitoring tools and, based on these experiences and feedback, should lead to adjustments and revisions.

Accordingly, the implementation of peacebuilding-related objectives can be understood as a recursive process allowing for the mutual learning of all participating actors, including international and domestic ones. In practice, as this book has shown, domestic political leaders have learned how to develop and consolidate their control of both institutions and society through the extraction of rents and the use of patronage networks to maintain (relative) social peace. With regard to the implementation of the internationally supported liberal peacebuilding framework, they have learned how to participate in the monitoring of policy implementation, reporting of agreed indicators, peer review and revision of plans, all while preserving their domestic power base.

International actors have also adapted to the local political context. Since the beginning of the peacebuilding process, they have endorsed two broad priorities: they have promoted institution-building, the development of civil society, the protection of human rights, the consolidation of the rule of law, the liberalization of the economy and other similar liberal objectives. Simultaneously, the pursuit of these objectives has coexisted with concerns about regional stability. Over time, however, experimentalist governance has led peacebuilders to modify the relative balance between these two broad goals. In substance, while in the first phase peacebuilders subscribed to grand transformation narratives and deployed intrusive missions to achieve radical restructuring of both political and economic institutions, eventually they veered towards less ambitious objectives, focusing increasingly on 'stability' as their underlying concern.

Stability concerns produced paradoxical effects. In the early phases of the peacebuilding transition, stability anxieties played into the hands of the very same domestic elites who were soon to be identified as the main obstacle to the implementation of the neo-liberal agenda. Two decades later, when citizens revolted against those political parties and domestic institutions, peacebuilders reacted by threatening to send in the troops to pacify troubled areas, as in Bosnia-Herzegovina, while adjusting only marginally their intervention approach in the attempt to appease citizens' calls for change. Unsurprisingly, widespread disillusionment with the peacebuilding process in general, and with EU accession dynamics in particular, increasingly took hold in the region.

Overall, the EU's member state-building in the Balkans has led to significant changes, but EU conditionality did not always function consistently and effectively in the process of accession (Džankić et al. 2019). Setting aside Slovenia, whose European future was never seriously questioned and which joined the EU as early as 2004, the other states proceeded towards EU membership at different speeds and with different results. Croatia officially joined the EU on 1 July 2013, while the other Western Balkan states made some progress towards that goal. Albania, FYROM, Montenegro and Serbia have obtained EU candidate status, with Albania, Montenegro and Serbia actually having started membership negotiations. Of the three countries, Montenegro is the furthest ahead but none of them expects the process to be completed in the immediate future. By contrast, FYROM has not yet started negotiations. The country was granted candidate status in 2005 but its progress towards membership has been blocked (primarily) by a long-standing dispute with its southern neighbour, Greece. The withdrawal of the Greek veto in mid-2018 resulted in the EU approval of the start of the accession talks with FYROM by June 2019 under the condition that country's constitutional name is changed to Republic of North Macedonia (Kitsantonis 2018). In the same period, accession negotiations will start for Albania as well.

Bosnia-Herzegovina and Kosovo constitute the most problematic cases. Bosnia-Herzegovina's internal political and economic struggles have been hindering its path towards closer links with European institutions. As discussed in Chapter 8, popular malcontent over corruption, poor governance and unemployment flared up in early 2014 and has raised alarm bells even among notoriously aloof EU bureaucrats. In an attempt to reboot EU–Bosnia-Herzegovina relations, the EU approved the SAA's entry into force on 16 March 2015, in exchange for a pledge by Bosnian authorities to adopt the reforms requested for European integration at a later stage. In February 2016 the country applied for EU membership but has not yet (as of early 2019) obtained the green light from the European Council. As for Kosovo, its independence is not recognized by Serbia or by five EU member states (Spain, Slovakia, Romania, Greece and Cyprus). This situation creates enormous obstacles for its progress towards EU membership, despite the fact that Kosovo, like all other Western Balkan states, is anchored to the framework of the Stabilisation and Association Process (Economides and Ker-Lindsay 2015).

9.2   Re-launching European Enlargement

The uncertainties related to the EU accession process, as well as growing levels of Euroscepticism, have favoured the development of a new geopolitical contest. Both regional powers, such as Turkey and Iran, and global ones, such as China and Russia, have taken advantage of the difficulties with the process of enlargement to the Western Balkans by attempting to shape domestic political and economic dynamics to their benefit. Bulgarian political scientist Ivan Krastev has warned how the Balkans have become the 'soft underbelly of Europe' (Krastev 2015).

In particular, it was the perception of an increasing Russian threat in the region that convinced Germany (supported by Austria, the United Kingdom, France, Italy and EU regional members Slovenia and Croatia) of the need for a more proactive presence in the area. Germany has been at the forefront in favour of a policy of continuing engagement with the Western Balkans, for example by attempting to sustain a reform process in Bosnia-Herzegovina through the so-called German–British Initiative (Jukić 2014). Germany has also taken a lead both in supporting further enlargement and in applying strict enlargement accession conditionality (Adenahr and Töglhofer 2017). It has criticized the Commission for presenting an unrealistic, too rosy picture of the situation in aspiring EU members, has clarified formerly unspecified conditions (for example by linking Serbia's accession to Serbia–Kosovo relations) and has stimulated the enlargement process in the most difficult cases as well as regionally by promoting cross-border collaboration on issues of common interest through the so-called 'Berlin process' (Flessenkemper 2017; Woelk 2019).

Germany's activism has facilitated the EU's renewed engagement vis-à-vis the Western Balkans, which is increasingly perceived in Brussels as a strategic region. In his 2017 State of the Union address, Commission President Juncker explained that the enlargement process continued to move forward despite the political difficulties that the EU has been experiencing, in particular after the outbreak of the economic and financial crisis in 2007–2008. Juncker reiterated that no new accessions will take place before the end of his mandate (that is, late 2019), but he added enlargement to both Serbia and Montenegro among the Union's objectives to reach by 2025. Along similar lines, French President Emmanuel Macron in his 'Initiative for Europe' speech on 26 September 2017, indicated that Western Balkan states could join the EU in a few years, after the Union has been substantially reformed. He also recognized the EU's strategic interest in preventing these states from aligning themselves with Russia, Turkey, or other semi-authoritarian powers (Macron 2017).

This re-affirmation of the enlargement prospect occurred in a political context very different from the optimistic period of the early 2000s, when the EU became the most important peacebuilding actor in the region. Indeed, rather than testifying to the EU's renewed commitment and reliance on its celebrated normative and transformative power, the re-affirmation of enlargement reflected a response to the regional dynamics of 'fear and uncertainty' (Belloni et al. 2019), including, among other issues, growing geopolitical competition, the difficulties related to increasing migration movements towards Europe, terrorist attacks in and outside Europe, and the related need to safeguard the EU's threatened ontological security. In proposing a revamped enlargement process, the EU has attempted to address its existential crisis by falling back on its established routines involving conditionality and the top-down assessment of domestic political, economic and social processes in the Western Balkans. This attempt remains controversial, since at a EU foreign ministers' meeting in February 2018 some countries claimed that a possible 2025 membership date for Serbia and Montenegro was too late, while others (above all the Netherlands and Austria) lamented the presence of continued problems with crime and corruption in the region (Baczynska and Maushagen 2018). Given these differences, this attempt is very likely to be misplaced.

The 2016 Global Strategy provided the EU with the new normative framework in foreign policy required to navigate the new, challenging international context. In particular, the Global Strategy elevated the concepts of 'principled pragmatism' and of 'resilience' as the guiding standards to address novel uncertainties and threats. While resilience, discussed below, still does not have a clear policy impact on the Balkans, 'principled pragmatism' has an intuitive appeal among policy-makers that makes it immediately relevant. In practice, 'principled pragmatism' has translated into the further sidelining of transformative ambitions. Particularly in Bosnia-Herzegovina and Kosovo, stabilization prevailed over emancipation or transformation (Cooley 2019). The Union is more concerned with immediate outcomes and less with its embedded liberal norms and identity. The EU's approach is mostly focused on achieving 'stability' through a leader-oriented method of engagement which favours the development of an 'unhealthy symbiotic relationship' (Bandović and Dimitrov 2017: 81) between Balkan strongmen and European political elites. The 2015–2016 refugee crisis along the so-called 'Balkan route' has been decisive in shaping this relationship. For the most part, EU member states interpreted the mass arrival of asylum-seeking persons as a threat to their security, identity and wellbeing, and decided to close their borders. As a result, the Commission could only take note of member states' unwillingness to accept asylum-seekers, and thus operated to block them along the frontiers of the Union by relying on the collaboration of domestic leaders.

Despite concerns about democratic backsliding, local governments, in particular the Serbian and Macedonian ones, could benefit from European support because of their role in closing the Balkan route. The EU praised regional leaders and elevated them to 'factors of stability,' while simultaneously downplaying normative and human rights concerns. The EU–Turkey Agreement, reached on 20 March 2016, testified to the Union's willingness to interpret 'principled pragmatism' by setting aside normative 'principled' issues in order to find a 'pragmatic' solution to the refugee problem. The EU provided Turkey with 3 billion euros, as well as with a more liberal visa policy for Turkish citizens travelling to Europe, to keep refugees from leaving from Europe (Amnesty International 2016), demonstrating the contingent and pragmatic nature of its commitment to liberal order norms (Smith and Youngs 2018). For their part, in addition to acting as border police, local leaders have skilfully exploited fears related to the rising influence of Russia and to simmering ethnic tensions in order to present themselves in Brussels as indispensable counterparts.

Overall, the EU approach has contributed to 'the rise of a regional "stabilitocracy,"' that is, weak democracies with autocratically minded leaders who govern through informal, patronage networks and claim to provide pro-Western stability' (BiEPAG 2017: 7; Börzel and Grimm 2018; Pavlović 2017). All major democracy indices (including Freedom House, Bertelsmann and World Bank) show that the Western Balkan states have been backsliding for about a decade. According to Freedom House (2018), there is no consolidated democratic regime in the region. Both Serbia and Croatia are considered as 'semi-consolidated' democracies in light of their extensive levels of corruption, the presence of an overwhelmed court system, and their limitations on media freedom, while Albania, Bosnia-Herzegovina, Kosovo, FYROM and Montenegro are ranked as 'transitional governments or hybrid regimes'. Patterns of semi-authoritarian political rule involving the exercise of power through party dominance and patron–client networks are ever more common (Keil 2018). Domestic leaders are both increasingly authoritarian and self-proclaimed pro-European democrats, while the EU is willing to turn a blind eye to local politicians' practices as long as they deliver on issues which represent a priority for member states, such as border control, fighting terrorism or regional stability (Stratulat 2017). The EU and its peacebuilding partners prefer a stable region dominated by oligarchs than one subjected to democratic protests and bottom-up mobilizations. The only exception to this deterioration in democratic life is found in FYROM where in 2017 citizens, enraged by the wire-tapping of thousands of citizens, opposition politicians, journalists and religious leaders, forced the resignation of a nationalist, corrupt and autocratic government (Mujanović 2018: 156–163).

In sum, Western Balkan leaders have learned that good relations with the EU are facilitated by the delivery of key EU needs, perhaps even more so than the adoption of those reforms required by the accession process. This situation cast doubt on the widely held assumptions that the EU's influence is higher the closer a candidate state gets to accession and that the accession perspective is a 'driver of transformation in the region' (European Commission 2018). Rather, the crisis of democracy in the region in the medium-long run could fuel popular discontent, damage the appeal of the EU (which is seen by pro-democracy movements in the region an impediment to democratization), and thus open the way to further Russian influence in the region.

9.3   Peacebuilding, R.I.P

The 'Liberalism of Restraint' adopted by the EU has only partially realized its ambitious objectives. While stability has been achieved and formally democratic institutions are in place everywhere in the Western Balkans, illiberal and semi-authoritarian values and practices continue to be common, while geopolitical competitors such as Russia exercise growing influence, in particular in those states with Orthodox populations. Both donors and local communities view peacebuilding activities with suspicion. For example, in Kosovo peacebuilding is considered obsolete and even associated with national disloyalty. Accordingly, civil society peacebuilding activities have gone underground both as a requirement of beneficiary groups and of the donors' strategic calculation (Visoka 2017: 173–174). As a result, liberal peacebuilding in the region, with its attendant linear understanding of political, economic and social processes, has been in crisis for while (Chandler 2017; Debiel et al. 2016).

The main lesson learned by the policy community with the waning of confidence in the possibility of achieving liberal institution-building has been the importance of pragmatism—either 'principled', as declared by the EU, or more commonly based on a realist matter-of-fact assessment of constraints and opportunities on the ground (Lake 2016). Pragmatism suggests the need to invert the international peacebuilding paradigm, 'starting from the problem rather than from the western or international provision of "solutions" or external goals' (Chandler 2017: 12–13). Rather than grounding intervention on liberal institutionalist assumptions, external involvement should focus on the context where peacebuilding takes place, in particular the complexity of personal and societal relations (Wiuff Moe and Stepputat 2018).

The so-called 'local turn' in the theory and practice of peacebuilding embodies the most common attempt to rethink the peacebuilding framework. The concern for the prerogatives and responsibilities of external actors have been replaced by a focus on the 'local' and its ability to shape, subvert, and deflect international intervention. From a policy perspective, the 'local turn' testifies to a 'post-liberal' understanding of the intervention process. No longer are conflict areas, both in the Balkans and more generally in the Global South, potentially amenable to constructive interference from the outside, if necessary through the assertion of coercive instruments over recalcitrant domestic elites. Rather, peacebuilding is understood as requiring a tailored, case-specific approach where advances and setbacks are inextricably linked and shaped by a complex web of personal and societal relationships.

As a result, notions of uncertainty, ambiguity and complexity increasingly permeate peacebuilding (Juncos 2018), changing policy-makers' approaches to intervention. In contrast with the type of liberal peacebuilding developed since the early 1990s, the notion of resilience moves away from the external provision of institutions, strategies, and policy frameworks in order to focus on communities' existing capacities to withstand destabilizing shocks (Menkahus 2012). It recognizes that there is no privileged external knowledge or pre-set model to address conflict situations. Resilience assumes that the local is permeated with legitimacy because of its congruence with domestic norms and practices. It further supposes that domestic situations of instability are not to be considered as exceptional circumstances, but normal conditions that can only be managed but not overcome. Accordingly, resilience stresses the importance of adaptability to adverse conditions and recovery. It entails coping with a state of affairs subjected to constant vulnerability and the threat of instability.

Consequently, rather than building democratic states, intervention should be focused on building 'resilient states' which are 'capable of absorbing shocks and transforming and channelling radical change or challenges while maintaining political stability and preventing violence' (OECD DAC 2011: 3). The focus on building resilient states is frequently accompanied by the commitment to the resilience of governments, communities and/or individuals, showing the wide and conceptually ambiguous agenda underpinning the concept. Whatever the primary target of intervention, the notion of resilience suggests the importance of internal capabilities as the most effective way to deal with risk (De Coning 2016; McCandless and Simpson 2015). The notion of resilience testifies to a shift from an understanding of peace, democracy and security as linear processes to a structural, non-linear, and long-term approach to vulnerabilities. Nonlinearity suggests that social systems do not follow a predictable, cause-and-effect path and thus, as opposed to linear social systems, they are not fully knowable, predictable and controllable (De Coning 2016: 170). For that reason, it entails coping with a state of affairs subjected to constant vulnerability and the threat of instability.

The notion of resilience has become central both for EU foreign policy and, more broadly, for donors' understandings of post-liberal intervention. In proposing resilience, the EU advocates a 'structural, long-term, non-linear approach to vulnerabilities, with an emphasis on anticipation, prevention, and preparedness' (European Commission and High Representative of the EU 2017: 2). From this perspective, policy-makers should be principally concerned with the protection of the population from systemic risks. Precisely because risk is difficult to predict and calculate, policy-makers should focus on the prevention of threats. Overall, resilience changes the peacebuilding perspective from a primary focus on transformation towards ever greater development of liberal democratic institutions, norms and practices, to self-management and the limitation of risk.

According to Rosa Balfour (2017: 17), the concept of resilience is of limited relevance to existing policies towards the Western Balkans. The operationalization of resilience discourses is still very limited, since it would require significant foreign policy reforms (Juncos 2018: 565). In addition, as argued in this book, intervention in the Balkans has increasingly focused on stability, not resilience. To the extent that stability is guaranteed, resilience may remain an academic and policy discourse with little local resonance. As long as domestic political elites are able to provide both the international community in general, and the EU in particular, with border control and regional stability and their patronage networks with the distribution of perks, the current stalemate may continue generally unperturbed.

However, there is no freezing or standstill in peacebuilding transitions (Pospisil 2019). Overtime stability may prove difficult to secure and resilience could emerge as the new conceptual and practical framework in the region. To begin with, the devastating floods that hit the region in 2014 are a remainder of the vulnerability of the Western Balkans to environmental disasters. More importantly, stability could be undermined by changing political conditions. If the ability of domestic elites to extract rents declines either because of decreasing levels of international aid or because of a new economic recession, then the situation of relative social peace in the region could be hard to sustain. Socio-economic difficulties, rising economic inequalities, and the perception of unacceptable corruption levels may reinvigorate citizens' protests and ultimately raise resilience to the level of principle coping mechanism to manage a condition of permanent crisis.

If so, the parable of peacebuilding would come full circle. The two central peacebuilding intervention targets discussed in this book—state institutions and civil society—have not developed according to the peacebuilders' expectations. The building of states' institutional capacity has generally proved ineffective: formal institutions have been captured by political parties, while informal ones continue to influence political and economic conditions. Similarly, civil society, understood as a set of professional NGOs, showed the same lack of capacity and social roots. Moreover, the likely growing inflexibility on fighting corruption may actually aggravate the situation. Local governments, pressured by more intransigent EU monitors, may invest more in the anti-corruption discourse, to strengthen state-level executive powers vis-à-vis institutions of deliberation and accountability, or vis-à-vis decentralized administrations. However, the trend to erosion of 'bureaucratic and inefficient' oversight mechanisms on the action of the executive power is unlikely to bring good news. More than one political transition in southeastern Europe has shown how a corruption-fighting radical-democrat leader can rapidly turn into a corrupt governing autocrat. The EU's support for reformist change agents ultimately has bolstered the power of political leaders who did not behave much differently from anti-reformist actors (Mendelski 2016).

The type of intervention which characterized peacebuilding since the 1990s has reached its logical end (Pospisil and Kühn 2016). This does not represent the end of intervention per se but rather the emergence of a mode of governance that sets aside indefinitely a transformative agenda and its liberal aspiration of progress and human betterment in favour of a drastic reduction of expectations vis-à-vis war-torn and conflict-affected states. Not only would emergency and crisis be normalized, but also responsibility for managing this condition would be placed squarely on local populations, thus allowing a shift in blame for missteps away from international peacebuilders onto local actors. Because the causality of intervention and its effects are completely decoupled, the responsibility of external actors becomes disguised (Juncos 2018). In sum, with the rise of resilience, the international community would finally succeed in withdrawing from any responsibilities towards conflict-affected states, in the Balkans as elsewhere in the Global South.

References

Adenahr, C., & Tőglhofer, T. (2017). Firm supporter and severe critic: Germany's two-pronged approach to EU enlargement in the Western Balkans. *Southeast European and Black Sea Studies, 17*(4), 523–539.

Amnesty International. (2016, June 3). *No safe refuge: Asylum seekers and refugees denied affective protection in Turkey.* EUR 44/3825/2016.

Baczynska, G., & Maushagen, P. (2018, February 15). *EU split over expansion into Western Balkans.* Reuters.

Balfour, R. (2017). Enlargement: What role for resilience? In S. Lange, Z. Nechev, & F. Trauner (Eds.), *Resilience in the Balkans* (pp. 17–22). Paris: EU Institute for Security Studies.

Bandović, I., & Dimitrov, N. (2017). Balkan strongmen and fragile institutions. In S. Lange, Z. Nechev, & F. Trauner (Eds.), *Resilience in the Balkans* (pp. 81–85). Paris: EU Institute for Security Studies.

Belloni, R., Della Sala, V., & Viotti, P. R. (Eds.). (2019). *Fear and uncertainty in Europe: The return to realism?* Houndmills: Palgrave.

BiEPAG (Balkans in Europe Policy Advisory Group). (2017). *The crisis of democracy in the Western Balkans: Authoritarianism and EU stabilitocracy.* Graz: BiEPAG.

Börzel, T., & Grimm, S. (2018). Building good 'enough' governance in post-conflict societies & areas of limited statehood: The European Union & the Western Balkans. *Daedalus, 147*(1), 116–127.

Chandler, D. (2017). *Peacebuilding: The twenty years' crisis, 1997–2017.* Houndmills: Palgrave.

Cooley, L. (2019). *The European Union's approach to conflict resolution: Transformation or regulation in the Western Balkans?* London and New York: Routledge.

Debiel, T., Held, T., & Schneckener, U. (Eds.). (2016). *Peacebuilding in crisis: Rethinking paradigms and practices of transnational cooperation.* Abingdon and New York: Routledge.

De Coning, C. (2016). From peacebuilding to sustaining peace: Implications of complexity for resilience and sustainability. *Resilience, 4*(3), 166–181.

Džankić, J., Keil, S., & Kmezić, M. (Eds.). (2019). *The Europeanisation of the Western Balkans: A failure of EU conditionality?* Houndmills: Palgrave.

Economides, S., & Ker-Lindsay, J. (2015). 'Pre-accession Europeanization': The case of Serbia and Kosovo. *Journal of Common Market Studies, 53*(5), 1027–1044.

European Commission. (2018). *A credible enlargement perspective for an enhanced EU engagement with the Western Balkans.* Strasbourg, 6.2.2018, COM (2018) 65 final.

European Commission and High Representative of the EU. (2017, June 7). *Joint communication to the European Parliament and the Council: A strategic approach to resilience in the EU's external action.* Brussels, JOIN (2017) 21 final.

Flessenkemper, T. (2017). The Berlin process: Resilience in the EU waiting room. In S. Lange, Z. Nechev, & F. Trauner (Eds.), *Resilience in the Balkans* (pp. 23–29). Paris: EU Institute for Security Studies.

Freedom House. (2018). *Nations in transit 2018: Confronting illiberalism.* Washington, DC: USAID.

Jukić, E. M. (2014, November 5). *UK, Germany, launch joint initiative on Bosnia-Herzegovina.* Balkan Insight.

Juncos, A. (2018). Resilience in peacebuilding: Contesting uncertainty, ambiguity, and complexity. *Contemporary Security Policy, 39*(4), 559–574.

Keil, S. (2018). The business of state capture and the rise of authoritarianism in Kosovo, Macedonia, Montenegro and Serbia. *Southeastern Europe, 42*(1), 59–82.

Kitsantonis, N. (2018, June 17). FYROM and Greece sign historic deal on name change. *The New York Times.*

Krastev, I. (2015, January 14). The Balkans are the soft underbelly of Europe. *Financial Times.*

Lake, D. A. (2016). *The statebuilder's dilemma: On the limits of foreign intervention.* Ithaca and London: Cornell University Press.

Macron, E. (2017, September 26). *Initiative for Europe: Speech by Emmanuel Macron*. President of the French Republic. www.elysee.fr.

McCandless, E., & Simpson, G. (2015). *Assessing resilience for peacebuilding*. New York: Interpeace.

Mendelski, M. (2016). Europeanization and the rule of law: Towards a pathological turn. *Southeastern Europe, 40*(3), 346–384.

Menkahus, K. (2012). *Making sense of resilience in peacebuilding contexts: Approaches, applications, implications* (Geneva Peacebuilding Forum, paper no. 6). Geneva.

Mujanović, J. (2018). *Hunger and fury: The crisis of democracy in the Balkans*. London: Hurst & Co.

OECD DAC. (2011). *Supporting statebuilding in situations of conflict and fragility: Policy guidance*. Paris: OECD.

Paris, R. (2004). *At war's end: Building peace after civil conflict*. Cambridge: Cambridge University Press.

Paris, R. (2010). Saving liberal peacebuilding. *Review of International Studies, 36*(2), 337–365.

Pavlović, S. (2017, May 5). *West is best: How 'stabilitocracy' undermines democracy building in the Balkans*. London School of Economics, European Politics and Policy (Resource document). http://blogs.lse.ac.uk/europpblog/2017/05/05/west-is-best-how-stabilitocracy-undermines-democracy-building-in-the-balkans/. Accessed 10 June 2018.

Pospisil, J. (2019). *Peace in political unsettlement: Beyond solving conflict*. Houndmills: Palgrave.

Pospisil, J., & Kühn, F. (2016). The resilient state: New regulatory modes in international approaches to state building? *Third World Quarterly, 37*(1), 1–16.

Sabel, C. F., & Zeitlin, J. (2012). Experimentalism in the EU: Common ground and persistent differences. *Regulation and Governance, 6*(3), 410–426.

Smith, M. H., & Youngs, R. (2018). The EU and the global order: Contingent liberalism. *The International Spectator, 53*(1), 45–56.

Sørensen, G. (2011). *A liberal world order in crisis: Choosing between imposition and restraint*. Ithaca and London: Cornell University Press.

Stratulat, C. (2017). Democratisation via European integration: Fragile resilience and resilient fragility. In S. Lange, Z. Nechev, & F. Trauner (Eds.), *Resilience in the Balkans* (pp. 11–16). Paris: EU Institute for Security Studies.

Visoka, G. (2017). *Shaping peace in Kosovo: The politics of peacebuilding and statehood*. Houndmills: Palgrave.

Wiuff Moe, L., & Stepputat, F. (2018). Introduction: Peacebuilding in an era of pragmatism. *International Affairs, 94*(2), 335–364.

Woelk, J. (2019). From enlargement perspective to 'waiting for Godot': Has the EU lost its transformative power in the Balkans? In L. Antoniolli, L. Bonatti, C. Ruzza (Eds.), *Highs and lows of European integration* (pp. 27–48). Cham: Springer.

Index